COMPUTER CONCEPTS FOR LIBERIAN SCHOOLS JR. & SR. HIGH EDITION

1ST EDITION

Computer Concepts for Liberian Schools, Jr.&Sr. High Edition Fundamentals, First Edition

Emmanuel Clarke

President/CEO
Emmanuel Clarke
Author and Professor

Vice President
Miatta Stella Herring
School Publishing & Marketing

Managing Editor
Michael Dundas

Visual Artist
Laura Cuevas

Sales and Marketing Rep.
Mustapha Kallon

Senior Production Editor
Candrick Clarke

Graphic Artist
Oudvin Cassell

Market Rep.
Jonathan Reeves

PREFACE

The Clarke Publishing and Consulting Group Technology Learning Series® offers the finest textbook in computer and technical education. This book is our answer to the many requests we have received from the Ministry of Education, instructors, students and education authorities in Liberia for a textbook that provides a succinct, yet thorough, introduction to computers and emerging technologies.

In *Computer Concepts for Liberian Schools: Fundamentals, First Edition,* you will find an educationally sound, highly visual, and easy-to-follow pedagogy that presents a complete, yet to the point, treatment of introductory computer and technology subjects. Students will finish the course with a solid understanding of computers and emerging technologies, how to use computers, and how to access information on the World Wide Web here in Liberia and wherever they go.

OBJECTIVES OF THIS TEXTBOOK

Computer Concepts for Liberian Schools: Fundamentals, First Edition is intended for use as a stand-alone textbook or in combination with an application in a one-quarter or one-semester introductory computer course for senior high school students in Liberia. No experience with computer is assumed. The objectives of this book are to:

- Provide a concise, yet comprehensive introduction to computers and technologies
- Present the most-up-to-date technology in an ever-changing discipline
- Give students an understanding of why computers are essential components in business and society
- Teach the fundamentals of computers and computers nomenclature, particularly with respect to personal computer hardware and software, the World Wide Web, and information security
- Present the material in a visually appealing and exciting manner that motivates students to learn
- Present strategies for pursuing career in information technology, as well as making sound purchasing decision in terms of computers and technologies
- Offer alternative learning techniques and reinforcement via the World Wide Web
- Offer distance-education providers a textbook with meaningful and exercise-rich examples

DISTINGUISHING FEATURES

To date, more than a hundred thousand students in Liberia thirst for computer knowledge. With the explosion of the World Wide Web, this textbook comes equipped with extraordinary step-by-step visual drawings and photographs, unparalleled currency, and the Clarke Publishing and Consulting Group Technology Learning Series® touch. This book will make your computer concepts course exciting and maybe dynamic. Distinguishing features of this book include:

A Proven Pedagogy

Careful explanations of complex concepts, educationally-sound elements, and reinforcement highlight this proven method of presentation.

Essential Computer Concepts Coverage

This book offers the same breadth of topics as other well-known Western computer textbooks have done; but a contrast here is that this textbook is Liberia and Africa centered. The depth of coverage focuses on the basic knowledge required to be computer literate in today's digital world.

A Visually Appealing Book that Maintains Student Interest

The latest technology, pictures, drawing, and text are combined artfully to produce a visually appealing and easy-to-understand book. Many of the figures include a step-by-step presentation (see page 118), which simplifies the more complex computer concepts. Pictures and drawings reflect the latest trends in computer technology.

Latest Technologies and Terms

The technologies and terms you the student will see in this book are those they will encounter when they start using computers. Only the latest application software packages are shown throughout the book.

Preface

World Wide Web Enhanced

This book uses the World Wide Web as major supplement. The purpose of integrating the World Wide Web into the book is to (1) offer students additional information and currency on important topics; (2) use its interactive capabilities to offer creative reinforcement and online quizzes; (3) make available alternative learning techniques with Web-based learning games, practice tests, and many other learning resources; (4) underscore the relevance of the World Wide Web as a basic information tool that can be used in all facets of society; (5) introduce students to doing research on the Web; and (6) offer instructors the opportunity to organize and administer their traditional campus-based or distance-education-based courses on the television or the Web using some online-learning application. This textbook, however, does not depend on Web access to be used successfully. The Web access adds to the already complete treatment of topics within the book.

Extensive End-of-Chapter Materials

A notable strength of this book is the extensive student activities at the end of each chapter. Well-structured student activities can make the difference between students merely participating in a class and student retaining the information they learn. The activities in this book include: Chapter Review, Key Terms, Checkpoint, Web Research and Learn How To.

ORGANIZATION OF THIS TEXTBOOK

Computer Concepts for Liberian Schools: Fundamentals, First Edition Provides a thorough, but succinct, introduction to computers. The material is divided into five chapters, Appendix A, a glossary/index, Answer sheet for Checkpoint questions, and a Student Notebook

Chapter 1 – Introduction to Computers In Chapter 1, students are introduced to basic computer concepts, such as what a computer is, how it works, and what makes it a powerful tool.

Chapter 2 – The Internet and World Wide Web In Chapter 2, students learn about the Internet, World Wide Web, browsers, e-mail, FTP, and instant messaging.

Chapter 3 – Application Software In Chapter 3, students are introduced to a variety of business software, graphics and multimedia software, home/personal/educational software, and communications software.

Chapter 4 – The Components of the System Unit In Chapter 4 students are introduced to the components of the system unit; how memory stores data, instructions, and information; and how the system unit executes an instruction.

Chapter 5 – Input and Output Chapter 5 describes the various methods of input and output, and commonly used input and output devices.

Chapter 6– Storage (Note! Chapter 6 is not included in this textbook. It is downloadable from publisher's website) In Chapter 6, students are introduced to magnetic disk and are going to differentiate the various types of storage devices as well as the methods used to store data and instructions and many others.

About the Author

Emmanuel Clarke, AAS, BS, MSc, MSc, OCP, PM

Emmanuel is currently the President and CEO of Clarke Publishing and Consulting Group, Inc., a textbook publishing company he started in 2007. Emmanuel is also a faculty member at Mercer County Community College in Trenton NJ, Burlington County College in Burlington New Jersey, and the United Methodist University in Monrovia, Liberia. He holds a B.S. in Engineering from the New Jersey Institute of Technology, NJIT, a Master's in Information System, and another Master's in Project Management from this same institution. He also holds an AAS in Computer Programming from Mercer County Community College and a Certificate in Project Management (PM) from this same institution. Mr. Clarke holds a certificate in Instruction and Curriculum Design and Development from Langevin Learning Services. He is current pursuing a doctorate in Human Centered Computing from the New Jersey Institute of Technology.

Clarke holds several professional certificates which include: Oracle Certified Professional (OCP) from Oracle University and Training Center in NYC, Certified Information Systems Implementer from NJIT, and a Certificate in Customer Service Trainer from the State of New Jersey Division of Human Services.

After a successful career working for the State of New Jersey Department of Health and Human Services, Child Care Networks and Mental Health Agencies as a MIS Director and Database Analyst as well as doing consultant work for Bullrun Financial LLC, a subsidiary of Merrill Lynch as a Financial Data Analyst and Bank of America as a Quality Control Special Representative, Emmanuel finally finds that his true calling was education. He has been teaching since 2005 at Mercer County Community College as well as training the college's corporate clients in various applications software. Clarke is also an Adjunct Information Technology Professor at Burlington County College in New Jersey.

Emmanuel serves on the Mercer County Community College Advisor Commission on Information Technology. He is a Distinguished Lecturer and does corporate training for companies such as: Bristol-Myers Squibb, the State of New Jersey Department of Banking and Insurance, Educational Testing Service, ETS, Firmenich, just to name a few. He loves singing, reading, running, hacking, fishing, making new friends, sleeping and bunchy jumping. He is the author of more than fourteen books, "The Fraternal Deception", "In Tears and Blood", "The City of Hopeless Romantics", "How the West Lost Africa to China: A Critical Analysis of Western Exploitation and China's Emerging Opportunities (to be released 2014)", "Computer Concepts for Liberian Schools" (currently being used by the Ministry of Education and schools in Liberia), "Growing Up With Technology, Primary Edition", "Computer Lab Manual For Elementary Schools", " Computer Lab Manual For Jr. High", " Computer Lab Manual For Sr. High", "Project Management for a Modern Liberia", "Management Information Systems for Liberian Colleges and Universities", "Computer Concepts for Liberian Colleges and Universities", "Computer Lab for Colleges and Universities", "So Far to Run (ghost wrote)" just to name a few.

Acknowledgements

As always, I would like to thank my students. I constantly learn from them while teaching and they are a continual source of inspiration and new ideas.

I could never have written this book without the loving support of my family. My partner in romance, Wante Saygbe, and my four loving children, Regina (Baby E), Eukey, Emmaree, and Emmanuella. Thanks for making the sacrifices (mostly in time not spent with me) to permit me to make this dream into reality.

My heartfelt thanks go to the hard working instructional designers at McGraw Hill for their guidance during the development of this book, it was quite a learning experience. Thanks to Samuel H. Taylor for inspiring me during my information technology career journey. To Marthalene Logan, your sense of humor is what I will not forget; thanks for making me laugh and forgetting about my long arduous journey to the finish-line.

This book wouldn't have been completed had it not been for the inputs from computer teachers at various schools in Liberia, staff at the Ministry of Education, Curriculum and Texbook Division, especially Esther Mulbah, as well as the instructors that are teaching computer courses at various public and private institutions around the nation. Thanks for your insight, I listened and I have come to deliver as promised. I would have been running in circle hadn't it been for David Sewon of the Monrovia Consolidate School System, MCSS, John Gbozee of the University of Liberia and Tarkolo Miller of Tubman University guidance on how to tailor this textbook specifically for Jr. and Sr. high schools in the country. My gratitude goes to my brother Mr. J. Frederick Clarke, and my two mothers, Regina W. Gaye, and Twon Bowo Clarke, for constantly praying for me. I also want to thank my many friends and admirers for your moral support. And to those unsung contributors that made this project possible, I owe you my gratitude.

TABLE OF CONTENTS

Table of Contents

Table of Contents

COMPUTER CONCEPTS FOR LIBERIAN SCHOOLS, JR. AND SR. HIGH EDITION

COMPUTER CONCEPTS FOR LIBERIAN SCHOOLS, JR. AND SR. HIGH EDITION

COMPUTER CONCEPTS FOR LIBERIAN SCHOOLS, JR. AND SR. HIGH EDITION

CHAPTER 1
INTRODUCTION TO COMPUTER

OBJECTIVE

After completing this chapter you will be able to:

1. Recognize the importance of computer literacy
2. Identify the components of a computer
3. Discuss the uses of the Internet and World Wide Web
4. Identify the categories of software
5. Describe the categories of computers
6. Identify the types of computer users
7. Discuss various computers uses in society

CONTENTS

A WORLD OF COMPUTERS

WHAT IS A COMPUTER?

- Data and Information
- Advantages and Disadvantages of Using Computer
- Information Processing Cycle

THE COMPONENTS OF A COMPUTER

- Input Devices
- Output Devices
- System Unit
- Storage Devices
- Communication Devices

NETWORKS AND INTERNET COMPUTER SOFTWARE

- Application Software
- Installing and Running Programs
- Software Development

CATEGORIES OF COMPUTERS

PERSONAL COMPUTERS

- Desktop Computers

MOBILE COMPUTERS AND MOBILE DEVICES

- Notebook Computers
- Mobile Devices

GAME CONSOLE SERVERS
MAINFRAME
SUPERCOMPUTERS
EMBEDDED COMPUTERS

EXAMPLES OF COMPUTER USAGE

- Home User
- Small Office/Home Office User
- Mobile User, Power User
- Large Business User

COMPUTER APPLICATIONS IN SOCIETY

- Education
- Finance Government
- Health Care Science
- Publishing
- Travel Manufacturing

CHAPTER SUMMARY

COMPANIES ON THE CUTTING EDGE

- Dell
- Apple Computers

TECHNOLOGY TRAILBLAZERS

- Bill Gates
- Ursula Burns

A WORLD OF COMPUTERS

Computers are everywhere; at work, at school, and at home (Figure 1-1), they are the primary means of communication for billions of people around the world. In Liberia, employees correspond with clients, students with teachers and family with friends and other special people. Through computers, society has instant access to information from around the globe. Local and national news, weather reports, sports scores, airlines schedules, telephone directories, maps and directions, job listing, and countless forms of educational material always are accessible. From the computer you can meet new friends, share photographs and videos, shop and take courses. Liberia has now become a part of the global technological revolution with the help of computers. In the next 10 years, it will be very much impossible for anyone to be successful in Liberia without a computer knowledge—Information and Communications Technology, ICT, is now a way of life in the 21st Century.

In the workplace, employees use computers to create correspondence such as e-mail messages, memos and letters; calculate payroll; track inventory; and general invoices. Some applications such as automotive design and weather forecasting use computers to perform complex mathematical calculations. At school, teachers use computer to assist with classroom instructions. Students use computers to complete assignments and research. People also spend hours of leisure time using a computer. They play games, listen to music, watch videos and movies, read books and magazines, research genealogy, compose music and video, retouch photographs, and plan vacations.

FIGURE 1-1 People use computers in their daily activities.

Many people in Liberia believe that computer literacy is vital to success. **Computer literacy** involves having knowledge and understanding of computers and theirs uses. This book will present the knowledge you need to be computer literate as a student here in Liberia. As you are reading this chapter, keep in mind it is an overview. Many of the terms and concepts introduced in this chapter will be discuss in more depth later in the book.

WHAT IS A COMPUTER?

A **computer** is an electronic device, operating under the control of instructions stored in its own memory, that can accept data, process that data according to specified rules, produce results, and store the results for future use. Depending on who you ask here in Liberia, every individual has their own definition of Computer.

Data and Information

Everywhere you turn and look, you will be greeted by data or some sort of fact. If you listen to the radio and read the Sport Page in the Daily Observer Newspaper or the Inquirer Newspaper, you will be given tons and tons of data about Invincible Eleven or Mighty Barrolle's positions on the LFA League Table. Even worse, you will see statistical data from the European Football leagues and others. For one fact, computers process data into information. **Data** is a collection of unprocessed items, which can include text, numbers, images, audio, and video. **Information** conveys meaning and is useful to people.

FIGURE 1-1a People use computers in their daily activities.

As shown in figure 1-2 for example, computers process several data items to print information in the form of a payroll check. How do you currently process data into information at your office or school in Liberia?

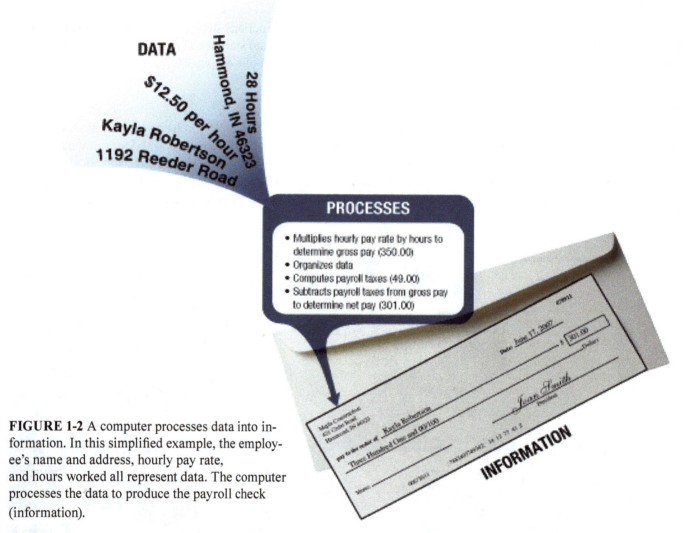

FIGURE 1-2 A computer processes data into information. In this simplified example, the employee's name and address, hourly pay rate,
and hours worked all represent data. The computer processes the data to produce the payroll check (information).

FAQ 1-1

Is data a singular or plural word?

The word data is a plural for datum. With respect to computers, however, it is accepted as a common practice to use data in both the singular and plural context. For more information, visit the Internet and check on Google Web site.

A FAQ (frequently asked question) helps you find answers to commonly asked questions. Many websites on the Internet will help you find answer for these FAQ section. In this textbook, each chapter includes FAQ boxes related to topics in the text. This is one of the unique features students will appreciate from using Computer Concepts for Liberian Colleges and Universities.

Advantages and Disadvantages of Using Computers

Society has reaped many benefits from using computers. Both business and home users can make well-informed decisions because they have instant access to information from anywhere in the world. A **user** is anyone who communicates with a computer or utilizes the information it generates. Students, another type of user, has
more tools to assist them in the learning process. Read looking into the future with technology 1-1 for a look at the next generation of benefits from using computers. This technology may also benefit people in Liberia.

Advantages of Using Computers

The benefits of computers are possible because computers have the advantages of speed, reliability, consistency, storage, and communication. Many students in Liberia are currently seeing some of these benefits of using computer.

- **Speed:** Computer operations occur through electronic circuits. When data, instructions, and information flow along these circuits, they travel at incredibly fast speeds. Many computers process billions or trillions of operations in a single second.

- **Reliability:** The electronic components in modern computers are dependable and reliable because they rarely break or fail.

- **Consistency:** Given the same input and processes, a computer will produce the same results – consistently. Computers generate error-free results, provided that the input is correct and the instructions work.

- **Storage:** Computers store enormous amount of data and make this data available for processing when it is needed.

- **Communications:** Most computers today can communicate with other computers, often wirelessly. Computers allow users to communicate with one another.

Disadvantages of Using Computers

Some disadvantages of computers relate to the violation of privacy, the impact on the labor force, health risks, and the impact on the environment.

- **Violation of Privacy:** It is crucial that personal and confidential records stored in computers be protected properly. In many instances, where these records were not properly protected, individuals have found their privacy violated and identities stolen.

- **Impact on Labor Force:** Although computers have improved productivity and created an entire industry with hundreds of thousands of new jobs, the skills of millions of employees have been replaced by computers. Thus, it is crucial that workers keep their education up-to-date. A separate impact on the labor force is that some companies are outsourcing jobs to foreign countries instead of keeping their homeland labor force employed.

- **Health Risks:** Prolonged or improper use can lead to health injuries or disorders. Computer users can protect themselves from health risks through proper workplace design, good poster while at the computer, and appropriately spaced work breaks.

- **Impact on Environment:** Computer manufacturing processes and computer waste are depleting natural resources and polluting the environment. Strategies that can help protect the environment include recycling old computers, regulating manufacturing processes, extending the life of computer, and immediately donating replaced computers.

Looking Ahead 1-1
Medical Breakthroughs with Computer Implants, Devices

Our ability to see is the result of a process very similar to that of a camera. With a camera, light rays pass through a series of lenses which focus images onto film. The eye performs a similar function in that light rays pass through the cornea and crystalline lens, which focus images onto the retina—the layer of light sensing cells that lines the back of the eye. The area of the retina that receives and processes the detailed images—and then sends them via the optic nerve to the brain—is referred to as the macula. The macula is of significant importance in that this area provides the highest resolution for the images we see. The macula is comprised of multiple layers of cells that process the initial "analog" light energy entering the eye into "digital" electro-chemical impulses.

Information Processing Cycle

Computers process data (input) into information (output). A computer often holds data, information, and instructions in storage for future use. Instructions are the steps that tell the computer how to perform a particular task. Some people refer to the series of input, process, output, and storage activities as the **information processing cycle.** Recently, communications also has become an essential element of the information processing cycle.

THE COMPONENTS OF COMPUTER

A computer contains many electrical, electronic and mechanical components known as **hardware**. These components include input devices, output devices, a system unit, storage devices, and communications devices. Figure 1-3 shows some common computer hardware components

Input Devices

An input device is any hardware component that allows you to enter data and instructions into a computer. Six widely used input devices; keyboard, mouse, microphone, scanner, digital camera, and PC video camera (figure 1-3). A computer keyboard contains keys you press to enter data into the computer. A mouse is a small handheld device. With the mouse, you can control movement of a small symbol on the screen, called the pointer, and you can make your selections from the screen. A microphone allows a user to speak into the computer to enter data and instructions. A scanner convert's printed material (such as text and picture) into a form the computer can use. With digital camera, you take pictures and then transfer the photographed images to the computer or printer instead of storing the images on traditional film. A PC video camera is a digital video camera that allows users to create a movie or take still photographs electronically.

Output Devices

An output device is any hardware component that conveys information to one or more people. Three commonly used output devices are a printer, a monitor, and speakers (Figure 1-3). A printer produces text and graphics on a physical medium such as paper. A monitor displays text, graphics, and video on a screen. Speakers allow you to hear music, voice, and other audio (sounds).

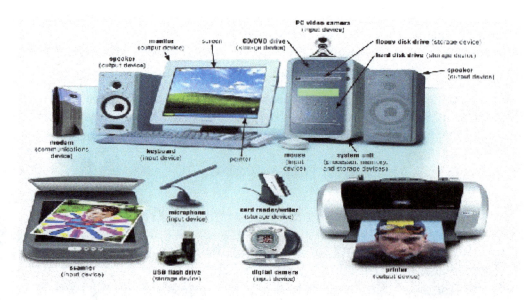

FIGURE 1-3 Some computer hardware components include the keyboard, mouse, microphone, scanner, digital camera, PC video camera, printer, monitor, system unit, speaker, modem, USB flash drive, card reader/writer, floppy disk drive, and hard disk drive.

System Unit

The **system unit** is a case that contains electronic components of the computer that is used to process data (figure 1-3). The circuitry of the system unit usually is part of or is connected to a circuit board called the motherboard. Two main components on the motherboard are the processor and the memory. The processor, also called the **central processing unit (CPU),** is the electronic component that interprets and carries out the basic instructions that operates the computer. **Memory** consists of electronic components that store instructions waiting to be executed and data needed by those instructions. Most memory keeps the data as instructions temporarily, which means its contents are erased when the computer is turned off.

Storage Devices

Storage holds data, instructions, and information for future use. For example, computers can store hundreds or millions of customer names and addresses. Storage holds these items permanently. A computer

keeps data, instructions and information on **storage media.** Examples of storage media are floppy disks, USB flash drives, hard disk drives, CDs, DVDs, and memory cards.

A **storage device** records (write) and/or retrieves (read) items to and from storage media. Storage devices often function as a source of input because they transfer items from storage to memory.

A **floppy disk** consists of a thin, circular, flexible disk enclosed in a square-shaped plastic shell. A typical floppy disk can store up to about 1.4 million characters. You insert the floppy disk in and remove it from a floppy disk drive. Some computer manufacturers are no longer including floppy disk drive with the computers because of the emergence of USB flash drives.

FIGURE 1-4 A Computer Hard Disk also known as Hard Drive.

A **USB flash drive** is a portable storage device that has much more storage capacity than a floppy disk but is small and lightweight enough to be transported on a keychain or in a pocket (figure 1-3).

A hard disk provides much greater storage capacity than a floppy disk or USB flash drive. The average hard disk can hold more than 100 billion characters. Hard disks are enclosed in an airtight, sealed case. Although some are external or removable, most are housed inside the system unit (figure 1- 4). In chapter six (6), we will discuss storage devices such as: CD-ROM, DVD-ROM, and memory card in a greater detail.

Communications Devices

A **communications device** is a hardware component that enables a computer to send (transmit) and receive data, instructions, and information to and from one or more computers. A widely used communications device is a modem (Figure 1-3 on page 6). Communications occur over cables, telephone lines, cellular radio networks, satellites, and other transmission media. Some transmission media, such as satellites and cellular radio networks, are wireless, which means they have no physical lines or wires.

Test your knowledge of pages 2 through 7 in Quiz Yourself 1-1.

QUIZ YOURSELF 1-1

Instructions: Find the true statement below. Then rewrite the remaining false statement so they are true.
1. A computer is a motorize device that processes output into input.
2. A storage device records (read) and/or retrieves (write) items to and from storage media.
3. An output device is any hardware component that allows you to enter data into a computer.
4. Computer literacy involves having knowledge and understanding of computers and their uses.
5. Three commonly used input devices are a printer, a monitor, and speaker.
Quiz Yourself Online: To further test your knowledge of computer literacy, visit www.clarkepublish.com or visit the Internet and then search www.google.com for more information.

NETWORKS AND THE INTERNET

A **network** is a collection of computers and devices connected together via communications devices and transmission media. When a computer is connected to a network, it is online. Networks allow computers to share resources, such as hardware, software, data, and information. Sharing resources saves time and money.

The **Internet** is a worldwide collection of networks that connects millions of business government agencies, education institutions, and individuals (figure 1-6). More than one billion people around the world use the Internet daily for a variety of reasons, including the following: to communicate with and meet other people; to access a wealth of information, news, and research finding, to shop for goods and services; to bank and invest; to take classes; to access sources of entertainments and leisure, such as online games, music, videos, books, and magazines; to download music; and to share information. Figure 1-7 shows examples in each of these areas.

Figure 1-5 A Global view of the Internet's network.

Communicate

Access Information

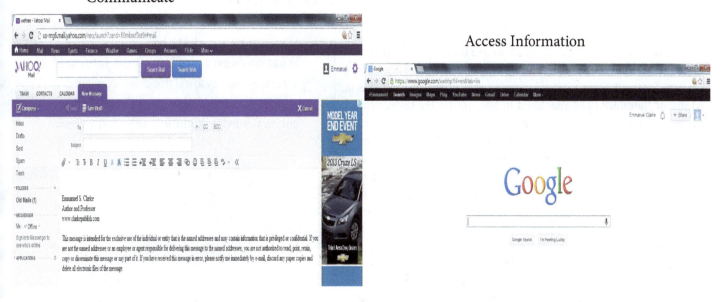

Shop

Bank and Invest

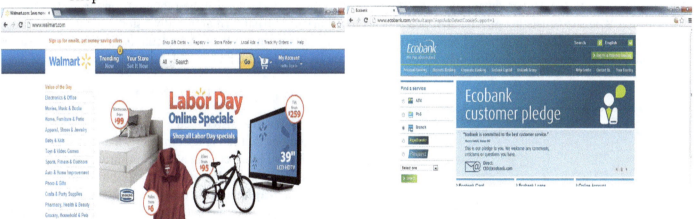

Take Classes

Entertainment

FIGURE 1-6 Users access the Internet for a variety of reasons.

People in Liberia connect to the Internet to exchange information with others around the world. Social media and E-mail allow a person to send messages to other users. With instant messaging, you can have a live conversation with another connected user. In a chat room, you can communicate with multiple users all at the same time–much like a group discussion.

Businesses that offer the Internet are called access providers; some charge a fee while others have it for free. There are several Internet access providers currently operating in Liberia. Many of them are headquartered in Monrovia. By subscribing to an access provider, you can use your computer and modem to connect to many services on the Internet. The **Web**, short for World Wide Web, is one of the more popular services on the Internet. The Web contains billions of documents called Web pages. A **Web page** can contain text, graphics, audio, and video. The eight screens shown in Figure 1-7 on the previous page are examples of Web pages. Web pages often have built-in connections, or links, to other documents, graphics, and other Web pages or Web sites. A **Web site** is a collection of related Web pages. Some Web sites allow users to access music that can be downloaded, or transferred to storage media in a computer or digital audio players, and then listen to the music through speakers, headphones, or earphones. Anyone can create a Web page and then make it available, or publish it, on the

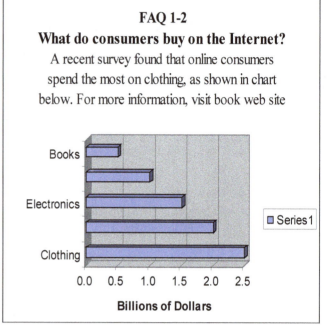

FAQ 1-2

What do consumers buy on the Internet?

A recent survey found that online consumers spend the most on clothing, as shown in chart below. For more information, visit book web site

Internet for other to see. Hundreds of thousands of people today use blogs to publish their thoughts on the Web. A **blog** is an informal Web site consisting of time-stamped articles in a diary or journal format, usually listed in reverse chronological order. Podcasts are a popular way people verbally share information on the Web. A **Podcast** is recorded audio stored on a Web site that can be downloaded to a computer or a portable digital audio player such as an iPod.

FIGURE 1-7 The graphical user interface of Windows 7.

COMPUTER SOFTWARE

Software, also called a **program**, is a series of instructions that tells the computer what to do and how to do it. You interact with a program through its user interface. Software today often has a graphical user interface. With a **graphical user interface** (GUI) pronounced gooey), you interact with the software using text, graphics, and visual images such as icons (Figure 1-8). An icon is a miniature image that represents a program, an instruction, or some other object. You can use the mouse to select icons that perform operations such as starting a program. The two categories of software are system software and application software. The following sections describe these categories of software.

System Software

System software consists of the programs that control or maintain the operations of the computer and its devices. System software serves as the interface between the user, the application software, and the computer's hardware. Two types of system software are operating system and utility programs.

OPERATING SYSTEM

An **operating system** is a set of programs that coordinates all the activities among computer hardware devices. It provides a means for users to communicate with the computer and other software. Many of today's computers use Microsoft's operating system, called Windows 7 (figure 1-7). When a user logs onto a computer part of the operating system loads itself into memory from the computer's hard disk. It remains in memory while the computer is on.

UTILITY PROGRAM

A **utility program** allows a user to perform maintenance-type task usually related to managing a computer, its devices, or its programs. Most operating systems include several utility programs for managing disk drives, printers, and other devices. You can also buy utility programs that allow you to perform additional computer management functions.

Application Software

Application software consists of programs designed to make users more productive and/or assist them with personal tasks. A widely used type of application software related to communications is a Web browser, which allows users with an Internet connection to access and view Web pages. Other popular application software includes word processing software, spreadsheet software, database software, and presentation graphics software.

Many other types of application software exist that enables users to perform a variety of tasks. These include personal information management, note taking, project management, accounting, document management, computer-aided design, desktop publishing, paint/image editing, audio and video editing, multimedia authoring, Web page authoring, personal finance, legal, home design-landscaping, education, reference, entertainment (e.g., game, simulation) and tax preparation (used in the US and Europe).

As shown in figure 1-9, you often purchase application software from a store that sells computer products. Read Discussion 1-1 for related discussion. Currently in Liberia, there are few stores that offer application software. To solve this problem Clarke Publishing and Consulting Group, Inc. has a wide-range of application software that meets the needs of education institutions and other business.

FIGURE 1-8 A Computer Software and Hardware Store in Monrovia, the capital of Liberia.

DISCUSSION 1-1
Is Computer Gaming More Good Than Bad?

Currently, computer games are not that big in Liberia but it is a discussion worth having. Many kids in Liberia will soon turn to computer gaming as a way of entertaining themselves.

Grand Theft Auto 5: is one of today's most popular computer games. In the game, players advance through the mafia by conveying secret packages, following alleged snitches, and planting car bombs. Since its release, shoppers around have bought millions of copies of Grand Theft Auto 5. Purchaser's praise the game's vivid graphic, edgy characters and wide range of allowable behaviors. Recently, the game was found to contain hidden adult content accessible by using a special code. Some parents and politicians condemn the game's explicit violence and rewards it gives players for participating in illegal acts. The fear that game like Grand Theft Auto 5 eventually could lead to antisocial or criminal behavior. Even worse, critics fear that the game's popularity may influence future developers of computer games aimed at younger children. Despite the fears, research has shown that playing violent games has no impact on behavior or increased by 50 percent in America. Some researchers and parents note the positive aspects of gaming, such as increased dexterity for players, use of critical thinking skills to solve problems in games, meeting goals, and following rules. What impact, if any, do violent computer games or games that include unacceptable acts have on individual behavior? On the balance, is computer gaming good or bad for people here in Liberia since many of us were witnesses to more than 10 years of volent civil wars?

What other motivations might parents have who limit their children's computer gaming? Do you think children below the age of 10 should be allowed into gaming booth in liberia even if they do not play volent games? Why or Why not?

Installing and Running Programs

The instructions in a program are store on storage media such as hard disk or compact disc. When purchasing software from a computer store, you typically receive a box that includes a CD(s) or DVD(s) that contains the program. You may also receive a manual or print instruction explaining how to install a use the software.

Installing is the process of setting up software to work with the computer, printer, and other hardware components. When you buy a computer, it usually has some software preinstalled on its hard disk. This enables you to use the computer the first time you turn it on. To begin installing additional software from a CD or DVD, insert the program disc in a CD or DVD drive. The computer then copies the program from the disc to the computer's hard drive. Once the software is installed it gives you the option to use or **run** it. When you instruct the computer to run an installed program, the computer loads it, which means the program is copied from storage to memory. Once in memory, the computer can carry out, or **execute**, the instructions in the program. Figure 1-10 illustrates the steps that occur when a user installs and runs a greeting card program.

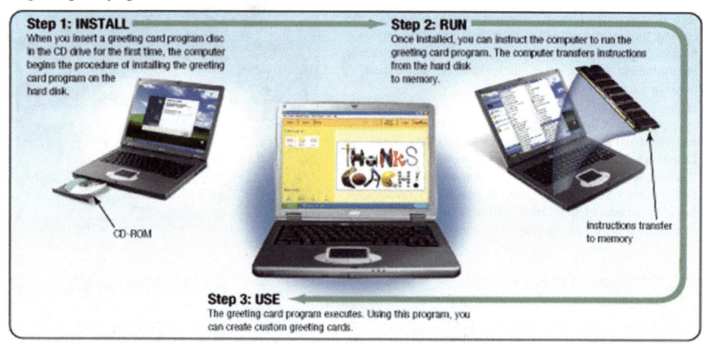

FIGURE 1-9 A Step-By-Step Instructions on How to Install and Run a Software Program.

Software Development

A **programmer**, sometimes called a developer, is someone who develops software or writes the instructions that direct the computer to process data into information. The author of this book has a degree in Programming. He is one of the few Liberians with a degree in Computer Programming. Complex programs can require thousands to millions of instructions.

Programmers use a programming language or program development tool to create computer programs. Popular programming languages include .NET, C++, Visual C# 2005, Visual Basic 2010, JavaScript, Python, and Java.

Figure 1-11 shows part of a JavaScript program.

```
<SCRIPT language=JavaScript src="http://a56.g.akamai.net/7/56/7207/fbf4d2c45e2b03/www.united.com/
<SCRIPT language=javascript>
function fCalendarPopup_dep() {
        var calendarCurl = '/homepage/cal/0,6740,FlightSearch,00.html';
        if (calendarWinDep==null||calendarWinDep.closed) {
        //calendarCurl = calendarCurl+"?posted_mon=-1&posted_year=-1&me=0";
        var chosen_mon = document.FlightSearch.elements[7].selectedIndex;
        var today = new Date();
        var chosen_year = today.getFullYear();
        calendarCurl = calendarCurl+"?posted_mon="+chosen_mon+"&posted_year="+cho
                var openCmd = "calendarWinDep = window.open('" + calendarCurl + "
                eval(openCmd);
        } else {
                calendarWinDep.focus();
                document.who_opened.whowho.value="departure";
        }
    }
function fCalendarPopup_return(calendarCurl1) {
        var calendarCurl = '/homepage/cal/0,6740,FlightSearch,00.html';
        if (calendarWinDep==null||calendarWinDep.closed) {
        //calendarCurl = calendarCurl+"?posted_mon=-1&posted_year=-1&me=1";
        var chosen_return_mon = document.FlightSearch.elements[10].selectedIndex;
        var today_return = new Date();
        var this_year = today_return.getFullYear();
        calendarCurl = calendarCurl+"?posted_mon="+chosen_return_mon+"&posted_yea
                var openCmd = "calendarWinDep = window.open('" + calendarCurl + "
                eval(openCmd);
        } else {
                calendarWinDep.focus();
                document.who_opened.whowho.value="return";
        }
    }
function validateFare (frm) {
    var msg = '';
    var cr = 'n';
    if (frm.depart.value.replace(/(^ *)/,"").length == 0) {
        msg = "Departing location is a required field.";
        alert(msg);
```

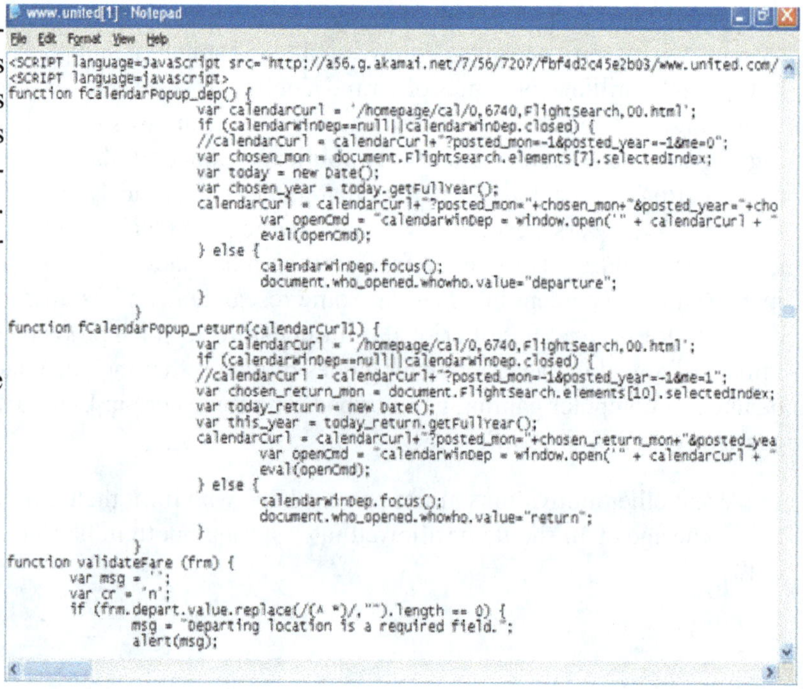

FIGURE 1-10 Some of the instructions in a JavaScript program code.

Test your knowledge of pages 8 through 12 in Quiz Yourself 1-2.

QUIZ YOURSELF 1-2

Instructions: Find the true statement below. Then rewrite the remaining false statement so they are true.

1. A resource is a collection of computer and devices connected together via communication devices and transmission media.
2. Installing is the process of setting up software to work with the computer, printer, and other
3. hardware components.
4. Popular system software includes Web browser, word processing software, spreadsheet software, database software and presentation graphics software.
5. The Internet is one of the more popular services on the Web.
6. Two types of application software are the operating system and utility programs.

Quiz Yourself Online: To further test your knowledge of computer literacy, visit www.clarkepublish.com or visit the Internet and then search www.google.com for more information.

CATEGORIES OF COMPUTERS

Industry experts typically classify computers in seven categories: personal computers, mobile computers and mobile devices, game consoles, servers, mainframes, supercomputers, and embedded computers. A computer's size, speed, processing power, and price determine the category it best fits. Due to rapidly changing technology, however, the distinction among categories is not always clear-cut; Figure 1-12 summarizes the seven categories of computers. This page and the following pages discuss the computer and devices that fall in each category.

CATEGORIES OF COMPUTERS

Category	Physical Size	Number of Simultaneously Connected Users	General Price Range
Personal computers (desktop)	Fits on a desk	Usually one (can be more if networked)	Several hundred to several thousand dollars
Mobile computers and mobile devices	Fits on your lap or in your hand	Usually one	Less than a hundred dollars to several thousand dollars
Game consoles	Small box or handheld device	One to several	Several hundred dollars or less
Servers	Small cabinet	Two to thousands	Several hundred to a million dollars
Mainframes	Partial room to a full room of equipment	Hundreds to thousands	$300,000 to several million dollars
Supercomputers	Full room of equipment	Hundreds to thousands	$500,000 to several billion dollars
Embedded computers	Miniature	Usually one	Embedded in the price of the product

FIGURE 1-11 This table summarizes some of the differences among the categories of computers.

Currently in Liberia, there are not that many companies using some to the computers that are listed in the table above. Only few companies and organizations are using servers. Examples of such companies are: Ecobank, Lonestar Communications Corporation, Clarke Publishing and Consulting Group, Inc., the Ministry of Finance, National Social Security and Welfare Corporation, LBDI, AccelorMittal of Liberia, just to name a few. The named companies and organizations are all using powerful servers to share resources in a network environment. We will discuss Networking and Security later on in this book. Mainframe computers and Supercomputers are currently not available in Liberia, but may soon be.

PERSONAL COMPUTERS

A **personal computer** is a computer that cannot perform all of its input, processing, output, and storage activities by itself. A personal computer contains a processor, memory, and one or more input, output, and storage devices. Two popular styles of personal computers are the PC (Figure 1-13) and the Apple (Figure 1-14). These two types of computers use different operating systems. PC and PC-compatible computers usually use a Windows operating system. Apple computers use a Macintosh operating system (Mac OS). The term, PC-compatible, refers to any personal computer based on the original IBM personal computer design. Companies such as Dell, Gateway, and Toshiba sell PC-compatible computers.

Two types of personal computers are desktop computers and notebook computers.

FIGURE 1-12 The PC and compatible computers usually use a Windows operating system.

FIGURE 1-13 The Apple computers such as iMac, use a Macintosh operating system.

Desktop Computers

A **desktop computer** is designed so the system unit, input devices, output devices, and any other devices fit entirely on or under a desk or table. The more popular styles of system unit are the tall and narrow tower, which can sit on the floor vertically.

MOBILE COMPUTERS AND MOBILE DEVICES

A **mobile computer** is a personal computer you can carry from place to place. Similarly, a mobile device is a computing device small enough to hold in your hand. The most popular type of mobile computer is the notebook computer.

Notebook Computers

A **notebook computer,** also called a **laptop computer,** it is a portable, personal computer designed to fit on your lap. Notebook computers are thin and lightweight yet can be as powerful as the average desktop computer. Notebook computers are more expensive than desktop computers with equal capabilities. On a typical notebook computer, the keyboard is on top of the systems unit, and the display attaches to the system unit with hinges (Figure 1-15). These computers weigh on average between 2.5 and 9 pounds, which allows users to easily transport the computers from place to place. Most notebook computers can operate on batteries or a power supply or both. Many students in Liberia and other parts of Continental Africa.

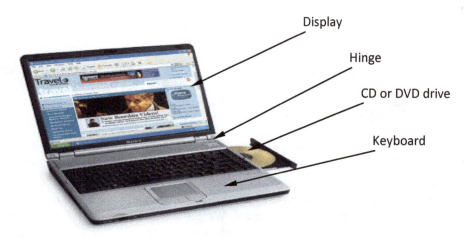

Display

Hinge

CD or DVD drive

Keyboard

FIGURE 1-14 On a typical notebook computer, the keyboard is on top of the system unit, and display attaches to the system unit with hinges.

TABLET PC

Resembling a letter-size slate, the **Tablet PC** is a special type of notebook computer that allows you to write on the screen using a digital pen (Figure 1-16). For users who prefer typing instead of handwriting, you can attach a keyboard to Tablet PCs if one was already not include. Tablet PCs are useful especially for taking notes in tight locations where the standard notebook computer is not practical. For the past five years, the use of Tablet PCs have been on the increase. Currently, there are more and more people buying Tablet PCs than are Notebook computers. In fact a recent Survey conducted by Clarke Publishing and Consulting Group, Inc., of college students, about 85% would buy a Tablet PC than a regular notebook or Laptop computer.

FIGURE 1-15 A Picture of one of the new Tablet PCs that are becoming students' favorite computer mobile device in Liberia and many parts of the world.

Mobile Devices

Mobile devices, which are small enough to carry in a pocket, usually store programs and data permanently on memory inside the system unit or on small storage media such as memory cards. You can often connect a mobile to a personal computer to exchange information. Some mobile devices are **Internet-enabled,** meaning they can connect to the Internet wirelessly. Three popular types of mobile devices are handheld computers, PDAs, and smart phones.

HANDHELD COMPUTER

A **handheld computer**, sometimes referred to as an **ultra personal computer (uPC)** or a **handtop computer**, is a computer small enough to fit in one hand. Because of their reduced size, the screens on handheld computers are small. Industry-specific handheld computers serve mobile employees, such as parcel delivery people, whose jobs require them to move from place to place. Apple iPad is another example of uPC.

PDA

A **PDA** (personal digital assistant) provides personal organizer functions such as a calendar, an appointment book, a calculator, and a notepad (Figure 1-16). Most PDAs also offer a variety of other application software such as word processing, spreadsheet, personal finance, and games.

Many PDAs are Internet-enable so a user can check e-mail and access the Web. Some also provide camera and telephone capabilities. The primary input device of a PDA is the **stylus**, which looks like a small ballpoint pen, but uses pressure of ink to write and draw

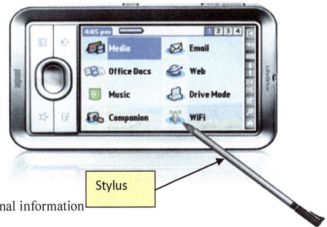

Stylus

FIGURE 1-16 A PDAs provides personal information management function.

SMART PHONE

Offering the convenience of one-handed operation, a **smartphone** is an Internet-enabled telephone that usually also provides PDA capabilities. In additional to basic telephone capabilities, a smart phone allows you to send e-mail messages, access the Web, listen to music, and share photographs or videos (Figure 1-17 on the next page).

With technology advancing at the speed of light and sound, so will the users of smartphone in Liberia. In fact, traditional phones are being replaced with smartphones in Liberia. If you took a walk on Randall Street or Broad Street, you will realize that many of the phones being sold are all Smart Phone.

As smartphones and PDAs continue a trend of offering similar functions, it is becoming increasingly difficult to differentiate between the two devices. This trend, known as convergence, has led manufacturers to refer to PDAs and smartphones simply as **handhelds**. Some factors that affect a consumer's purchasing decision include the device's size, screen size, and capabilities of available software.

GAME CONSOLES

A **game console** is a mobile computing device that is designed for single-players or multiple-players video gamers (Figure 1-18). Standard game consoles use a handheld controller(s) as an input device(s); a television screen as an output device; and hard disks, CDs, DVDs, and/or memory cards for storage. The compact size and lightweight of game consoles makes them easy to use at home, in car, in a hotel, or any location that has electrical outlet. Two popular models are the Microsoft Xbox 360 and Sony's PlayStation 4.

FIGURE 1-17 A PDAs provides personal information management function.

FIGURE 1-18 Game console provide hours of video game entertainment.

A handheld game console is small enough to fit in one hand. With the handheld game console, the controls, screen, and speakers are built into the device.

Some models use cartridges to store games, others use a miniature type of CD or DVD. Many handheld game consoles can communicate wirelessly with other similar consoles for multiplayer gaming. Two popular models are Nintendo's Game Boy Micro and Sony's PlayStation Portable (PSP). In addition to gaming, many console models allow users to listen to music, watch movies, and connect to the Internet.

SERVERS

A **server** controls access to the hardware, software, and other resources on a network and provides a centralized storage area for programs, data, and information (Figure 1-20). Servers support from two to several thousand connected computers at the same time.

People use personal computers or terminals to access data, information, and programs on a server. A terminal is a device with a monitor, a keyboard and memory.

According to the needs of an organization, a server comes in many shapes, sizes, speed, and capabilities. Usually, the speed and capacity of a server plays a determining role in its price. The government of Liberia and many businesses use servers to control access to resources on their network.

FIGURE 1-19 A server controls access to resources on a network.

MAINFRAMES

A **mainframe** is a large expensive powerful computer that can handle hundreds or thousands of connected users simultaneously (Figure 1-21). Mainframes store huge amount of data, instructions, and information. Most major corporations use mainframes for business activities. With mainframes, large businesses are able to bill millions of customers, prepare payroll for thousands of employees, and manage thousands of items in inventory. One study reported that mainframes process more than 83 percent of transactions around the world.

Servers and other mainframes can access data and information from a mainframe. People can also access programs on the mainframe using terminals or personal computers. There is currently no mainframe computer in Liberia.

SUPERCOMPUTERS

A **supercomputer** is the fastest, most powerful computer – and the most expensive (Figure 1-22). The fastest supercomputers are capable of processing more than 100 trillion instructions in a single second.

Applications requiring complex, sophisticated mathematical calculations use supercomputers. Large-scale simulations and applications in medicine, aerospace, automotive design, online banking, weather forecasting, nuclear energy research, and petroleum exploration use supercomputers.

EMBEDDED COMPUTERS

An **embedded computer** is a special-purpose computer that functions as a component in a larger product. A variety of everyday products contain embedded computers:

- Consumer electronics
- Home automation devices and appliances
- Automobiles
- Process controllers and robotics
- Computer devices and office machines

FIGURE 1-20 Mainframe computers can handle thousands of connected users and process millions of instructions per second.

FIGURE 1-21 This supercomputer simulates various environmental occurrences such as global climate changes, pollution and earthquakes.

EMBEDDED COMPUTERS

An **embedded computer** is a special-purpose computer that functions as a component in a larger product. A variety of everyday products contain embedded computers:

- Consumer electronics
- Home automation devices and appliances
- Automobiles
- Process controllers and robotics
- Computer devices and office machines

Because embedded computers are components in large products, they usually are small and have limited hardware. Embedded computers perform various functions, depending on the requirements of the product in which they reside. Embedded computers in printers, for example, monitor the amount of paper in the tray; check the ink or toner level; signals if a paper jam has occurred, and so on. Figure 1-22 shows some of the many embedded computers in cars.

Can you name any embedded computer you've used or seen here in Liberia? Recently, one of my students at the Burlington County College asked me if we had computers and Smart Phone in Liberia. Not surprised, I do him we did and that our market is flooded with a lot of fancy but substandard Chinese electronic, especially Smart Phone, Tablets and other consumer electronics.

Adaptive cruise control systems detect if cars in front of you are too close and, if necessary, adjust the vehicle's throttle, may apply brakes, and/or sound an alarm.

Advanced airbag systems have crash-severity sensors that determine the appropriate level to inflate the airbag, reducing the chance of airbag injury in low-speed accidents.

Tire pressure monitoring systems send warning signals if tire pressure is insufficient.

Cars equipped with wireless communications capabilities, called telematics, include such features as navigation systems and Internet access.

Drive-by-wire systems sense pressure on the gas pedal and communicate electronically to the engine how much and how fast to accelerate.

FIGURE 1-22 This supercomputer simulates various environmental occurrences such as global climate changes, pollution and earthquakes.

EXAMPLES OF COMPUTER USAGE

Everyday, people around the world rely on different types of computers for a variety of applications. To illustrate the range of uses for computers, this section takes you on a visual and narrative tour of five categories of users: a home user, a small office/home office (SOHO) user, a mobile user, a power user, and a large business user.

Home User

In an increasing number of homes in the west, the computer is a basic necessity. Each family members, or **home user**, spend time on the computer for different reasons. These include budgeting and personal financial management, Web access, communications, and entertainment (Figure 1-24). On the Internet, home users access a huge amount of information, take college classes, pay bills, manage investments, shop, listen to the radio, watch movies, read books, play games, file taxes, book airline reservations, and make telephone calls. They also communicate with others around the world through e-mail, blogs, instant messaging, and chat rooms. Read Discussion 1-2 for related discussions. Home users are increasing in Liberia and other parts of Africa.

Many home users have a portable digital audio player (this may not currently be the with home users case here in Liberia), so they can listen to downloaded music and/or podcasts at a later time through earphones attached to the player. They also usually have one or more game consoles to play video games. Today's home typically have one or more desktop computers. Some home users network multiple desktop computers throughout the house, often wirelessly. These small networks allow family members to share an Internet connection and a printer. Home users have a variety of software. They type letters, homework assignments, and other documents with word processing software. Personal finance software assists with preparing taxes, keeping a household inventory, and setting up maintenance schedules.

Reference software, such as encyclopedias, medical dictionaries, or a road atlas, provides valuable information for everyone in the family. With entertainment software, the home user can play games, compose music, research genealogy, or create greeting cards. Educational software helps adults learn to speak a foreign language and youngsters to read, write, count and spell.

FIGURE 1-23b (Web access).   **FIGURE 1-23a** (personal financial management).

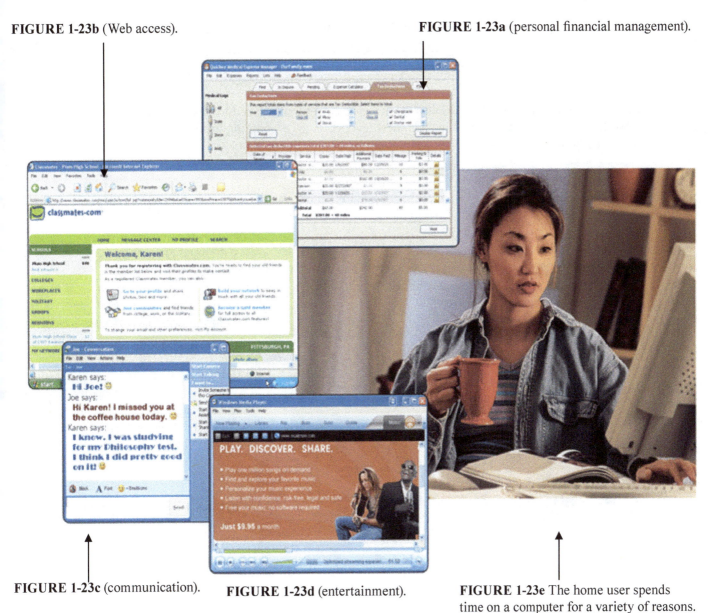

FIGURE 1-23c (communication).   **FIGURE 1-23d** (entertainment).   **FIGURE 1-23e** The home user spends time on a computer for a variety of reasons.

DISCUSSION 1-2

Does Facebook and Other Internet Dating Really Work?

Back in the day in Liberia, people met dates through family, friends, co-workers and community, religious, and recreational activities. Facebook and other social networks sometimes resulted in a perfect match, but often, they become time constraints. The limited pool of participants and infrequent meetings made it difficult to find a potential partner in churches, library or at school. Today, many people in Liberia and all over the world are turning to other resources – Facebook and Internet dating, also called online dating or e-dating. In the U.S. Internet dating is a two-billion dollar industry and the market for these services has grown almost 40 percent in the past year. Many Liberians have found their husbands and wives on Facebook and other Internet dating sites. Internet dating services supply members basic information about their appearance, and usually offer advanced options such as live chat, voice mail and computer matchmaking. On the other hand, in an Internet dating service it can be difficult to judge the truthfulness of the profiles of the other members or the claims made in live chat or e-mail. With Facebook, one is able to see the picture of their date.

Is Facebook and Internet dating services worth it? Why or why not? How is Facebook and Internet dating changing the way people meet in Liberia? If you used an Facebook or Internet dating service, what precautions might you take to protect yourself from deceptive acts of other members? Will you marry a person you met on Facebook? Why or Why Not?

Small Office/Home Office User

Computers assist small business and home office users in managing their resources effectively. Currently in Liberia, there are not that many small businesses using computer as an effective device to run the organization's activities. But within the next 10 years, we're going to see more small business owners using computer or Information and Communications Technology to solve business' problem as well as to service their customers.

A **small office/home office (SOHO)** includes any company with fewer than 50 employees, as well as the self-employed who work from home. Small offices include local law practices, accounting firms, travel agencies, and florists. SOHO users typically use a desktop computer. Many may also use PDAs.

SOHO users access the Internet – often wirelessly – to look up information such as address, directions (Figure 1-25), postal codes, flights, package shipping rates and to make telephone calls.

Nearly all SOHO users communicate through e-mail. Many are entering the e-commerce arena and conduct business on the Web. Their Web sites advertise products and service and may provide a means for taking orders. To save money on hardware and software, small offices often network their computers. For example, the small office connects one printer to a network for all employees to share. SOHO users often have basic business software such as word processing and spreadsheet software to assist with document preparation and finances (Figure 1-25b). They are likely to use other industry-specific types of software. A candy shop, for example, will have software that allows for taking orders and payments, updating inventory, and paying vendors.

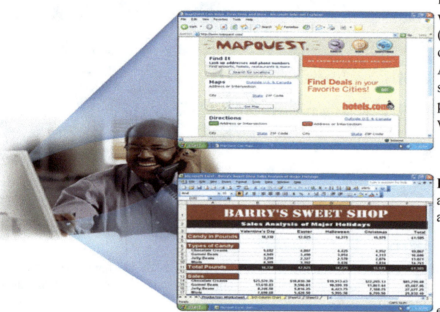

FIGURE 1-24 People with a home office and employees in small offices typically use a personal computer.

Mobile User

Today, businesses and schools are expanding to service people across the country and around the world. Thus, increasingly more employees and students are **mobile users,** who work on a computer while away from a main office or school. (Figure 1-26). Some examples of mobile users are sales representatives, real estate agents, insurance agents, meters readers, package delivery people, journalists, government officials and students.

Mobile users often have a notebook computer, Internet-enabled PDA, or smart phone. With these computers and devices, the mobile user can connect to other computers on a network or the Internet, often wirelessly accessing services such as e-mail and the Web. Mobile users can transfer information between their mobile devices and another computer. The mobile user works with business software such as word processing and spreadsheet software. With presentation graphics software, the mobile user can create and deliver presentation to a large audience by connecting to a mobile computer or device to a video projector that displays the presentation on a full screen. As a mobile user in this Liberia, how do you use your mobile device?

Besides LIBTELCOM, Blink wireless modem, Lonestar's wireless modem also know as Lonestar Edge, or Cellcom's 4G Modem, that users often attach to the notebook or laptop via the USB port in order to access the Internet, is there any company in Liberia that offers a wireless Internet connection without having to plug in a LIBTELCO, Leonstar or Cellcom Modems into a user's computer? I am sure there might be a few out there since technology is so dynamic and Liberians are so innovative, technologically.

FIGURE 1-25 Mobile users have notebook computers, Tablet PCs, PDAs, and smartphones so they can work, do homework, send messages, or connect the Internet while away from a wired connection.

FIGURE 1-26 A Power Users at their desk reading X-ray of a patient in a hospital. Very soon, doctors in Liberia are going to be reading X-ray result on computer screen.

Power User

Another category of user, called a **power user,** requires the capabilities of a powerful desktop computer, called a workstation (Figure 1-27). Examples of power users include engineers, scientist, architects, desktop publishers, and graphics artists. Power users typically work with multimedia, combining text, graphics, audio, and video into one application. These users need computers with extremely fast processor because of the nature of their work. Power users are on the rise in Liberia.

The power user's workstation contains industry-specific software. For example, engineers and architects use software to draft and design floor plans, mechanical assemblies, or vehicles. A desktop publisher uses software to prepare marketing literature such as newsletters, brochures, and annual reports. A geologist uses software to study the earth's surfaces. This software usually is expensive because of its specialized design.

Power users exist in all types of businesses. Some also work at home. Their computers typically have network connections and Internet access. I can tell you outright that technology is going to improve in Liberia such that there are going to be a lot of power users in the country within the next 7 years. This statement is not something that I cannot not guarantee. The reason is due to the fact that more and more foreign investors are coming into the country to invest and many of them are going to be retraining many of the people they're going to be employing. On a more positive note, Liberians themselves are embracing technology in a way as never before seen. More and more Liberians are studying Information and Communications Technology, ICT, related courses at home and abroad. As such, some of them are going to create the next big thing in the ICT Market.

Large Business User

A large business has hundreds or thousands of employees or customers that work in or do business with offices across a region, the country, and the world. Each employee or customer who uses a computer in the large business is a **large business user** (Figure 1-28). Many large companies use the words, **enterprise computing,** to refer to the huge network of computers that meets their diverse computing needs.

The network facilitates communications among employees at all locations. users access the network through desktop computers, mobile computers, PDAs, and smart phones. Large businesses use computers and the computer network to process high volumes of transaction in a single day. Although they may differ in size and in the products or services offered, all generally use computers for basic business activities. For example, they bill millions of customers or prepare payroll for thousands of employees. Some large businesses use blogs to open communications among employees and/or
customers. Large businesses typically have e-commerce Web sites, allowing customers and vendors to conduct business online. The Web site showcases products, services, and other company information. Customers, vendors, and other interested parties can access this information on the Web.

FIGURE 1-27 A large business can have hundreds of thousands of users in offices across a region, the country and the world.

The Production Department at Clarke Publishing Group, Inc. uses desktop publishing software to prepare marketing literature. The accounting department uses software for accounts receivable, accounts payable, billing, general ledger, and payroll activities. Other users work with word processing, spreadsheet, database, and presentation graphics software. They may also use calendar programs to post their schedules on the network, and they might use PDAs or smart phones to maintain contact information. E-mail and Web browsers enable communications among employees, vendors, and customers. Many employees of large businesses today telecommute (Figure 1-28).

Telecommuting is a work arrangement in which employees work away from the companies standard workplace environment often communicating with the office through the computer. Employees who telecommute have flexible work schedules so they can combine work and personal responsibilities, such as childcare. With the coming of a broadband Internet to Liberia, many workers will begin telecommuting in various industries around the country.

FIGURE 1-28 Many employees of large businesses telecommute. While this practice is not prevalent in Liberia, with the coming of a high-speed Internet, many Liberian professionals will soon begin telecommuting to their office or virtual work office as it is called.

COMPUTER APPLICATIONS IN SOCIETY

The computer has changed society today as much as the industrial revolution changed society in the eighteenth and nineteenth centuries. People interact with computers in field such as education, finance, government, health care, science, publishing, travel, and manufacturing. In addition, they can reap the benefits from breakthroughs and advances in these fields. The following pages describe how computers have made a difference in people's interactions with these disciplines. Read Looking Ahead 1-2 for a look at the next generation of computer applications in society.

Looking Ahead 1-2

Robots Perform Mundane Tasks, Entertain and Learn New Things

Playwright Karel Cape created the name, robot, for his humanoid machines that turned against their creators. Today, mobile, intelligent robots perform task typically reserved for humans in a $5 billion dollar global market. Each day, the iRobot Roomba self-propelled vacuum cleans homes, and the da Vinci Surgical System's robotic hands drill through bones and make incisions. Sony's home robot, QRIO, responds to voices and faces, displays emotions, and walks and dances fluidly.

Tomorrow's practical and versatile robots will serve a variety of personal and industrial needs. By 2020, the expected $34 billion dollar market should include products to care for senior citizens, transport people in major cities, and perform hundreds or thousands of mobile utility jobs, such as picking up and delivering items. For more information visit www.google.com.

Education

Education is the process of acquiring knowledge. In the traditional model, people learn from other people such as parents, teachers, and employers. Many forms of printed material such as book and manuals are used as learning tools. Today, educators are also turning to computers to assist with education (Figure 1-29). Many schools and companies equip labs and classrooms with computers. Some schools require students to have a notebook computer or PDA to access the schools network or Internet wirelessly.

Students often use computer software to assist them with learning or to help complete homework assignments. To promote education by computers, many vendors offer substantial student discounts on software as well as hardware. Sometimes they delivery of education occurs at one place while the learning occurs at other locations. For example, students can take a class on the Web. More than 90 percent of colleges in the Western World offer some type of distance learning classes. A few even offer entire degrees online. In Liberia many college administrators have not embraced the idea of distance learning. The author of this textbook once met the President of the United Methodist University on Ashmun Street so as to implement an online course management application as

FIGURE 1-29 In some schools, students have notebook computers on their desks during classroom lectures. These children at CDA in Monrovia use computer to perform various tasks.

an alternative to some of their courses that were being offered but the University's president refused the idea of an online alternative to for his student. Often, the behavior of a leader within an institution can somehow determine the success of that entity. Many educators in Liberia with a traditional backgrounds often resist the use of technology as a value adding productivity tool for the institution.

While this college's president may have denied his students the benefit of taking online classes the would help the students and college safe money, within the next 10 years, Liberian colleges will all offer online classes.

Finance

Many people and companies in Liberia use computers to help manage their finances. Some use finance software to balance checkbooks, pay bills, track personal income, expenses, manage investments, and evaluate financial plans. This software usually includes a variety of online services. For example computer users can track investments and do **online banking** (Figure 1-31).

With online banking, users access account balances, pay bills, and copy monthly transactions from the bank's Web site. Investors often use **online investing** to buy and sell stocks and bonds–without using a broker. With online investing, the transaction fee for each trade usually is much less than when trading through a broker. All of the banks in Liberia have Web sites but only few are truly offering online banking—LBDI and Ecobank are among the few.

FIGURE 1-30 Banking institution like LBDI has a website is e-banking enable. Many financial institutions' Web sites offer online banking. As the Internet becomes popular in Liberia and through out Africa, many people will opt for online banking.

Government

A government provides society with direction by making and administering policies. To provide citizens with up-to-date information, most government offices have Web sites. About 10 years ago, the Government of Liberia did not have a website that would provide information to citizens as well as her international partners. In the U.S., people access government Web sites to apply for permits and licenses, pay-parking tickets, report crimes, apply for financial aid, and renew vehicle registration and driver licenses. In 2007, several Liberian government ministries have Web sites but many of them lacked the basic interactive functionalities—this too might soon change as Web Technology is repidly improves.

Employees of government agencies use computers as part of their daily routine. Military and other agency officials use the U.S. Department of Homeland Security's network of information about domestic security threats to help protect the U.S. Law enforcement officers have online access to the FBI's National Crime Information Center (NCIC) in police cars they have computers and finger-printed scanners which can be used through PDAs (Figure 1.31). The NCIC contains more than 100 millions missing persons and criminals records, including names, fingerprints, parole/probation records, mug shots, and other information.

While the Government of Liberia, GOL, may not have this now, it is not a givens that the GOL, law enforcers will not have access to such in the future.

FIGURE 1-31 Law enforcement officials in the U.S. have in-vehicle computers and PDAs to access records. Pretty soon in Liberia, our law enforcement official might begin using in-vehicle computers.

Health Care

Nearly every area of health care uses computers. If you take a visit or the J.F.K or Jackson F. Doe Hospital, you will see what I am talking about. Computer is changing the face of health care in Liberia. Whether you are visiting a family doctor for a regular checkup, having lab work, outpatient test, or being rushed in for emergency surgery, the medical staff around you will be using computer for various purposes:

- Hospitals and doctors use computers to maintain patient records.
- Computer monitors patients' vital signs in hospital rooms and at home.
- Doctors use the Web and medical software to assist with researching and diagnosing health conditions.
- Doctors use e-mail to correspond with patients.
- Pharmacists use computers to file insurances claims.
- Computer and computerized devices assist doctors, nurses and technicians with medical test (Figure 1-33).
- Surgeons implant computerized devices, such as pacemakers, that allow patients to live longer.
- Surgeons use computer-controlled devices to provide them with greater precision during operation, such as for laser eye surgery and robot-assisted heart surgery.

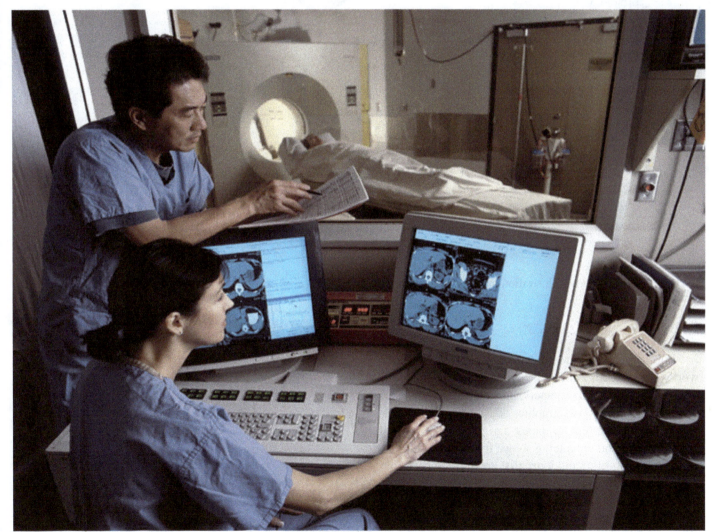

FIGURE 1-32 Doctors and nurses use computer related technology to help patients.

An exciting development in health care is telemedicine, which is a form of long-distance health care. Through **telemedicine**, health-care professionals in separate locations conduct live conferences on the computer. For example, a doctor at one location can have a conference with a doctor at another location to discuss a bone X-ray. Live images of each doctor, along with the X-ray, are displayed on each doctor's computer screen. If hospitals in Liberia embrace this new technology, it could change the face of medicine and the way doctors work and interact with each other. This technology will reduce the time it takes for patients to have their X-Rays, and other labs results read by a specialist by more than 90%.

Science

All branches of science, from biology to astronomy to meteorology, use computers to assist them with collecting, analyzing, and modeling data. Scientists also use the Internet to communicate with colleagues around the world. Breakthrough in surgery, medicine, and treatments often result from scientists' use of computers. Tiny computers now imitate functions of the central nervous system, retina of the eye, and cochlea of the ear. A cochlear implant allows a deaf person to listen. Electrodes implanted in the brain stop tremors associated with Parkinson disease. Cameras that are small enough to swallow sometimes call a camera pill—take pictures inside your body to detect polyps, cancer, and other abnormalities (Figure 1-33).

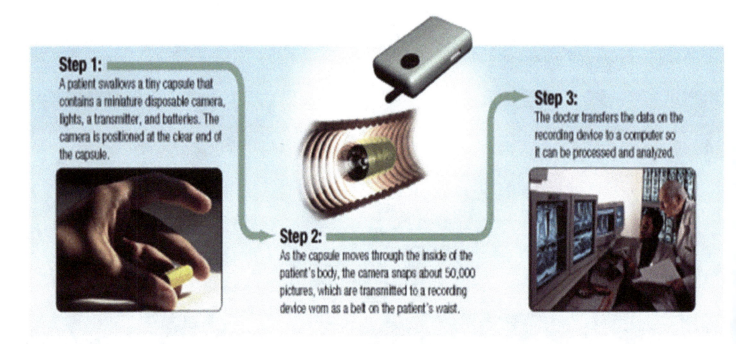

Step 1:
A patient swallows a tiny capsule that contains a miniature disposable camera, lights, a transmitter, and batteries. The camera is positioned at the clear end of the capsule.

Step 2:
As the capsule moves through the inside of the patient's body, the camera snaps about 50,000 pictures, which are transmitted to a recording device worn as a belt on the patient's waist.

Step 3:
The doctor transfers the data on the recording device to a computer so it can be processed and analyzed.

FIGURE 1-33 The above illustration show you how a camera pill works.

Publishing

Publishing goes through a process as it makes the works available for public views. These works include books, magazines, newspapers, music, film, and video. Special software assists graphics designers in developing pages that include text, graphics, and photographs; artists in composing and enhancing songs; filmmakers in creating and editing film; and journalist and mobile users in capturing and modifying video clips.

Many publishers make their work available online (Figure 1-34). Some Web sites allows you to copy the work, such as a book or music to your desktop computer, handheld computer, PDA, notebook computer, or smart phone. At Clarke Publishing and Consulting Group, Inc., the company is adding these functionalities to their Web site for our students' access. Soon, student will be able to access resources on various subjects and topics.

FIGURE 1-34 Many news organizations bring contents online. Clarke Publishing also has several of its books online.

Travel

Many vehicles manufactured today include some types of onboard navigation system. Airlines are now providing online access allowing their passengers to connect a mobile computer or device to the Internet (Figure 1-35). In preparing for a trip, you may need to reserve a car, hotel, or flight. Many Web sites offer these services to the public. For example, you can order airline tickets on the Web, or if you plan to drive somewhere and are unsure of the roads to take, you can look and print directions right from the Web. Back in the day in Liberia, one had to go to an airlines' office before buying a ticket. Now if you want to book a trip to Ghana or the United States, you can do this on your own as long as you have a credit or an ATM card from one of the local banks. We will talk about the Internet and Electronic Commerce or E-commerce in the next chapter.

FIGURE 1-35 Airlines today offer in-flight Internet connections to passengers. Liberian businessmen and women use computer while travelling.

Manufacturing

Computer-Aided Manufacturing (CAM) refers to the use of computers to assist with manufacturing processes such as fabrication and assembly. Often, robots carry out processing a CAM environment. CAM is used by a variety of industries, including oil drilling, power generation, food production, and automobile manufacturing. Automobile plants, for example, have an entire line of industrial robots that can assemble a car (Figure 1-36).

FIGURE 1-36 Automotive factories use industrial robots to weld car bodies as well as to make accessories parts.

Test your knowledge of pages 13 through 27 in Quiz Yourself 1-3.

QUIZ YOURSELF 1-3

Instructions: Find the true statement below. Then rewrite the remaining false statement so they are true.

1. A desktop computer is a portable personal computer designed to fit on your lap.
2. A personal computer contains a processor, memory, and one or more input, output, and storage devices.
3. Each large business user spends time on the computer for different reasons that include budgeting
4. and personal financial management, Web access, communications, and entertainment.
5. A home user requires the capabilities of a workstation or other powerful computer.
6. Mainframes are the fastest, most powerful computers – and the most expensive.
7. With embedded computers, users access account balances, paying bills, and copy monthly transactions from the bank's computer right into their personal computers.

Quiz Yourself Online: To further test your knowledge of computer literacy, visit www.clarkepublish.com or visit the Internet and then search www.google.com for more information.

CHAPTER SUMMARY

Chapter 1 introduced you to basic computer concepts. You learned about the components of a computer. Then the chapter discussed networks, the Internet, and computer software. The many different categories of computers, computer users, and computer applications in society were also presented. This chapter was an overview. Many of the terms and concepts introduced will be discussed further in later chapters. For a variety of hardware and

COMPANIES ON THE CUTTING EDGE

Dell

Computers Your Way

As a leading manufacturer of personal computers, Dell prides itself on its direct approach to computer sales. In 1984, Michael Dell, built Dell up to the company that it is today. The company deals openly with customers one at a time. This direct approach eliminates retailers that add cost and time to the ordering process.

Dell uses the Internet to enhance its advantages of direct marketing and host one of the world's largest volume e-commerce Web Sites. Customers can configure and price computers, order systems, and track their order online.

In response to the U.S. Environmental Protection Agency's estimate, those 500 million computers will be discarded from 2012 to 2017. Dell began an aggressive campaign to increase the amount of computer equipment it recycled by 85 percent. For more information visit www.dell.com or visit www.clarkepublish.com.

Apple Computer

Introducing Innovative Technologies

Millions of computer users in more than 180 countries loyally use Apple Computer's hardware and software with a passion, usually reserved for sport team or musical group.

Steve Jobs who died October 5, 2011 and Stephen Wozniak founded Apple in 1976 when they marketed the Apple I, a circuit board they had developed in Job's garage. In 1977, Apple computer incorporated and introduced the Apple II, the first mass-marketed personal computer. Apple introduced the Macintosh product line in 1984, which featured a graphical user interface.

Under Job's direction as CEO, Apple introduced the iMac, the iBook, the Power Mac G5, the iPod digital audio player, the iPhone, the iPad, and the Mac OS X; a strong demand for the iPod, the iPhone and the iPad helped boost the company's earnings. Many people in Liberia use Apple's products daily. Product sales jumped after Apple introduced its pay-per-download iTune online music store in 2003. For more information visit www.apple.com or visit www.clarke-publish.com.

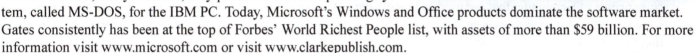

COMPANIES ON THE CUTTING EDGE

Bill Gates

Microsoft's Founder

Bill Gates, the founder and chief software architect of the Microsoft Corporation, suggests that college students should learn how to learn, by getting the best education they can. Because he is considered by many as the most powerful person in the computing industry, it might be wise to listen to him.

Gates learned to program computers when he was 13. Early in his career, he developed the BASIC programming language for the MIT Altair, one of the first microcomputers. He founded Microsoft in 1975 with Paul Allen, five years later, they provided the first operating system, called MS-DOS, for the IBM PC. Today, Microsoft's Windows and Office products dominate the software market. Gates consistently has been at the top of Forbes' World Richest People list, with assets of more than $59 billion. For more information visit www.microsoft.com or visit www.clarkepublish.com.

Ursula Burns

Xerox CEO

Color printing and consultant services are the two areas where the Xerox Corporation can make a difference, according to Ursula Burns, the company's CEO and chairman of the board. She should know the nature of the business, having starting her career with the Xerox as a Mechanical Engineering Summer Intern in 1980 more than 30 years ago.

As she later assumed roles in product development and planning, the company was securing its leadership position in digital document technologies. From 1992 through 2000, Burns, at a pivotal point in the company's history, led several business teams including the company's color business and office network printing business. In 2000, Burns was named senior vice president, Corporate Strategic Services, heading up manufacturing and supply chain operations.

In April 2007, Burns was named president of Xerox, expanding her leadership to also include the company's IT organization, corporate strategy, human resources, corporate marketing and global accounts. At that time, she was also elected a member of the company's Board of Directors. On May 20, 2010, Burns became chairman of the company, leading the 140,000 people of Xerox who serve clients in more than 160 countries. Building on Xerox's legacy of innovation, they're enabling workplaces – from small businesses to large global enterprises -- to simplify the way work gets done so they can focus more on what matters most: their real business. Under her leadership, sales have approached $23 billion.

Personal Computer Salesperson

CAREER CORNER

When you decide to buy or upgrade a personal computer, the most important person with whom you interact with will be a personal computer salesperson. This individual will be a valuable resource to you in providing the information and expertise you will need to select a computer that meet your requirements. Computer retailers that sell various kinds of computers need competent salespeople.

A Personal computer salesperson must be computer literate and have a specific knowledge of the computers he or she sells. The salesperson must also have a working knowledge of computer peripherals (printers, scanners, cameras, etc.). In addition, a successful salesperson has a friendly, outgoing personality that helps customer feel comfortable.

Computer salespeople typically have at least a high school diploma. Before reaching the sales floor, however, salespeople usually complete extensive company training program. Personal computer salespeople in the United States, generally earn about $60,000 dollars a year. This salary may not be the same for computer salespeople in Liberia or other African countries. Top salespeople can be among a company's more highly compensated employees, earning in excess of $110,000 dollars. For more information, check the Internet.

Chapter Review

The Chapter Review section summarizes the concepts presented in this chapter. To obtain help from other students regarding any subject in this chapter, visit the book's Web site.

1. **Why is Computer Literacy Important?**

   Compute literacy involves having a knowledge and understanding of computers and their uses. As computers become an increasingly important part of daily living, many people believe that computer literacy is vital to success.

2. **What Are the Components of a Computer?**

   A **computer** is an electronic device, operating under the control of instructions stored in its own memory, which can accept data, process that data according to specified rules, produce results, and store the results for future use. The electric, electronic, and mechanical components of a computer, or **hardware**, include input devices, a system unit, storage devices, and communication devices. An **input device** allows you to enter data or instructions in a computer. An **output device** conveys information to one or more people. The **system unit** is a case that contains the electronic components of a computer that are used to process data. A **storage device** records and/or retrieves items to and from storage media. A **communications device** enables a computer to send and receive data, instructions, and information to and from one or more computers.

3. **How are the Internet and World Wide Web Used?**

   The **Internet** is a worldwide connection of networks that connect millions of businesses, government agencies, educational institutions, and individuals. People use the Internet to communicate with and meet other people, access news and information, shop for goods and services, bank and invest, take classes, entertainment and leisure, download music, and share information. The **Web**, short for World Wide Web, is one of the more popular services on the Internet.

4. **What Are the Categories of Software?**

   Software, also called program, is a series of instructions that tells the computer what to do and how to do it. The two categories of software are system software and application software. **System software** consists of programs that control or maintain the operation of a computer and its hardware devices. Two types of system software are **operating system,** which coordinates activities among computer hardware devices, and **utility programs,** which perform maintenance-type tasks usually related to a computer, its devices, or its programs. **Application software** consists of programs designed to make users more productive and/or assist them with personal task. Popular application software includes Web browser, word processing software, spreadsheet software, database software, and presentation graphics software.

5. **What Are the Categories of Computers?**

   Industry experts typically classify computers into seven categories: personal computers, mobile computers, and mobile devices, game consoles, servers, mainframes, supercomputers, and embedded computers. A **personal computer** is a computer that can perform all of its input, processing, output, and storage activities by itself. A **mobile computer** is a computer that you can carry from place to place, and a mobile device is a computing device small enough to hold in your hand. A **game console** is a mobile computing device designed for single-player or multiplayer video games. A **server** controls access to the hardware, software, and other resources on a network and provides a centralized storage area for programs, data, and information. A **mainframe** is a large expensive powerful computer that can handle hundreds or thousands of connected users simultaneously and can store huge amounts of data, instructions, and information. A **supercomputer** is the fastest, most powerful, and most expensive computer and is used for applications requiring complex, sophisticated mathematical calculations. An **embedded computer** is a special-purpose computer that functions as a computer in a larger product.

6. **What Are the Types of Computers Users?**

   Computer users can be separated in five categories: home users, small office/home office users, mobile users, power users, and large business user. A **home user** is a family member who uses computer for a variety of reasons, such as budgeting and personal financial management, Web access, communications, and entertainment. A **small office/ home office (SOHO)** user is a small company or self-employed individual who works from home and use basic business software and sometimes industry specific software. **Mobile users** are employees and students who work on a computer while away from a main office or school. A **power user** can exist in all types of businesses and uses powerful computers to work with industry specific software. A **large business user** works in a company with many employees and uses a computer and computer network to process high volumes of transactions.

7. **What Computer Applications Are Used in Society?**

You may interact directly with computers in areas such as education, finance, government, health care, society, publishing, travel, and manufacturing. In education, students use computers and software to assist with learning or take distance-learning classes. In finance, people use computers for **online banking** to access information and **online investing** to buy and sell stocks and bonds. Government offices have Web sites to provide citizens with up-to-date information, and government employees use computers as part of their daily routines. In health care, computers are used to maintain patient records, assist doctors with medical test and research, file insurance claims, provide greater precision during operations, and implants. All branches of science use computers to assist with collecting, analyzing, and modeling data and to communicate with scientists around the world. Publishers use computers to assist in developing pages and make their works available online. Many vehicles use some type of online navigation system to help people travel more quickly and safely. Manufacturers use **computer-aided manufacturing (CAM)** to assist with the manufacturing process.

For more info, visit www.clarkepublish.com.

Key Terms

You should know the Key Terms. Use the list below to help focus your study. To further enhance your understanding of the Key Terms in this chapter, visit the book's Web site and click the chapter 1 link.

application software (11)
blog (10)
central processing unit (7)
communication devices (7)
computer (3)
computer literacy (3)
computer-aided manufacturing (27)
data (3)
desktop computer (14)
developer (12)
embedded computer (17)
enterprise computing (22)
execute (12)
FAQ (4)
game console (16)
graphical user interface (GUI) (10)

handheld computer (15)
handhelds (15)
handtop computer (15)
hardware (6)
home user (18)
information (3)
information processing cycle (5)
input device (6)
installing (12)
Internet (8)
Internet-enabled (15)
laptop computer (14)
large business user (22)
mainframe (17)
memory (7)
mobile computer (15)
mobile device (15)

mobile users (20)
network (8)
notebook computer (14)
online (8)
online banking (23)
online investing (24)
operating system (11)
output devices (6)
PDA (15)
personal computer (14)
podcast (10)
power user (22)
processor (7)
program (10)
programmer (12)
run (12)
server (16)
salesperson (29)

small home/home office (SOHO) (20)
smart phone (15)
software (10)
storage device (7)
storage media (7)
stylus (15)
supercomputer (17)
system software (10)
system unit (11)
Tablet PC (15)
telecommuting (22)
telemedicine (25)
UPC (15)
user (4)
utility program (11)
Web (10)
Web page (10)

32

Checkpoint

Use the Checkpoint exercises to check your knowledge level of the chapter.

True/False Mark T for True and F for False. (see page numbers in parentheses.)

_____ 1. Most people do not believe that computer literacy is vital to success.
_____ 2. Hardware consists of a series of instructions that tells the computer what to do and how to do it.
_____ 3. A user is anyone who communicates with a computer.
_____ 4. A network is a collection of computers and devices connected together via communication device and transmission media.
_____ 5. Some Web sites allow users to access music that can be downloaded.
_____ 6. Software is a series of instructions that tells the computer what to do.
_____ 7. System software serves as the interface between the user, the application software, and the computer's hardware.
_____ 8. A notebook computer is a computer small enough to fit in one hand.
_____ 9. A power user requires the capabilities of a powerful desktop computer.
_____ 10. Through telemedicine, health-care professionals in separate locations conduct live conferences on the computer.

Multiple Choice Select the best answer (see page numbers in parentheses.)

1. Computer literacy involves having knowledge and understanding of _____.
   a. computer programming
   b. computers and their uses
   c. computer repair
   d. all of the above

2. Three commonly used _____ devices are key board, a mouse, and a microphone.
   a. input
   b. output
   c. storage
   d. mobile

3. _____ allow(s) people to share thoughts and information with others over the Internet.
   a. blogs
   b. podcasts
   c. Web pages
   d. All of the above

4. The term, PC-compatible, refers to any personal computer _____.
   a. with processors having the same architecture as processor in Apple computers
   b. base used on the original IBM personal design
   c. that uses the Macintosh operating system (Mac OS)
   d. all of the above

5. Two types of _____ are desktop computer and notebook computer.
   a. personal computers
   b. servers
   c. mainframe computers
   d. supercomputers

6. Three popular types of _____ are handheld computers, PDAs, and smart phones.
   a. mobile devices
   b. notebook computers
   c. desktop computers
   d. tower computers

7. A _____ is a mobile computing device designed for single or multiplayer game
   a. Media Center PC
   b. Gaming desktop computer
   c. Game console
   d. Mobile devices

8. When using ¬¬¬ _____, users access account balances, pay bills, and copy monthly transactions from a bank's computer right into their PCs
   a. e-commerce
   b. personal finance software
   c. online banking
      accounting software

Matching   **Match the terms with their definitions. (see page numbers in parentheses.)**

_____ 1. information processing cycle

_____ 2. processor

_____ 3. memory

_____ 4. network

_____ 5. Internet-enabled

a. collection of computers connected together
b. electronic components that store instructions or program
c. mobile devices that connect to the Internet wirelessly
d. series of input, process, output, and storage activities
e. system that attempts to illustrate behavior of human brain
f. electronic component that interprets and carries out the basic instructions for a computer

Short Answer   **Write a brief answer to each of the following questions.**

1. What are some ways people use computers in the home, at work, and at school? _____

2. What does it mean to be computer literate? ¬¬¬_____

3. How is hardware different from software? _____

4. What is installing software? _____

5. How is an input device different from output device? _____

6. What are commonly used input and output devices? _____

7. What are six common storage devices? _____ How are they different? _____

8. What are seven categories of computers? _____ What determines how a computer is categorized? _____

Working Together   **Working in a group with your classmates, complete the following team exercise.**

1. Computers are everywhere. Watching television, driving or riding in a car anywhere in Liberia, using a charge ATM card from your local bank here in Liberia (like they do in the US and other countries), ordering fast food, and the more obvious activity of typing a term or research paper on a personal computer, all involve interaction with computers. For one day, have each member of your team make a list of every computer he or she encounters (be careful not to limit yourselves just to the computer you see.) Meet with the members of your team and combine your lists. Consider how each computer is used. How were the task done before computers were invented? Use Microsoft PowerPoint to create a group presentation and share your findings with the instructor and class.

Web Research

Use the Internet-based Web Research exercises to broaden your understand of the concepts presented in this chapter. Visit the book's www.clarkepublish.com site to obtain more information pertaining to each exercise. To discuss any of the Web Research exercises in this chapter with other students, post your thoughts or questions at the forum.

1. Journaling - Respond to your readings in this chapter by writing at least one page about your reactions, evaluations, and reflections about computer usage in your school. For example, how many students have high-speed Internet access at home or at on-campus housing? Are students without this Internet access at a disadvantage for completing homework assignments and research papers? Do electronic materials in the classroom get students more encourage in learning? You can also write about the new terms you learned by reading this chapter. If required, submit your journal to your instructor or teacher.

2. Scavenger Hunt - Use one of the search engines listed in Figure 2-8 in Chapter 2 on page 46 or your own favorite search engine to fine the answers to the question below. Copy and past the Web address from the Web page where you found the answer. Some questions may have more than one answer. If required, submit your answer to your instructor or teacher.

    1. What are three accredited online colleges or universities that offer a bachelor's degree in computer infor mation technology?

    2. In the United States, two National Science Foundation (NSF) programs were established in 1997 to inter connect 50 universities and scientific computing sites. What colleges host these two sites? What were the locations of the five original NSF-financed supercomputer centers?

    3. Personal finance software helps you balance your checkbook and manage your finances. What is the name of a popular personal finance software or program?

    4. What is the name of the first spreadsheet program?

    5. A programming language developed by the U.S. Department of Defense was name to honor a famous woman mathematician. What is the name of this programming language?

3. Search Sleuth - Visit the Google Web site (google.com) and then click the about Google link at the bottom of the page. Using your word processing program, answer the following questions and if required, submit your answer to your instructor or teacher.

    1. Below Our Company, click Corporate Info. Who are the founders of Google?

    2. Click the Technology link on the left side of the page. Provide a summary on the steps Google takes to complete query.

    3. Click your browser's Back button twice or press the BACKSPACE key two times to return to the About Google page. Below Our Search, click the Google Web Search Features link. How is Google including books in its search result? What are some of Goggle's newest features? What weather information is available?

    4. Click your browser's Back button two times to return to Google home page. In the Google Search text box, type computer and click the Google Search button. Approximately how many hits resulted? Do any definitions appear? If so, list the definitions. How much time did it take to complete the search?

    5. In the Google Search text box, type personal computer and click the Search button. Compare this to your earlier search. Are there more or fewer hits? How much time did it take to complete the second search?

    6. Click one of the resulting personal computer links and review the information. Write a 50-word summa ry. Using the information contained within the Web site, do you think you have sufficient knowledge to purchase a computer intelligently?

Learn How To

Use the Learn How To activities to learn fundamental skills when using a computer and accompanying technology. Complete the exercises and submit them to your instructor or teacher.

LEARN HOW TO 1:

Start and Close an Application

An application accomplishes task on a computer. You can start any application by using the start button. Complete these steps to start the Web browser application called Internet Explorer:

1. Click the start button at the left of the Windows taskbar on the bottom of the screen. The *Start menu is displayed.*

2. Point to All Programs on the Start menu. The *All Programs submenu appears (figure 1-38).*

3. Click the program name, Internet Explorer, on the All Programs submenu. The *Internet Explorer browser window opens* (Figure 1-39).

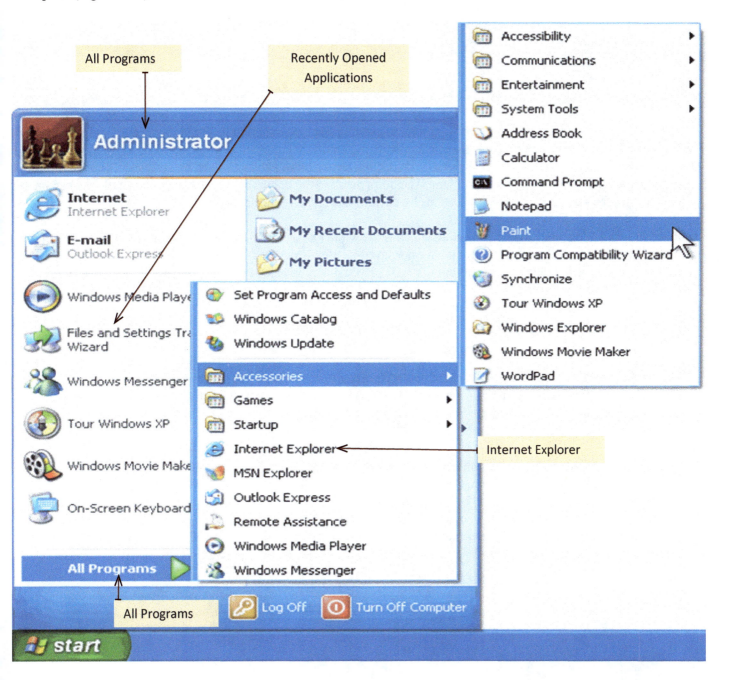

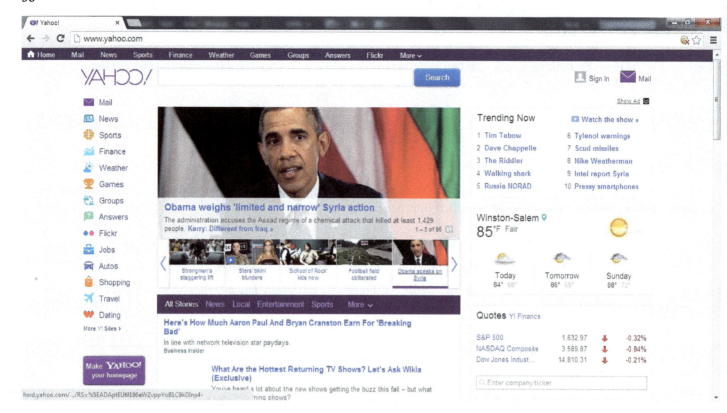

An item on the All Programs submenu might have a small right arrow next to it. When this occurs, point to the item and another submenu will appear. Click the application name on this submenu to start the application. Some application names might appear on the Start menu itself. If so, click any of these names to start the corresponding application. Below the line on the left side of the start Menu, Windows displays the names of the applications recently opened on the computer. You can start any of these applications by clicking the name of the application.

To close an application, click the Close button, which is the white (X) in the red square, in the upper-right corner of the window. If you have created a document but have not saved it, Windows will ask if you want to save the document. If you do not want to save it, click the No button in the displayed dialogue box. If you want to save it, refer to Learn How To number 1 in Chapter 3 on page 130.

Exercise

1. Using the Start button, start the application name WordPad found on the Accessories submenu of the All Programs submenu. WordPad is a word processing application. Type the following: To start an application, click the application name on the All Programs submenu and then type your name. Click the Print button on the toolbar. Submit the printout to your instructor or teacher.

2.

3. Close the WordPad application. If you are asked if you want to save changes to the document, click the No button. Start the WordPad application again, type some new text, and then close the WordPad application. When the dialogue box is displayed, click Cancel button. What happened? Now, close the WordPad window without saving the document. Submit your answer to your instructor or teacher. Using the start button, start the e-mail program on the computer. What is the name of the e-mail program? In the program window, what menu names are displayed on the menu bar at the top of the window? Close the e-mail program. Submit your answer to your instructor or teacher.

CHAPTER 3

THE INTERNET AND THE WORLD WIDE WEB

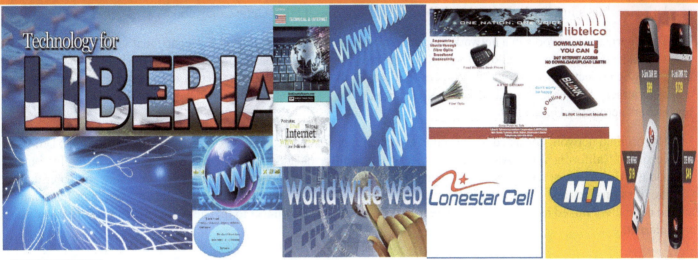

OBJECTIVE

After completing this chapter you will be able to:

Explain how to access and connect to the Internet

Explain how to view pages and search for information on the Web

Describe the types of Web sites

Identify the steps required for Web publishing

Describe the types of e-commerce

Describe how Internet communication work

Identify the rule of Netiquette

CONTENTS

THE INTERNET

One of the major reasons Liberian businesses, homes, and other users purchase computers is for Internet access. The **Internet**, also called the **Net**, is a worldwide collection of networks that links millions of businesses, government agencies, educational institutions, and individuals. Through the Internet, society has access to global information and instant communication. Today, more than two billion users around the world access a variety of services on the Internet, some of which are shown in Figure 2-1. The World Wide Web and e-mail are two of the more widely used Internet services. Other services include social networks, chat rooms, instant messaging, and Internet telephony. The Internet has become a big phenomena in Liberia and other places in Africa. In fact, the Internet is going revolutionize things in Liberia due to the availability of High-Speed Fiber Optic Connection.

The Internet has its roots in a networking project started by an agency of the U.S. Department of Defense. The goal was to build a network that; (1) allowed scientist at different locations to share information and work together on military and scientific projects; and (2) could function even if part of the network were disabled or destroyed by a disaster such as a nuclear attack. That network, called ARPANET, became functional in September 1969, linking scientific and academic researchers across the United States.

The original network consisted of four main computers; one is located at each of the following institutions; University of California at Los Angeles, the University of California at Santa Barbara, the Stanford Research Institute, and the University of Utah. Each computer served as a host on the network. A **host** or **server** is any computer that provides services and connection to other computers on a network. By 1984, the network had more than 1,000 individual computers linked as hosts. Today, more than 350 million hosts connect to this network, which became know as the Internet.

Figure 2-1 (Web)

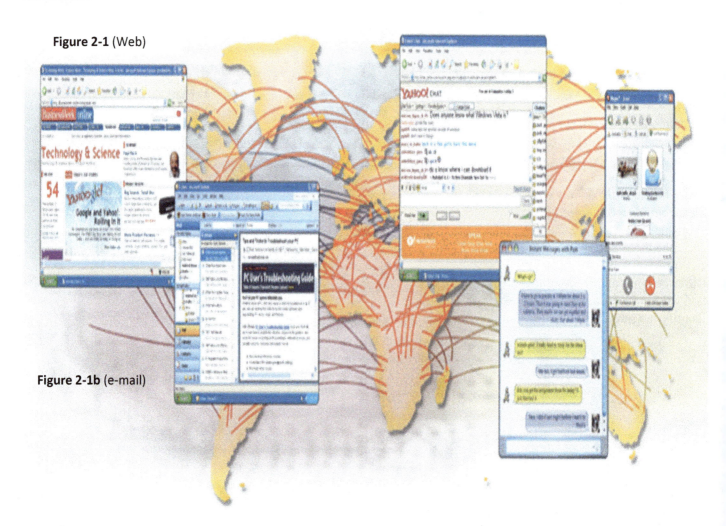

Figure 2-1b (e-mail)

FIGURE 2-1 People in Liberia and around the world use a variety of Internet services in daily activities. Internet services allow users to access the Web, send e-mail messages, chat on Facebook with friends or a group, or have a private conversation with friend(s) or family member(s) that are also online.

The Internet consists of many local, regional, national, and international networks. Both public and private organizations own networks on the Internet. These networks, along with the government, telephone companies, cable and satellite companies, are all contributors toward the internal structure of the Internet.

Each organization on the Internet is responsible only for maintaining its own network. No single person company, institution, or government agency controls or owns the Internet. The **World Wide Web Consortium (W3C),** however, oversees research and set standards and guidelines for many areas of the Internet. Nearly 2,000 institutions and organizations from around the world are members of the W3C.

HOW THE INTERNET WORKS

Data sent over the Internet travels via networks and communications media owned and operated by many companies. The following sections present various ways to connect to these networks on the Internet.

Connecting to the Internet

In Liberia, employees and students often connect to the Internet through a business or school network. Some homes and small businesses use dial-up access to connect to the Internet. **Dial-up access** takes place when the modem in your computer uses a standard telephone line to connect to the Internet. A dial-up connection, however, is slow-speed technology. In fact, most Internet connections are slow in Liberia. It is due to low bandwidth. With the approaching underwater fiber-optic broadband service, slowness will become history.

Figure 2-1c (chat)

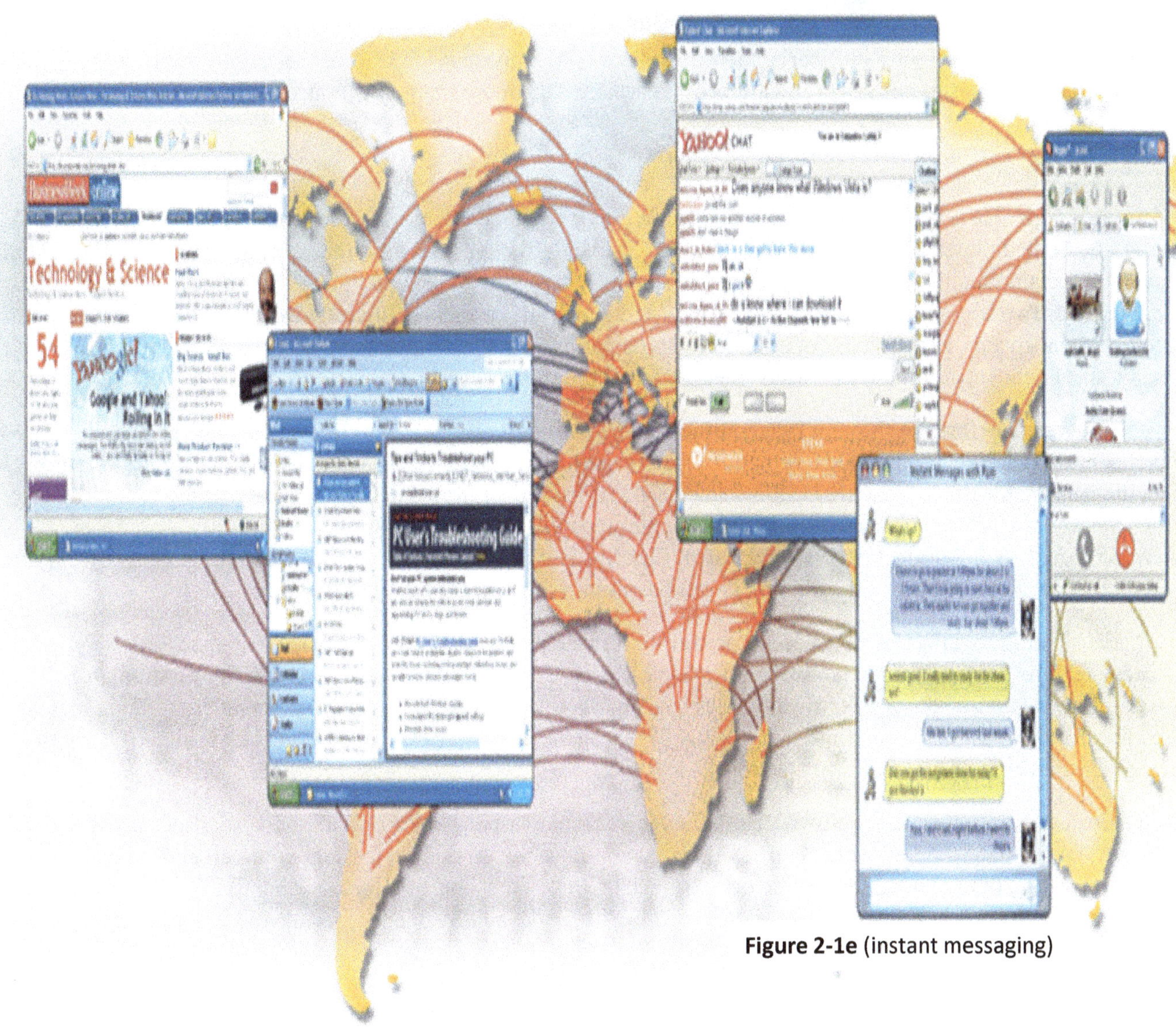

Figure 2-1d (Internet telephony)

Figure 2-1e (instant messaging)

FAQ 2-1

Do many people have Internet access in Liberia?
According to a recent 12-month study by Clarke Publishing and Consulting Group, Inc., the number of home and small business users with Internet access grew by more than 3 percent, resulting in a total of 925 thousand Internet access subscribers today in Liberia. The main reason for the increase is due to the reduction in fees by ISP due to the landing of the Fiber Optic Cable within the country. This number is going to jump by the year 2012 to 150 thousand. For more info, visit www.clarkepublish. com.

In the Western World, many home and small business users are opting for higher-speed Internet connections through DSL, cable television, radio signals, or satellite. **DSL**, (digital subscriber line) is a technology that provides high-speed Internet connections using regular telephone lines. A **cable modem** allows access to high-speed Internet services through the cable television network. **Fixed wireless** high-speed Internet connections use a dish-shaped antenna on your house or business to communicate with a tower location via radio signals. A **satellite modem** communicates with a satellite dish to provide high-speed Internet connections via satellite. As to-date, all of the Internet services in Liberia that were previously being provided by satellite companies—this was why Internet service were so expensive are now being replace for Fiber Optic Backed-Internet Connection within the country.

In most cases, DSL, cable television, fixed wireless, and satellite connections are always on, that is, connected to the Internet the entire time the computer is running. With dial-up access, by contrast, you must establish the connection to the Internet.

Mobile users access the Internet using a variety of technologies. Back in the old-days of the Internet, most hotels and airport provided dial-up or with a few offering high-speed Internet connections. Wireless Internet access technologies allows mobile users to connect to the Internet with notebook computers, iPad, Tablet PCs, PDAs, and smart phones while away from a telephone, cable, or other wired connection. Currently in Liberia, the three major Global System for Mobile Communication, GSM companies are all offering various types of wireless Internet services to the more than 2 million subscribers.

Access Providers

An **access provider** is a business that provides individuals and companies access to the Internet free or for a fee. In Liberia, the United States, Europe, and other Western countries, the most common fee arrangement for an individual account is a fixed amount, usually about $10 to $25 per month for dial-up access and $20 to $99 for high-speed access. In Liberia, the fee is two times higher than those in the Western World. For this fee, many providers offer unlimited Internet access. Others specify a set number of accessible hours per month. With the latter arrangement, the provider charges extra per hour of connection time that exceeds the allotted number of access hours.

Users access the Internet through ISPs, online service providers, and wireless Internet service providers. An **ISP (Internet service provider)** is a regional or national access provider. A regional ISP usually provides Internet access to a specific geographic area. A national ISP is a business that provides Internet access in cities and towns nationwide. National ISPs usually offer more services and have a larger technical support staff than regional ISPs. Examples of National ISPs are AT&T Worldnet Service and EarthLink. In Liberia, WEN Inc, Lonestar Communications Corporation, LIBTELCO, Cellcom GSM, Comuim, and others can be put into this category as regional ISPs.

In addition to providing Internet access, an **online service provider (OSP)** also has many members-only features. These features include special content and services such as news, weather, legal information, financial data, hardware and software guides, games, travel guides, e-mail, photo communities, online calendars, and instant messaging. The fees for using an OSP sometimes are slightly higher than fees for an ISP. The two more popular OSP are AOL (American Online) and MSN (Microsoft Network).

A **wireless Internet services provider (WISP)** is a company that provides wireless Internet access to users with wireless modems or wireless devices or Internet-enabled mobile computers or devices. the four cell phone companies in Liberia are all WISP. Internet-enabled mobile devices include PDAs and smart phones. Examples of U.S. wireless Internet service providers include Boingo Wireless, Sprint PCS, T-Mobile, and Verizon Wireless. In Liberia, all of the cell phone companies are providing their customers wireless Internet services along with the voice service that are currently being provided.

How Data Travel the Internet

Computers connected to the Internet work together to transfer data and information around the world. Several main transmission media carry the heaviest amount of traffic on the Internet. These major carriers of network traffic are known collectively as the **Internet backbone.**

In the United States, the transmission media that make up the Internet backbone exchange data at several different major cities across the country. When the High-Speed Fiber-Optic Internet cable lands in Liberia, the Internet backbone server will be hosted by the Liberia Telecommunications Authority or even LIBTELCO. That is, they will transfer data from one network to another until it reaches its destination (Figure 2-2).

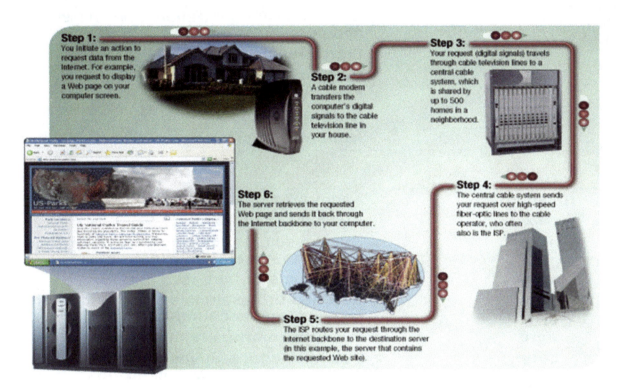

FIGURE 2-2 HOW A HOME USER'S DATA MIGHT TRAVEL THE INTERNET USING A CABLE MODEM CONNECTION

Internet Addresses

The Internet relies on an addressing system much like the postal service to send data to a computer at a specific destinations. An **IP address,** short for Internet Protocol address, is a number that uniquely identifies each computer or device connected to the Internet. The IP address usually consists of four groups of numbers, each separated by a period. In general, the first portion of each IP address identifies the network and the last portion identifies the specific computer.

These all-numeric IP addresses are difficult to remember and use. Thus, the internet supports the use of a text name that represents one or more IP addresses. A **domain name** is the text version of an IP address. Figure 2-3 shows an IP address and its associated domain name. As with IP address, the components of a domain name are separated by period.

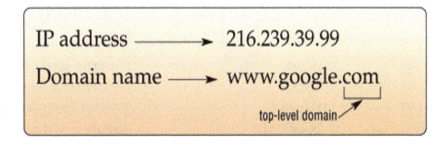

FIGURE 2-3 The IP address and domain name for the Google Web site

In Figure 2-3 on the previous page, the COM portion of the domain name is called the top-level domain. Every domain name contains a **top-level domain**, which identifies the type of organization associated with the domain. Figure 2-4 lists some top-level domains. For international Web sites outside the United States, the top-level domain also ends with a two-letter country code, such as au for Australia or fr for France.

When you specify a domain name, a server translates the domain name into its associated IP address so data can be routed to the correct computer. This server is an Internet server that usually is associated with an Internet access provider.

EXAMPLES OF TOP-LEVEL DOMAINS

Original Top-Level Domains	Type of Domain
com	Commercial organizations, businesses, and companies
edu	Educational institutions
gov	Goverment agencies
mil	Military organizations
net	Network provider
org	Nonprofit organizations
Newer Top-Level Domains	**Type of Domain**
museum	Accredited museums
biz	Businesses of all sizes
info	Businesses, organizations, or individuals providing general information
name	Individuals or families
pro	Certified professionals such as doctors, lawyers, and accountants
aero	Aviation community members
coop	Business cooperatives such as credit unions and rural electric co-ops
Proposed Top-Level Domains	**Type of Domain**
asia	Businesses that originate in Asian countries
cat	Catalan cultural community
jobs	Employment or human resource businesses
mail	Registries to control spam (Internet junk mail)
mobi	Delivery and management of mobile Internet services
post	Postal service
tel	Internet communications
travel	Travel industry
xxx	Adult content

FIGURE 2-4 With the dramatic growth of the Internet during the last few years, seven new top-level domains recently have been adopted an nine additional domains are being evaluated

Test your knowledge of pages 38 through 42 in Quiz Yourself 2-1

QUIZ YOURSELF 2-1

Instructions: Find the true statement below. Then rewrite the remaining false statement so they are true.

1. An access provider is a business that provides individuals and companies access to the Internet free or for a fee.

2. A WISP is a number that uniquely identifies each computer or device connected to the Internet.

3. An IP address, such as www.google.com, is the text version of a domain name.

4. Dial-up access takes place when the modem in your computer uses the cable television network to connect to the Internet.

Quiz Yourself Online: To further test your knowledge of computer literacy, visit www.clarkepublish.com or visit the Internet and then search www.google.com for more information.

THE WORLD WIDE WEB

The **World Wide Web (WWW)**, or **Web**, a widely used service on the Internet, consists of a worldwide collection of electronic documents. Each electronic document on the Web, called **Web pages,** can contain text, graphics, audio (sound), and video. Additionally, Web pages usually have built-in connections to other documents. A **Web site** is a collection of related Web pages and associated items, such as documents and pictures that are stored on a Web server. A **Web server** is a computer that delivers requested Web pages to your computer.

Browsing the Web

A **Web browser** or a **browser's** application software allows users to access and view Web pages. To browse the Web, you need a computer that is connected to the Internet and that has a Web browser. The most widely used Web browsers for personal computers are Internet Explorer, Netscape, Mozilla, Firefox, Opera, and Safari. With an Internet connection established, you can start a Web browsing. The browser retrieves and displays a starting Web page, sometimes called the browser's home page. Figure 2-5 shows how a Web browser displays a home page.

The more common usage of the term, **home page,** refers to the first page that a Web site displays. Similar to a book cover or a table of contents for a Web site, the home page provides information about the Web purpose and content. Often it provides connection to other documents, Web pages or Web sites which can be downloaded to a computer or to a mobile device. **Downloading** is the process of a computer receiving information, such as a Web page, from a server on the Internet. Depending on the speed of your Internet connection and the amount of graphics involved, a Web page download can take a few seconds to several minutes.

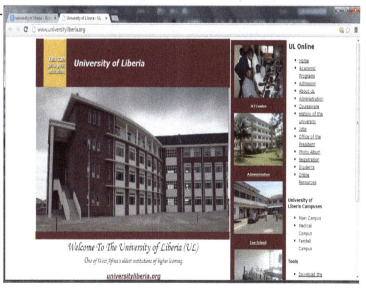

FIGURE 2-5 Home page of the University of Liberia. Does your school have a Web site? What is the address or URL?

FIGURE 2-5b HOW THE WEB BROWSER DISPLAYS A HOME PAGE

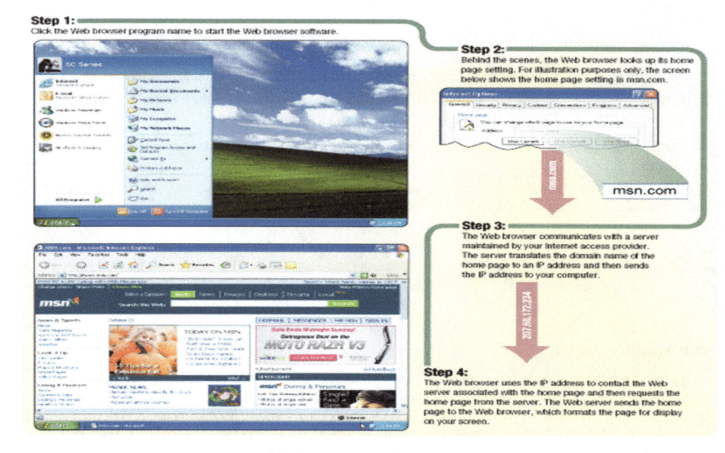

Web Addresses

A Web page has a unique address, which is called a **URL** (Uniform Resource Locator) or **Web address**. For example, the home page for the Liberian government Executive Mansion has a Web address of http://www.moe.gov.lr. A Web browser retrieves a Web page using its Web address. If you know the Web address of a Web page, you can type it in the Address box at the top of the browser window. If you type the Web address http://www.clarkepublish.com/meet.html in the Address box, and then press the ENTER key, the browser downloads and displays the Web page show in Figure 2.6.

A Web address consists of a protocol, domain name, and sometimes the path to a specific Web page or location on a Web page. Many Web page addresses begin with http://. The **http**, which stands for Hypertext Transfer Protocol, is a set of rules that defines how pages transfer on the Internet. The first portion of the domain name identifies the type of Internet server. For example, www indicates a Web server.

How many Web pages does the average user visit in a month?

More than one thousand? This and other interesting average Web usage statistics are in the table below. For more info, visit www.clarkepublish.com.

Web pages visited per month	1,036 pages
Web page visited per Internet session	34 pages
Time spent surfing per Internet session	51 minutes
Time spent viewing a single Web page	46 seconds

Source: The ClickZ Network

To help minimize errors, most browsers and Web sites do not require the http:// and www portion of the Web address. For example, typing clarkepublish.com/about.html, instead of the entire address, still accesses the Web site.

When you enter the Web address, http://www.clarkepublish.com/about.html in the Web browser, it sends a request to the Web server that contains the clarkepublish.com Web site. The server then retrieves the Web page name about.html and delivers it to your Web browser, which then displays the Web page on the screen. Protocol domain name and Web page name **http://clarkepublish.com/about.html** (the site below has been updated).

FIGURE 2-6 After entering the Web address http://www.clarkepublish.com in the Address box, this Web page at the author's Web site is displayed. Please note that the contents of this page has long been updated.

Navigating Web pages

Most Web pages contain links. A **link**, short for **hyperlink**, is a built-in connection to another related Web page or part of a Web page. Links allow you to obtain information in a nonlinear way. That is, instead of accessing topics in a specified order, you moved directly to the topic of interest. Branching from one related topic to another in a nonlinear fashion is what makes links so powerful. Some people use the phrase, **surfing the Web**, to refer to the activity of using links to explore the Web.

On the Web, a link can be text or an image. Text links may be underlined and/or displayed in a color different from other text on the Web page. Pointing or positioning to the pointer on, a link on the screen typically changes the shape of the pointer to a small hand with a pointing index finger. The Web page shown in Figure 2-7 contains a variety of link types, with the pointer on one of each of the links.

Each link on a Web page corresponds to another Web address. To activate a link, just **click** it, meaning point to the link with the mouse or a pointing device and then press the left mouse button. Clicking a link causes the Web page associated with the link to be displayed on the screen. The linked object might be on the same Web page, a different Web page at the same Web site, or a separate Web page at a different Web site in another city or country. Read Looking Ahead 2-1 for a look at the next generation of Web surfing.

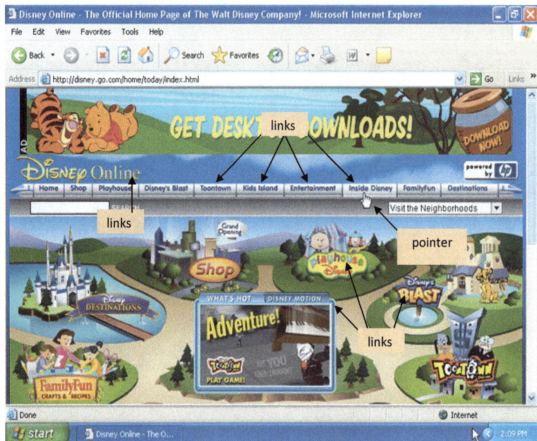

FIGURE 2-7 This Web page contains various types of links: text that is underlined, text in a different color, and images.

Looking Ahead 2-1

Internet Speed into the Future

The Internet of the future will be much larger and faster. According to some Internet experts, in the next 20 years, Web surfers will be able to browse more than 205 million Web sites. This increase in volume will be based, in part, on Internet2. This not-for-profit project connects more than 206 educational and 60 research institutions via a high-speed private network. When used solely as a research tool, Internet2 applications process massive amounts of data, such as linking observatories with Hawaii's tallest mountains and videoconferences from 20 remote sites across the world. Recently, the recording industry charged scores of college students with copyright infringement for trading millions of copyrighted songs through Internet2 privileged access. For more info, visit the book's Web site and then click Internet2.

Searching for Information on the Web

The Web is a global resource of information. One primary use of the Web is to research for specific information, including text, graphics, audio, and video. The first step in successful searching is to identify the main idea or concept in the topic about which you are seeking information. Determine any synonyms, alternate spellings, or variant word forms for the topic. Then, use a search tool to locate the information.

The two most commonly used search tools are subject directories and search engines. A **subject directory** classifies Web pages in an organized set of categories, such as sports or shopping, and related subcategories. A **search engine** is a program that finds Web sites and Web pages. Some Web sites offer the functionality of both a subject directory and a search engine. Yahoo! Bing, and Google, for example, are widely used search engines that also provide subject directories. To use Yahoo! Bing, or Google, you enter the Web address (yahoo.com, msn.com or google.com) in the address box of the browser window. The table in Figure 2-8 lists the Web addresses of several popular general-purpose subject directories and search engines. Many people in Liberia preferred Google as their search engine for its huge databases that give out many search results on a single topic.

WIDELY USED SEARCH TOOLS

Search Tool	Web Address	Subject Directory	Search Engine
A9.com	a9.com		X
AlltheWeb	alltheweb.com		X
Alta Vista	altavista.com	X	X
AOL Search	search.aol.com		X
Ask Jeeves	ask.com	X	X
Dogpile	dogpile.com		X
Excite	excite.com	X	X
Gigablast	gigablast.com	X	X
Google	google.com	X	X
HotBot	hotbot.com		X
LookSmart	looksmart.com	X	X
Lycos	lycos.com	X	X
MSN Search	search.msn.com	X	X
Netscape Search	search.netscape.com	X	X
Open Directory Project	dmoz.org	X	X
Overture	overture.com		X
Teoma	teoma.com		X
WebCrawler	webcrawler.com		X
Yahoo!	yahoo.com	X	X

FIGURE 2-8 Popular subject directories and search engines.

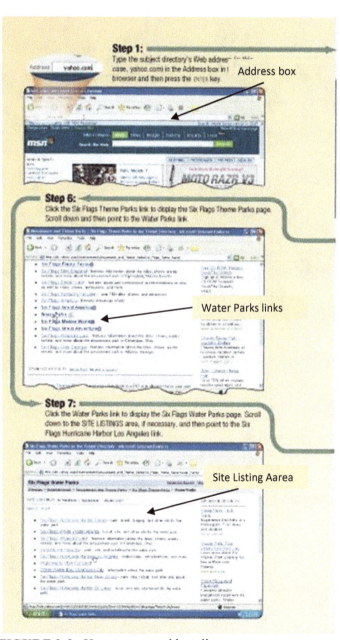

FIGURE 2-9a How to use a subject directory.

Subject Directories

A **subject directory** provides categorized list of links arranged by subject. Using this search tool, you can locate a popular topic by clicking links through different levels, moving from the general to the specific. Figure 2-9a and 9b on the previous page, shows how to use Yahoo's subject directory to search for information about Six Flags Hurricane Harbors Los Angeles. You can even search on the Noway Camp Mudslide that occurred in Bomi County in Western Liberia back in the 1980s. Using one of the subject directories in your favorite Search engine, try searching for resources on the West Africa Examination Council, WAEC tests so as to start preparing for your exam.

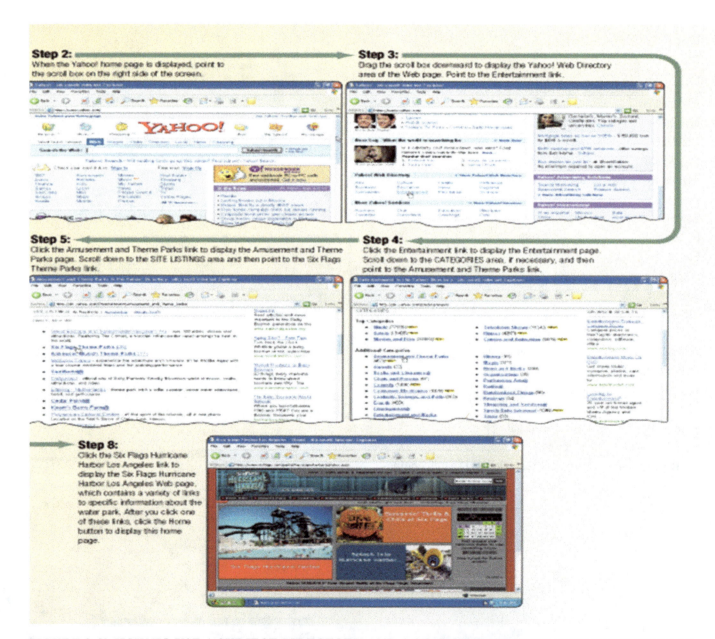

FIGURE 2-8b HOW TO USE A SUBJECT DIRECTORY AND A SEARCH ENGINE TO FIND INFORMATION

SEARCH ENGINE

A search engine is particularly helpful in locating Web pages about certain topics or in locating specific Web pages for which you do not know the exact Web address. Instead of clicking through links, search engines require that you enter a word or phrase, called **search text,** which defines the item about which you want information. Figure 2-10 shows how to use the Google search engine to search for the phrase, Six Flags Hurricane Harbor Los Angeles coupons.

The results shown in step 3 include about 90,000 links to Web pages, called hits that reference Six Flags Hurricane Harbor Los Angeles coupons. Each hit in the list has a link that, when clicked, displays an associated Web site or Web page. Most search engines sequence the hits based on how close the words in the search text are to one another in the Web page titles and their descriptions. Thus, the first links probably contain more relevant information.

FIGURE 2-10 HOW TO USE A SEARCH ENGINE

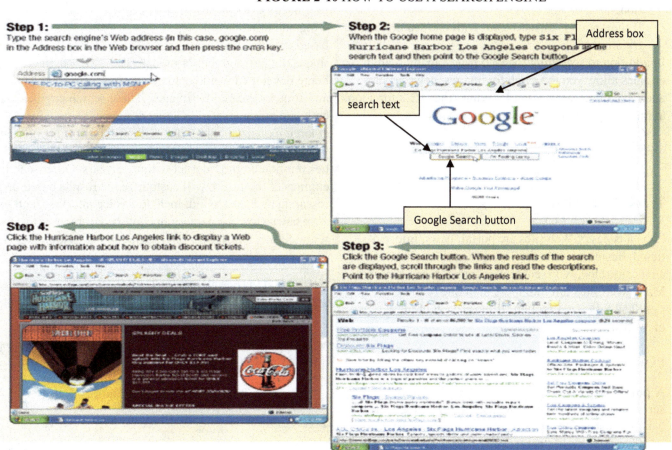

A search engine is very vital to surfing and finding information on the Internet. Google, the leading search engine worldwide, was founded in 1998 by Stanford University graduate students Larry Page and Sergei Brin. While at Stanford in 1996, Page and Brin began developing a search engine they eventually entitled BackRub. This search engine was designed to look at the connecting links between web pages in order to determine a site's authority. In 1998, Page and Brin set up their first data center in Page's dorm.

With the encouragement of fellow Stanford alum David Filo, who started Yahoo a few years earlier, Page and Brin decided to start a company and started looking for investors to back them. Andy Bechtolsheim, one of the founders of Sun Microsystems, invested $100,000 in the company after receiving a demo of their search technology. Eventually the pair raised over $1M. Google, Inc. was established on September 7, 1998 in a friend's garage in Menlo Park, California. Page and Brin hired their first employee, Craig Silverstein, who was later to become Google's Director of Technology.

In 2000, Google replaced Yahoo's own internal search engine as the provider of supplementary search results on Yahoo. Now, with more than 50% share of the total search market, Google provides search results for numerous search engines on the web. Google has become all-important to both search engines and search engine optimization specialists alike. The other search engines have a tendency to mimic any algorithmic changes made by Google. Likewise, search engine optimization specialists continually study the changes as well in order to provide their clients with the best search engine rankings.

If you enter a phrase with spaces between the words in the search text, most search engines return links to pages that include all of the words. Techniques you can use to improve your Web searches include the following:

- Use specific nouns and put the most important terms first in the search text.
- Use the asterisk (*) to substitute characters in words. For example, retrieve* returns retrieves, retrieval, retriever, and any other variation.
- Use quotation marks to create phrases so the search engine finds the exact sequence of words.
- List all possible spellings, for example, email, e-mail.
- Before using a search engine, read its Help information.
- If the search is unsuccessful with one search engine, try another.

In addition to searching for Web pages, many search engines allow you to search for images, news articles, and local businesses. Read Looking Ahead 2-2 for a look at the next generation of searching techniques.

Types of Web Sites

Eleven types of Web sites are portal, news, informational, business/marketing, educational, entertainment, advocacy, blog, wiki, content aggregator, and personal. Many Web sites fall into more than one of these categories. The following sections discuss each of these types of Web sites.

PORTAL

A **portal** is a Web site that offers a variety of Internet services from a single convenient location (Figure 2-11a). Most portals offer the following free services: search engine and/or subject directories; news, sports and weather; free Web publishing services; reference tools such as the yellow pages, stock quotes, and maps; shopping malls and auto auctions; e-mail and other forms of online communications.

When you connect to the Internet, the first Web page that is displayed often is a portal. Popular portals include AltaVista, AOL, Excite, GO.com, HotBot, LookSmart, Lycos, MSN, NBCi, Netscape, and Yahoo!

Looking Ahead 2-2

3-D Search Engine Gets the Picture

Conventional search engines, such as Google, use words to find information. But what happens when a computer user needs to locate a wing nut or camshaft based on a particular shape, not part number or model? The 3-D search engines being developed would help people who work with patterns and contours search for images. These search engines presently are being created to assist designers and engineer's at large industrial companies with millions of inventories parts, but university researchers predict image searches will be common on the Internet within 15 years. Other search engines of the future will customize the results based on the researcher's background, include a voice interface, and use a thesaurus to keep a query in context. For more info, visit www.clarkepublish.com or Google for 3-D Search Engines.

FIGURE 2-11a (portal) and FIGURE 2-11b (news)

FIGURE 2-11b Types of Web sites. (continues on next page)

FIGURE 2-11c (informational)

FIGURE 2-11d
(business/marketing)

FIGURE 2-11e
(education)

FIGURE 2-11f
(entertainment)

FIGURE 2-11g
(avocacy)

FIGURE 2-11h
(blog)

FIGURE 2-11 Types of Web sites. (continues on next page)

INFORMATIONAL An informational Web site contains factual information (Figure 2-11c). United States government agencies have informational Web sites providing information such as census data, tax codes, and the congressional budget. Other organizations provide information such as public transportation schedules and publish research findings.

BUSINESS/MARKETING A business/marketing Web site contains content that promotes or sells products or services (Figure 2-11d). Nearly every business has a business/ marketing Web site. Many companies also allow you to purchase their products or services online.

EDUCATIONAL An educational Web site offers exciting, challenging avenues for formal and informal teaching and learning (Figure 2-11e). For a more structural learning experience, companies provide online training to employees; while some colleges offer online classes and degrees. Instructors often use the Web to enhance classroom teaching by publishing course materials, grades, and other pertinent class information.

ENTERTAINMENT An entertainment Web site offers an interactive and engaging environment (Figure 2-11f). Popular entertainment Web sites offer music, videos, sports, games, and much more.

ADVOCACY An advocacy Web site contains content that describes a cause, opinion, or idea (Figure 2-11g). The purpose of an advocacy Web site is to convince the reader of the validity of the cause, opinion or idea. These Web sites usually present views of a particular group.

BLOG A blog, short for Weblog, is an informal Web site consisting of time-stamped articles, or posts in a diary or journal format, usually listed in reverse chronological order (Figure 2-11h). Blogs reflect the interests of the author and visitors. Read Discussion 2-1.

DISCUSSION 2-1

Smart Phone Photos -- an Invasion of One's Privacy or Public Service?

Camera-equipped smart phones are popular – at least 100 million were sold last year. A growing number of people use these phones to create online albums, called mobile Web blogs or moblogs, to share their visions of the world with thousands of people. Some smart phone cameras have been banned from health club locker rooms, movie screenings, and corporate offices. In the United States, Congress is even considering barring covert cameras from places where people should be able to expect some privacy. But, even in public, smart phone paparazzi photograph (unaware) people in private at emotional times. The subjects of these pictures often object to living in a fishbowl, where even personal moments can be captured and posted on the Web. Recognizing this, some Web sites that monitor moblogs refuse to show certain photos or encourage photographers to obtain permission from the photo subjects. On the other hand, in the interest of public awareness, mass-media outlets actively solicit smart phone pictures taken and using them as news- worthy events. What, if anything, should be done to protect personal privacy? Should laws be enacted to regulate smart phone photographers? Why? Must we accept that, outside of our homes, private moments no longer exist? Is it ethical for the news media to solicit smart phone pictures of newsworthy events?

WIKI   A **wiki** is a collaborative Web site that allows users to add to, modify, or delete the Web site content via their Web browser. Most wikis are open to modification by the general public. Wikis usually collect recent edits on a Web page so someone can review them for accuracy. The difference between a wiki and a blog is that users cannot modify original post made by the blogger. A popular wiki is Wikipedia, a free Web encyclopedia (Figure 2-11i).

CONTENT AGGREGATOR   A **content aggregator** is a business that gathers and organizes Web content and then distributes, or feeds, the content to subscribers for free or a fee. Examples of distributed content include news, music, video, and pictures. Subscribers select content in which they are interested. Whenever this content changes, it is downloaded automatically (pushed) to the subscriber's computer or mobile device. **RSS 2.0,** which stands for Really Simple Syndication, is a specification that content aggregators use to distribute content to subscribers (Figure 2-11j).

PERSONAL   A private individual or family not usually associated with any organization may maintain a personal Web site. People who publish personal Web pages do it for a variety of reasons. Some are job hunting as others just simply want to share life experiences with the world.

FIGURE 2-11i (Wiki)

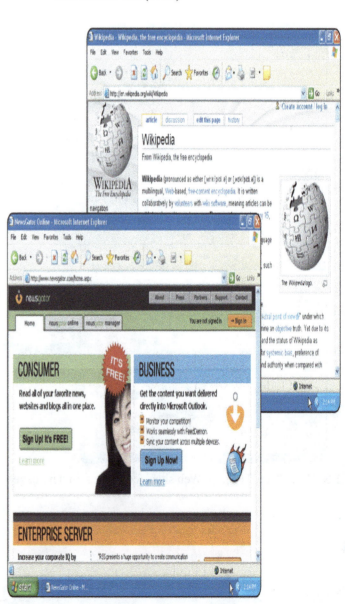

FIGURE 2-11j (content aggregator)

FIGURE 2-11 Types of Web sites. (continues on next page)

Evaluating a Web Site Do not assume that information presented on the Web is correct or accurate. Any person, company, or organization can publish a Web page on the Internet. No one oversees the contents of these Web pages. Figure 2-12 lists guidelines for assessing the value of a Web site or Web page before relying on its contents.

Multimedia on the Web Most Web pages include more than just a formatted text and links. The more exciting Web pages use multimedia. Multimedia refers to any application that combines text with graphics, animation, audio, and/ or virtual reality. This section discusses how the Web use these multimedia elements.

GRAPHICS

A **graphic**, or graphical image, is a digital representation of non-text information such as a drawing, chart, or photograph. Many Web pages use colorful graphical designs and images to convey messages (Figure 2-13).

Of the graphics formats that exist on the Web, the two most common ones are JPEG AND GIF formats. JPEG (pronounced JAY-peg) is a format that compresses graphics to reduce their file size, which means that the file will take up less storage space. The goal with JPEG graphics is to reach a balance between the image quality and file size. GIF format (pronounced jiff) graphics also use compression techniques to reduce file sizes. The GIF format works best for images that have only a few distinct colors. Some Web sites use thumbnails on their pages because graphics can be time-consuming to display. A **thumbnail** is a small version of a larger graphic. You usually can click a thumbnail to display the larger image.

GUIDELINES FOR EVALUATING THE VALUE OF A WEB SITE

Evaluation Criteria	Reliable Web Sites
Affiliation	A reputable institution should support the Web site without bias in the information.
Audience	The Web site should be written at an appropriate level.
Authority	The Web site should list the author and the appropriate credentials.
Content	The Web site should be well organized and the links should work.
Currency	The information on the Web page should be current.
Design	The pages at the Web site should download quickly and be visually pleasing and easy to navigate.
Objectivity	The Web site should contain little advertising and be free of preconceptions.

FIGURE 2-12 Criteria for evaluating a Web site.

FIGURE 2-14 Criteria for evaluating a Web site.

ANIMATION

Many Web pages use animation, in which is the appearance of motion created by displaying a series of still images in a sequence. Animation can make Web pages more visually interesting and draw attention to the more important information or links.

AUDIO

On the Web, you can listen to clips and live audio. Audio includes music, speech, and other types of sound. Simple applications on the Web consist of individual audio files available for downloading to a computer. Once the downloading process has finished you can play (listen to) the contents of these files. Audio files are also compressed to reduce their file sizes. For example, MP3 format reduces an audio file to about one-tenth of its original size, while preserving much of the original quality of the sound.

Some music publishers have Web sites that allow a user to download sample tracks free to persuade them to buy the entire CD. Other Web sites allow a user to purchase and download the entire music CD to the hard drive (see Figure 2-14 on the next page). Keep in mind that it is legal to download copyrighted music only if the song's copyright holder has granted permission for users to download and play a song.

To listen to an audio file on your computer, you will need special software called a **player**. Most current operating systems contain a player. Popular players include iTune, RealOne Player, and Windows Media Player. Some applications on the Web use streaming audio. **Streaming** is the process of transferring data in a continuous and even flow. Streaming allows users to access and use a file while it is transmitting. For example, streaming audio enables you to listen to music as it downloads to your computer.

Podcasting is another popular method of distributing audio. A **podcast** is recorded audio, usually an MP3 file, stored on a Web site that can be downloaded to a computer or a portable digital audio player such as an iPod. An example of podcast includes music, radio shows, news stories, classroom lectures, political messages, and television commentaries. Podcasters register their podcasts with content aggregators. Subscribers select podcast feeds as they want to be downloaded automatically whenever they connect to the Internet.

Step 1:
Display the music Web site on the screen. Search for, select, and pay for the music you want to purchase from the music Web site.

Step 2:
Download the music from the Web site's server to your computer's hard disk.

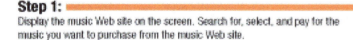

Step 3a:
Listen to the music from your computer's hard disk.

Step 3b: Download music from your computer's hard disk to a portable digital audio player. Listen to the music through headphones attached to the digital audio player.

FIGURE 2-14 HOW TO PURCHASE AND DOWNLOAD MUSIC

VIDEO

Video consists of full-motion images that are played back at various speeds. Just about all videos have accompanying audio that tags along with it. Instead of turning on the television, you can use the Internet to watch live and prerecorded coverage of your favorite programs or enjoy a live performance of your favorite vocalist.

Video files are often compressed because they are quite large in size. These clips also are quite short in length, usually less than 10 minutes, because they can take a long time to download. The Moving Picture Exchange Group (MPEG) defines a popular video compression standard, a widely used one called **MPEG-4.** As with streaming audio, streaming video allows you to view longer or live video images as they download to your computer or wireless device.

VIRTUAL REALITY

Virtual reality (VR) it is used in computer to simulate a real or imagined environment that appears as a three-dimensional (3-D) space. On the Web, VR involves the display of 3-D images that users explore and manipulate interactively. A VR site, for example, might show a room with furniture. Users walk through such a VR room by moving an input device forward, backward, or to the side.

PLUG-INS

Most Web browsers have the capability of displaying basic multimedia elements on a Web page. Sometimes, a browser might need an additional program; called a plug-in. A **plug-in** is a program that extends the capability of a browser. You can download many plug-ins at no cost from various Web sites (Figure 2-15).

POPULAR PLUG-IN APPLICATIONS

Plug-In Application	Description	Web Address
Acrobat Reader	View, navigate, and print Portable Document Format (PDF) files — documents formatted to look just as they look in print	adobe.com
Flash Player	View dazzling graphics and animation, hear outstanding sound and music, display Web pages across an entire screen	macromedia.com
QuickTime	View animation, music, audio, video, and VR panoramas and objects directly in a Web page	apple.com
RealPlayer	Listen to live and on-demand near-CD-quality audio and newscast-quality video; stream audio and video content for faster viewing; play MP3 files; create music CDs	real.com
Shockwave Player	Experience dynamic interactive multimedia, 3-D graphics, and streaming audio	macromedia.com
Windows Media Player	Listen to live and on-demand audio; play or edit WMA and MP3 files; burn CDs, watch DVD movies	microsoft.com

FIGURE 2-15 Most plug-ins can be downloaded for free from the Web.

Web Publishing

Before the World Wide Web, became a major means of sharing opinions and ideas with others, it was neither easy nor inexpensive; media was limited to classrooms, work, and social environments. Today, businesses and individuals convey information to millions of people by creating their own Web pages.

Web publishing is the development and maintenance of Web pages. To develop a Web page, one does not need to be a computer programmer. For small businesses and home users Web publishing is fairly easy as long as you have the proper tools.

The five major steps to Web publishing are as follows:

1.   Plan a Web site.
2.   Analyze and design a Web site.
3.   Create a Web site.
4.   Deploy a Web site.
5.   Maintain the Web site.

Figure 2-16 illustrates these steps with respect to a personal Web site.

FIGURE 2-16 HOW TO PUBLISH YOUR RESUME ON THE WEB.

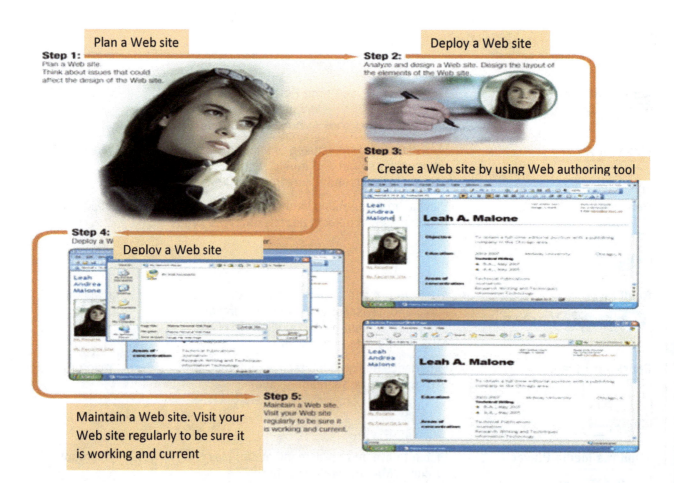

E-Commerce

E-Commerce, short for electronic commerce, is a business transaction that occurs over an electronic network such as the Internet. Anyone with access to a computer, an Internet connection, and a means to pay for purchased goods or services can participate in e-commerce. Three types of e-commerce are business-to-business (B2B), consumer-to-consumer (C2C), and business-to-consumer (B2C). Business-to-consumer (B2C) e-commerce consists of the sale of goods and services to the general public. For example, Dell has a B2C Web site. Instead of visiting a computer store to purchase a computer, customers can order one directly from Dell Web site. In the not too distance future, people in Liberia will participate in this efficient Internet trend especially with the expansion of global trade coupled with local banks issuing ATM Debit cards.

A customer (consumer) visits an online business through an **electronic storefront,** which contains product descriptions, graphics, and a shopping cart. The **shopping cart** allows the customer to collect purchases. When ready to complete the sale, the customer enters personal data and the method of payment, preferably through a secure Internet connection. Instead of purchasing from a business, consumers can purchase from each other. For example, with an **online auction,** users bid on an item being sold by someone else. The highest bidder at the end of the bidding period purchases the item. Consumer-to-consumer (C2C) e-commerce occurs when one consumer sells directly to another, such as an online auction. eBay is one of the most popular online auction Web site (Figure 2-17). Most of the e-commerce, transactions actually takes place between businesses, which is called business-to-business (B2B) e-commerce. Many businesses provide goods and services to other businesses, like online advertising, recruiting, credit, sales, market research, technical support, and training.

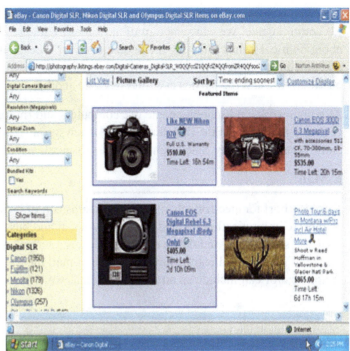

FIGURE 2-17 E-commerce activities include shopping for good at an online, such as eBay.

Test your knowledge of pages 43 through 57 in Quiz Yourself 2-2

QUIZ YOURSELF 2-2

Instructions: Find the true statement below. Then rewrite the remaining false statement so they are true.

1. A blog is a Web site that uses a Regular updated journal format to reflect the interest and opinions of the author and sometimes site visitors.

2. A Web browser classifies Web pages in an organized set of categories and related subcategories.

3. Business-to-consumer e-commerce occurs when one consumer sells directly to another, as done in on online auctions.

4. 19. The more widely used search engines for personal computers are Internet Explorer, Netscape, and Mozilla.

5. To develop a Web page, you have to be a programmer

Quiz Yourself Online: To further test your knowledge of computer literacy, visit www.clarkepublish.com or visit the Internet and then search www.google.com for more information.

OTHER INTERNET SERVICES

The Web is only one of the many services on the Internet. The Web and other Internet services have changed the ways we communicate. We can send e-mail messages to the president or legislaturesof Liberia, have discussions with experts about political issues affecting the people of River Gee County, chat with someone in another country about genealogy, and talk about homework with classmates via Facebook. Many times, these communications take place completely in writing – without the parties ever meeting one another.

At home, work, and school, people use computers and Internet-enabled mobile devices so they always have instant access to e-mail, FTP (File Transfer Protocol), newsgroups, message boards, mailing lists, chat rooms, instant messaging, and Internet telephony. The following pages discuss each of these Internet services.

E-Mail

E-mail (short for electronic mail) is the transmission of messages and files via a computer network. Today, e-mail is a primary communication method for both personal and business use. You use an **e-mail program** to create, send, receive, forward, store, print, and delete e-mail messages. Outlook and Outlook Express are two popular e-mail programs. The steps in Figure 2-18 illustrate how to send an e-mail message using Outlook as your e-mail client. The message can be simple text or can include an attachment such as word processing document, a graphic, an audio clip, or a video clip.

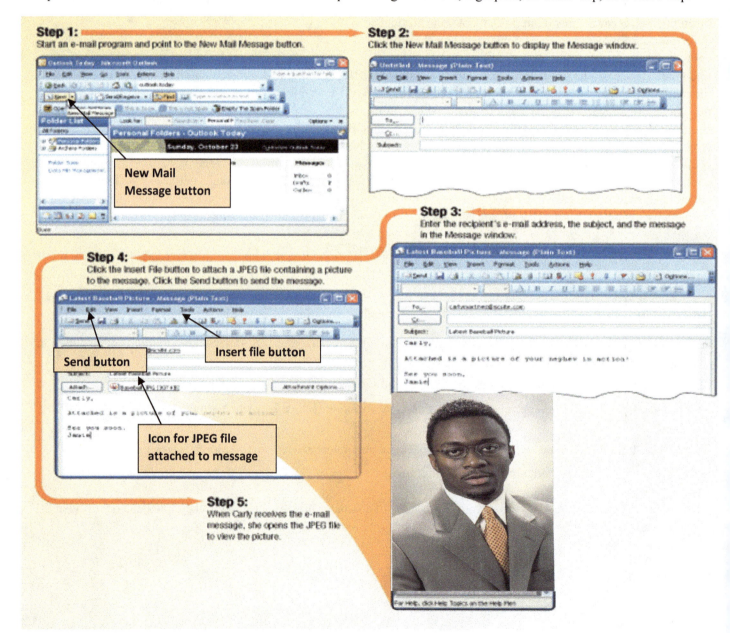

FIGURE 2-18 HOW TO SEND AN E-MAIL MESSAGE

Internet access providers typically supply an e-mail program as a standard part of their Internet access services. To use these Web-based e-mail programs, you connect to the Web site and set up an e-mail account, which typically includes an e-mail address and a password. Just as you address a letter when using the postal system, you must address an e-mail message with the e-mail address of your intended recipient. Likewise, when someone sends you a message, they must have your e-mail address. An **e-mail address** is a combination of a user name and a domain name that identifies a user so he or she can receive Internet e-mail (Figure 2-19).

info@clarkepublish.com

FIGURE 2-19 An e-mail address is a combination of a user Name and a domain name.

A **user name** is a unique combination of characters, such as letters of the alphabet and/or numbers that identifies a specific user. In an Internet e-mail address, an @ (pronounced at) symbol separates the user name from the domain name. Your service provider supplies the domain. Using the example in Figure 2-19, a possible e-mail address for author@ emmanuelclarke.com, which would be read as follows: info at Clarke Publish dot com. Most e-mail programs allow you to create an **address book,** which contains a list of names and e-mail addresses.

When you send an e-mail message, an outgoing mail server that is operated by your Internet access provider determines how to route the message through the Internet and then sends the message. As you receive e-mail messages, an incoming mail server – also operated by your Internet access provider – holds the messages in your mailbox until you use your e-mail program to retrieve them. Most e-mail programs have a mail notification alert that informs you via a message or sound when you receive a new mail. Figure 2-20 illustrates how an e-mail message may travel from sender to a receiver.

FAQ 2-3

Can My Computer Get Virus Through E-mail?

Yes. A virus is a computer program that can damage files and the operating system. One way that virus authors attempt to spread a virus is by sending virus-infected e-mail attachments. If you receive an e-mail attachment, you should use an antivirus program to verify that it is virus free. For more information, visit the book's Web site and the click Viruses. For more info, visit www. clarkepublish.com.

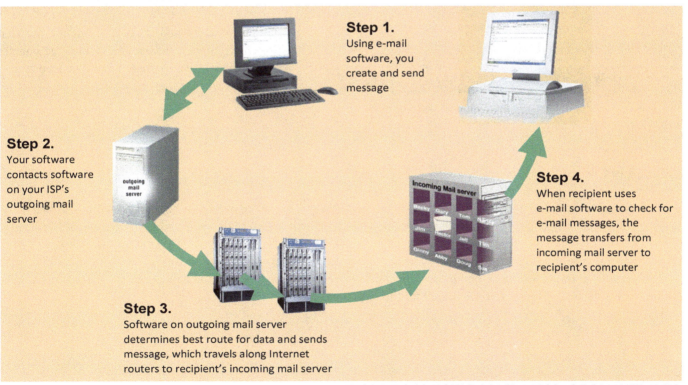

Step 1. Using e-mail software, you create and send message

Step 2. Your software contacts software on your ISP's outgoing mail server

Step 3. Software on outgoing mail server determines best route for data and sends message, which travels along Internet routers to recipient's incoming mail server

Step 4. When recipient uses e-mail software to check for e-mail messages, the message transfers from incoming mail server to recipient's computer

FIGURE 2-20 HOW E-MAIL MESSAGE MAY TRAVEL FROM SENDER TO A RECEIVER

FTP

FTP (File Transfer Protocol) is an Internet standard that permits the process of file uploading and downloading (transferring) with other computers on the Internet. **Uploading** is the opposite of downloading: in which uploading is the process of transferring documents, graphics, and other objects from your computer to a server on the Internet.

Many operating systems include FTP capabilities. An FTP site is a collection of files including text, graphics, audio clips, video clips, and program files that reside on an FTP server. Many FTP sites have anonymous FTP, whereby anyone can transfer some, if not all, available files. Some FTP sites restrict file transfers to those who have authorized accounts (user names and passwords) on the FTP server.

Newsgroups and Message Boards

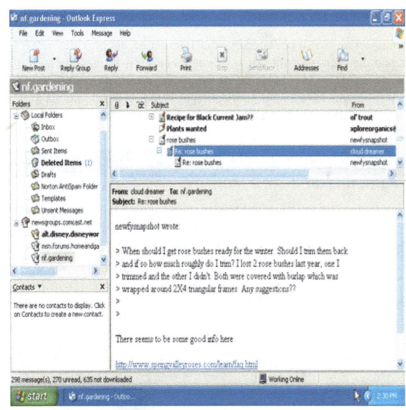

A **newsgroup** is an online area in which many users have written discussions about a particular subject (Figure 2-21). To participate in a discussion, a user sends a message to the newsgroup, for other users in the newsgroup to read and reply to the message. Some major topic areas include news, recreation, society, business, science, and computers.

Some newsgroups require you to enter a user name and password to participate in the discussions. Only authorized members can use this type of newsgroup. For example, a newsgroup for students taking a college course may require a user name and password to access the newsgroup. This ensures that only students in the course participate in the discussion. To participate in a newsgroup, typically you use a program called a newsreader.

A popular Web-based type of discussion group that does not require a newsreader is a **message board**. Many Web sites use message boards instead of a newsgroup because they are easier to use.

FIGURE 2-21 Users in a newsgroup read and reply to other users' Messages.

Mailing Lists

A **Mailing** list is a group of e-mail names and addresses given a one word names. When a message is sent to a mailing list, everyone on the list receives a copy of the message in his or her own mailbox. To add your e-mail and address to a mailing list, you will have to be a **subscriber** on that company's Web site mailing list. To remove your name, you will have to **unsubscribe** from the company' Web site mailing list. Thousands of mailing lists exist about a variety of topics in areas of entertainment, business, computers, society, culture, health, recreation, and education. To locate a mailing list dealing with a particular topic, you can search for the text mailing list, in a search engine.

Chat Rooms

A **chat** is a real-time typed conversation that takes place on a computer. **Real time** means that you and other people with whom you are conversing with are all online at the same time, like as if you all were on the phone together. A **chat room** is a location on an Internet server that permits users to chat with each other. Anyone in the chat room can participate in the conversation, which usually is specific to a particular topic.

As you are typing from your keyboard, a line of characters and symbols will display onto the computer screen. Others connected to the same chat server will also see what you are typing (Figure 2-22). Some chat rooms support voice and video chat, in which people will hear and/or see what each other are typing as they chat.

To start a chat session, you connect to a chat server through a program called a chat client. Today's browsers usually include a chat client. If your does not, you can download a chat client from the Web. Once you have installed a chat client, you can create or join a conversation on the chat server to which you are connected.

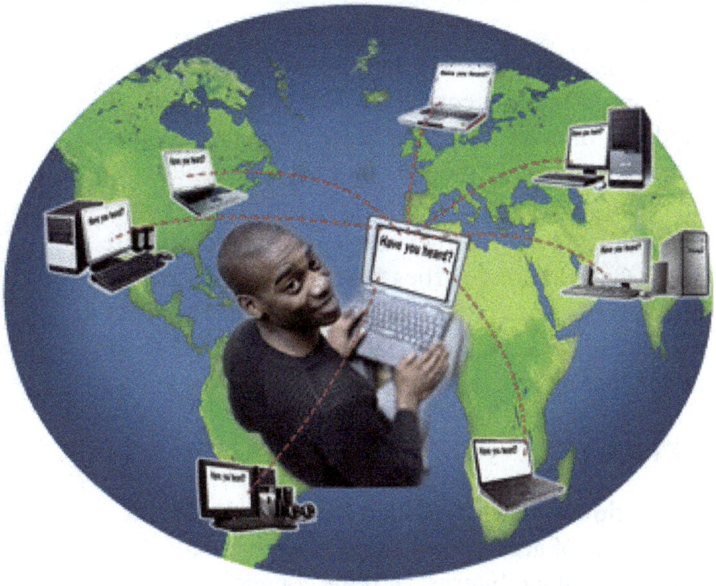

FIGURE 2-22 As you type, the words and symbols you enter are displayed onto the computer screens of other people in the chat room.

Instant Messaging

Instant messaging (IM) is a real-time Internet communications service that notifies you when one or more people are online and then allows you to exchange messages and files or join a private chat room with them (Figure 2-22). Some IM services support voice and video conversations. For IM to work, both parties must be online at the same time. Also, the receiver of a message must be willing to accept messages.

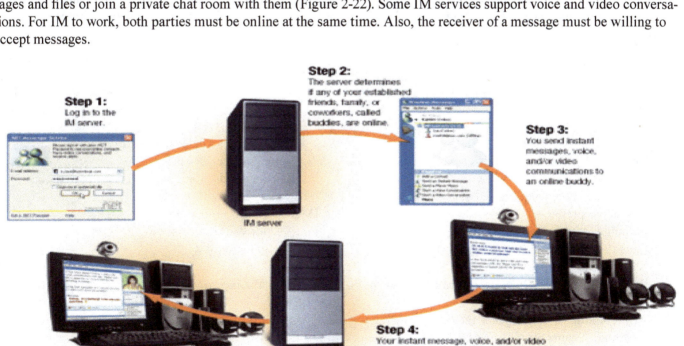

Step 1:
Log in to the IM server.

Step 2:
The server determines if any of your established friends, family, or coworkers, called buddies, are online.

Step 3:
You send instant messages, voice, and/or video communications to an online buddy.

Step 4:
Your instant message, voice, and/or video travels through a messaging server and then to the online buddy's computer.

Step 5:
Your online buddy replies.

IM server

messaging server

FIGURE 2-23 AN EXAMPLE OF AN INSTANT MESSAGE.

To use IM, you must install the instant messenger software onto your computer or device, (such as a smart phone) you're planning to use. Some operating systems, such as Windows Vista and XP, include an instant messenger. There are no standards currently exist for IM. To ensure successful communications all individuals on the contact list need to use the same or compatible instant messenger.

Internet Telephony

Internet Telephony also called **Voice over IP** (Internet Protocol), enables users to speak to other users over the Internet (instead of the public switched telephone network) using their desktop computer, mobile computer, or mobile device.

To place an Internet telephone call, you need a high-speed Internet connection (e.g., via cable or DSL modem); Internet telephone service; a microphone or telephone, depending on the Internet telephone service; and Internet telephone software or a telephone adapter, depending on the Internet telephone provider (Figure 2-24). Calls to other parties with the same Internet telephone service are often free, while calls that connect to the telephone network typically range from $13 to $15 dollars per month.

FIGURE 2-24 Equipment configuration for a user making a call via Internet telephony.

NETIQUETTE

Netiquette, which is short for Internet etiquette, is the code of acceptable behaviors users should follow while on the Internet; it is the conduct expected of individuals while online. Netiquette includes rules for all aspects of the Internet, including the World Wide Web, e-mail, FTP, newsgroup, message boards, chat rooms, and instant messaging. Figure 2-25 outlines some of the rules of netiquette.

NETIQUETTE
Golden Rule: Treat others, as you would like them to treat you. 1. In e-mail, newsgroups, and chat room • Keep messages brief. Use proper grammar, spelling, and punctuation. • Be careful when using sarcasm and humor, as it might be misinterpreted. • Be polite. Avoid offensive language. • Read the messages before you send it. • Avoid sending or posting flames, which are abusive or insulting messages. Do not participate in flame wars, which are exchanges of flames. • Avoid sending spam, which is the Internet version of junk mail. Spam is an unsolicited e-mail message or newsgroup posting sent to many recipients or newsgroups at once.	• Do not use all capital letters, which is like SHOUTING! • Use **emoticons** to express emotion: Examples, :) Smile :\ Undecided :| Indifference :(Frown :o Surprise • Use abbreviations and acronyms for phrases: BTW by the way IMHO in my humble opinion FYI for your information TTFN tat a for now FWIW for what it's worth TYVM thank you very much • Clearly identify a spoiler, which is a message that reveals a solution to a game or its ending. 2. Read the FAQ, if it exits. 3. Do not assume material is accurate. 4. Never read someone else's private e-mail

Test your knowledge of pages 58 through 62 in Quiz Yourself 2-3

QUIZ YOURSELF 2-3

Instructions: Find the true statement below. Then rewrite the remaining false statement so they are true.

1. A chat room is a location on an Internet server that permits users to chat with each other.

2. An e-mail address is a combination of a user name and an e-mail program that identifies a user so that he or she can receive Internet e-mail.

3. FTP uses the Internet (instead of the public switched telephone network) to connect a calling party to one or more called parties.

4. Netiquette is the code of unacceptable behaviors while on the Internet.

5. In a newsgroup, subscription consist of the original article and all subsequent related replies.

Quiz Yourself Online: To further test your knowledge of computer literacy, visit www.clarkepublish.com or visit the Internet and then search www.google.com for more information.

CHAPTER SUMMARY

This chapter presented the history and structure of the Internet. It discussed the World Wide Web in length, including topics such as browsing, navigating, searching, Web publishing, and e-commerce (read Discussion 2-2 for related discussion). It also introduced other services available on the Internet, such as e-mail, FTP, newsgroups, message boards, chat rooms, instant messaging, and Internet telephony. As the chapter narrowed down, it gave you a list of netiquette rules to follow when messaging to others, while on the Internet.

DISCUSSION 2-2

Should Companies Be Able to Track You Online Habits?

When you visit Web sites that include advertisements, someone probably is recording the fact that you visited that Web site and viewed the advertisement with your browser. Over time, companies that specialize in tracking who Views which online advertisements can a mass an enormous amount of information about your online Web surfing habits. This collection of information is considered to be part of your online profile. One company claims that through the use of advertisements on Web pages, it can track well over one billion Web page views per day. Through tracking the Web sites a user visits, the products they buy, and the articles they read, a company may attempt to profile the visitor's beliefs, associations, and habits. Although a user may think he or she is anonymous while navigating the Web, the company can attempt through various means to link the user's true identity with the user's online profile. The company can sell online profiles, with or without the user's true identity, to other advertisers or organizations. Should organizations be allowed to track your Web surfing habits? Why or why not? Should organizations be allowed to associate your real identity with your online identity and profit from the information? Should companies give you the option of not being tracked? What are the benefits and dangers of online tracking?

Web Developer

If you are looking for a job working with the latest Internet Technology, then Web Developer could be the career for you. A Web developer analyzes, designs, develops, implements, and supports Web Applications and functionality. Special programming skills required include HTML, JavaScript, Java, Perl, C++, PHP, Cold-fusion, and VBScript. Education requirements vary from company to company and can range from high school to four-year degree. A wide range of salary exists – from $35,000 to $70,000 dollars, depending on the educational background. This salary may not be the same for Web developers in Liberia or other countries. For more information visit the www.google.com.

COMPANIES ON THE CUTTING EDGE

Google

Popular Search Engine

The founders of Google, the leading Internet Search engine, state that their mission is to organize the world's information. Every day their Web site handles hundreds of millions of queries for information. In seconds, it can locate specific phrases and terms on four billion Web pages by using more than 10,000 connected computers.

Sergey Brin and Larry Page launched Google in 1998 in a friend's garage. The name is derived from "googol," which is the name of the number 1 followed by 100 zeros. Nearly 4,200 employees worldwide are employed for the Mountain View, California Corporation. In 2005, the company expanded its multi-lingual search capabilities, by partnering with the most-visited Spanish language Web site, Unvision.com. For more info, visit www.clarkepublish.com or www.google.com.

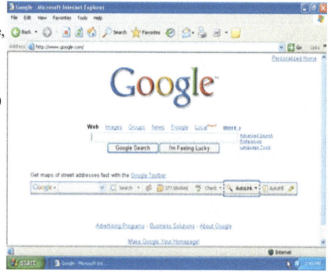

Yahoo!

Popular Web Portal

Yahoo! the first navigational portal to the Web, began as a hobby for Jerry Yang and David Filo when they were doctoral candidates in electrical engineering at Stanford University. They started creating and organization lists of their favorite Web sites in 1994. The following year, they shared their creativity Yahoo!, with fellow students and then released their product to the Internet community. Yahoo! Is an acronym, for Yet Another Hierarchical Officious Oracle. What makes Yahoo! so unique is the staff members that built the directory by assuming the role of a typical Web researcher. Yahoo! is recognized for its breadth of features; in 2005, it added an audio search service that lets users preview an individual song or artist with 16 different services and a job search engine located at HotJobs.com. For more information, visit www.clarkepublish.com or www.google.com.

Tim Berners-Lee

Create of the World Wide Web

The World Wide Web (WWW) has become one of the widely used Internet services, and its roots are based from Tim Berners-Lee's work. Berners-Lee is credited with creating the first Web server, browser, and URL addresses. He developed his ideas in 1989 while working at CERN, the European Particle Physics Laboratory in Geneva, Switzerland, and based his work on a program he had written for his own use to track random associations. Today, he works quietly in academia as director of the World Wide Web Consortium (W3C) at the Massachusetts Institute of Technology. In 2005, Berners-Lee told the British Broadcasting Corporation (BBC) that he is please to see that blogging is becoming a creative medium that resembles his original idea of the World Wide Web. For more info, visit the book's Web site and then click Tim Berners-Lee.

John J. Donahoe

eBay President and CEO

John J. Donahoe has been a director of Intel since 2009 and President and CEO of eBay Inc., a global online marketplace in San Jose, California, since 2008. Mr. Donahoe joined eBay in 2005 as President of eBay Marketplaces, and was responsible for eBay's global e-commerce businesses. In this role, he focused on expanding eBay's core business, which accounts for a large percentage of the company's revenue. Prior to joining eBay, Mr. Donahoe was the Worldwide Managing Director from 2000 to 2005 for Bain & Company, a global management consulting firm based in Boston, Massachusetts, where he oversaw Bain's 30 offices and 3,000 employees. More than 250 million people worldwide were part of the eBay community in 2012, and Donahoe is looking to expand the marketplace, especially in China. he predicts the number of Chinese users will surpass the number of American users by 2015. For more info, visit www.clarkepublish.com or www.google.com.

Chapter Review

This Chapter Review section summarizes the concepts presented in this chapter. To obtain help from other students regarding any subject in this chapter, visit the book's Web site.

1. **How Cay You Access and Connect to the Internet?**

   The **Internet** is a worldwide collection of networks that links millions of businesses, government agencies, educational institutions, and individuals. Employees and students often connect to the Internet through a business or school network. Some home and small businesses connect to the Internet with **dial-up access**, which uses a modem in the computer and a standard telephone line. Many home and small business users opt for higher-speed connections, such as DSL, cable television, radio signal, or satellite. **DSL** provides higher-speed Internet connections using regular copper telephone lines. A **cable modem** allows access to high-speed Internet service through the cable television network. **Fixed wireless** high-speed Internet connections use a dish-shaped antenna to communicate via radio signals. A **satellite modem** communicates with a satellite dish to provide high-speed Internet connections. An **access provider** is a business that provides access to the Internet free or for a fee. An **ISP (Internet service provid-**

er) is a regional or national access provider. An **online service provider (OSP)** provides Internet access in addition to members-only features. A **wireless Internet service provider (WISP)** provides wireless Internet access to users with wireless modem or Internet-enabled mobile computer or devices.

2. **How Can You View a Web Page and Search for Information on the Web?**

A **Web browser**, or **browser**, is an application software that allows users to access and view Web pages. When you type a Web address in the Address box of a browser window, web page link called a **Web server** delivers the requested Web page to your computer. Most Web pages contain links. A **link** is a built-in connection that, when clicked, display related Web pages or part of a Web page. Two commonly used search tools are subject directories and search engine. A **subject directory** classifies Web pages in an organized set of categories. A **search engine** finds Web sites and Web pages related to a word phrase, called search text that defines items about the information you were searching for.

3. **What Are the Types of Web Sites?**

A **portal** is a Web site that offers a variety of Internet from a single location. A news Web site contains newsworthy material. An informational Web site contains factual information. A business/marketing Web site promotes or sells products or services. An educational Web site offers avenues for teaching and learning. An advocacy Web site describes a cause, opinion, or idea. A **blog** is an informal Web site consisting of time-stamped articles, or posts, in a diary or journal format, usually listed in reverse chronological order. A **wiki** is a collaborative Web site that allows users to add to modify, or delete the Web site content via Web browser. A **content aggregator** is a business that gathers and organizes Web content and then distributes, or feeds, the content to subscribers for free or a fee. The individual who creates a personal Web site is usually the person who will maintain it.

4. **What are the Steps Required for Web Publishing?**

Web publishing is the development and maintenance of Web pages. The five steps to Web publishing are: (1) plan a Web site, (2) analyzed and design a Web site, (3) create a Web site, (4) deploy a Web site, and (5) maintain a Web site.

5. **What are the Types of E-Commerce?**

E-commerce, short for electronic commerce, is a business transaction that occurs over an electronic network such as the Internet. Business-to-consumer (B2C) e-commerce consists of the sales of goods and services to the general public. Consumer-to-consumer (C2C) e-commerce occurs when one consumer sells directly to another, from an **online auction**. Business-to-business (B2B) e-commerce takes place when two businesses that exchange goods and services.

6. **How Do E-Mail, FTP, Newsgroups and Message Boards, Mailing Lists, Chat Rooms, Instant Messaging, and Internet Telephony Work?**

E-mails (short for electronic mail) is the transmission of message and files via a computer network. **FTP** (File Transfer Protocol) is an Internet standard that permits file uploading and downloading with other computers on the Internet. A **newsgroup** is an online area in which users have written discussions about a particular subject. A message board is a popular Web-based type of discussion group that is easier to use than a newsgroup. A **mailing** list is a group of e-mail names and addresses given a single name, so that everyone on the list receives the same message all at the same time. A **chat room** is a location on an Internet server that permits users to chat, or conduct real-time conversations. **Instant messaging (IM)** is a real-time Internet communications service that notifies you when one or more people are online. **Internet telephony** enables users to speak over the Internet using a computer or mobile device.

(7) **What Are the Rules of Netiquette?**

Netiquette, which is short for Internet etiquette, is the code of acceptable behavior users should follow while on the Internet. Keep messages short, be polite and read the FAQ if ones exists. Do not assume all the material is accurate or up-to-date, and never read someone else's private e-mail.

Key Terms

You should know the Key Terms. Use the list below to help focus your study. To further enhance your understanding of the Key Terms in this chapter, visit book's Web site and click the chapter 2 links.

access provider (40)
address book (59)
animation (53)
audio (53)
blog (51)
cable modem (40)
chat (61)
click (46)
content aggregator (52)
dial-up access (39)
domain name (41)
downloading (43)
DSL (40)
e-commerce (57)
electronic storefront (57)
e-mail (58)
e-mail address (59)
e-mail program (58)
emoticons (62)
fixed wireless (40)

FTP (60)
graphic (53)
home page (43)
host (38)
http (44)
hyperlink (45)
instant messaging (61)
Internet (38)
Internet backbone (41)
IP address (41)
Internet telephony (62)
ISP (Internet service Provider) (40)
link (45)
mailing list (60)
message board (60)
MPEG 4 (55)
multimedia (53)
net (38)
netiquette (62)

newsgroup (60)
online auction (57)
online service provider (OSP) (40)
player (54)
plug-in (55)
podcast (54)
portal (50)
real-time (61)
satellite modem (40)
search engine (47)
search text (49)
server (38)
shopping cart (57)
streaming (54)
subject directory (47)
subscriber (60)
surfing the web (45)
thumbnail (53)
top-level domain (42)

unsubscribe (60)
uploading (60)
URL (44)
user name (59)
video (55)
virtual reality (55)
Voice over IP (62)
Web (43)
Web address (44)
Web browser (43)
Web developer (64)
Web page (43)
Web publishing (56)
Web server (43)
Web site (43)
wiki (52)
WISP (40)
(WWW) (43)
World Wide Web Consortium (W3C) (39)

Checkpoint

Use the Checkpoint exercises to check your knowledge level of the chapter.

True/False	Mark T for True and F for False. (see page numbers in parentheses.)

_____ 1. No single person, company, institution, or government agency controls or owns the Internet.

_____ 2. DSL is a technology that provides high-speed Internet connections over the cable television network.

_____ 3. A domain name is the text version of an IP address.

_____ 4. Each electronic document on the Web is called a Web site.

_____ 5. Downloading is the process of receiving information for a server on the Internet.

_____ 6. A search engine is a program that finds Web sites and Web pages.

_____ 7. An educational Web site contains content that describes a cause, opinion, or idea.

_____ 8. A podcast is a collaborative Web site that allows users to add to, modify, or delete the Web site content via their Web browser.

_____ 9. A chat room is a location on an Internet server that permits users to chat with each other.

_____ 10. Internet telephony is an online service in which users have written discussion.

Multiple Choice Select the best answer (see page numbers in parentheses.)

1. Although it is slow-speed technology, some homes and small businesses use _____ to access the Internet.
   a. a satellite modem
   b. cable modem
   c. DSL
   d. dial-up access

2. An IP address usually consists of _____.
   a. two groups of numbers separated by commas
   b. two groups of numbers separated by periods
   c. four groups of numbers separated by commas
   d. four groups of numbers separated by periods

3. Many Web addresses begin with http, which is _____.
   a. path
   b. domain name
   c. protocol
   d. page name

4. A _____ is recorded audio stored on a Web site that can be downloaded to a computer or a portable digital audio player.
   a. blog
   b. wiki
   c. portal
   d. podcast

5. _____ format reduces the size of an audio file to about one-tenth its original size.
   a. JPEG
   b. GIF
   c. MPEG-4
   d. MP3

6. _____ is the development and maintenance of Web pages.
   a. Web server
   b. Web addressing
   c. Web publishing
   d. Web browsing

7. In _____ e-commerce, customer purchase from other consumers.
   a. consumer-to-consumer
   b. business-to-business
   c. consumer-to-business
   d. business-to-consumer

8. The _____ standard permits uploading and downloading of files on the Internet.
   a. e-commerce
   b. personal finance software
   c. online banking
   d. accounting software

Matching Match the terms with their definitions. (see page numbers in parentheses.)

_____ 1. home page

_____ 2. RSS 2.0

_____ 3. streaming

_____ 4. e-mail address

_____ 5. uploading

a. combination of a user name and a domain name that identifies user
b. process of transferring data in a continuous and even flow
c. specification used by content aggregators to distribute content
d. first page that a Web site displays
e. built-in connection to a related Web page
f. process of transferring documents, graphics and other objects from your computer to an Internet server

Short Answer Write a brief answer to each of the following questions.

1. How is a regional ISP different from a national ISP? _____ How are an ISP, OSP and WISP different? _____

2. How is a Web page different from a Web site? _____ How can you use a Web address to display a Web page? _____

3. What are the differences between blogs, wikis, and podcasts? _____ When might you use each of them? _____

4. How do you use a subject directory to find information? _____ What is a search engine? _____

5. What is FTP? _____ What is anonymous FTP? _____

Short Answer Write a brief answer to each of the following questions.

1. How is a regional ISP different from a national ISP? _____ How are an ISP, OSP and WISP different? _____

2. How is a Web page different from a Web site? _____ How can you use a Web address to display a Web page? _____

3. What are the differences between blogs, wikis, and podcasts? _____ When might you use each of them? _____

4. How do you use a subject directory to find information? _____ What is a search engine? _____

5. What is FTP? _____ What is anonymous FTP? _____

Working Together Working in a group of your classmates, complete the following team exercise.

1. This chapter lists eleven types of Web sites: portal, news, informational, business/marketing, educational, entertainment, advocacy, blog, content aggregator, and personal. Working as a team, use the Internet to find at least two examples of each type of Web site. For each Web site, identify the Web address, the multimedia elements used, the purpose of each Web site, and the type of Web site. Explain why you classified each site as you did. Then, keeping in mind the purpose of each Web site, rank the sites in terms of their effectiveness. Share your findings in a report and/ or a PowerPoint presentation with the class.

Web Research

Use the Internet-based Web Research exercises to broaden your understanding of the concepts presented in this chapter. Visit the book's Web site to obtain more information pertaining to each exercise. To discuss any of the Web Research exercises in this chapter with other students, post your thoughts or questions at the forum.

1. **Journaling**   Respond to your readings in this by writing at least one page about your reactions, evaluations, and reflections about using the Internet. For example, how many e-mail messages do you send and receive daily? How many Web pages do you visit each month? Have you ever shopped online? Has your instructor require you to access the Internet for class projects? Which search engines have you used? You can also write about the new terms you've learned from reading this chapter. If required, submit your journal to your instructor or teacher.

2. **Scavenger Hunt**   Use one of the search engines listed in Figure 2-8 in Chapter 2 on page 46 on your own favorite search engine to find the answers to the question below. Copy and paste the Web address from the Web pages where you found the answer. Some questions may have more than one answer. If required, submit your answer to your instructor or teacher. (1) Microsoft Internet Explorer and Google Chrome are the two more popular Web browsers. What is the name of the first graphical Web browser? (2) What cable company was established in 1858 to carry instantaneous communications across the ocean that eventually would be used for Internet communication? (3) Under which Liberian president's administration did Maryland County become part of the Republic of Liberia in 1857? (4) What is the location of Microsoft's headquarters? (5) How many Web pages is Google currently searching?

3. **Search Sleuth**   The Internet has provided the opportunity to access encyclopedias online. One of the more comprehensive encyclopedia search sites is Encyclopedia.com. Visit this Web site and then use your word processing program to answer the following questions. Then, if required, submit your answers to your instructor or teacher. (1) The site's home page lists the top five searches for the day. What are today's top searches? Click one of these links. What magazines and newspapers contain information on this topic? (2) Type in World Wide Web in the search text box. How many articles discussing the World Wide Web are found on the Encyclopedia.com Web site? (3) In the search results list, click the first link. What is the definition of the World Wide Web according to the first sentence of the article? Who is the American computer consultant who promoted the idea of linking documents via hypertext during the 1960's? What words are hyperlinks within this article? (4) Type multimedia as a keyword in the Search text box. In the search results list, click the multimedia link. What hardware typically is required to work with multimedia according to this article? (5) Type personal computer as the keyword in the Search text box. Click one of the personal computer links, review the material, and, if required, submit to your instructor or teacher fifty-word summary of the information you read.

Learn How To

Use the Learn How To activities to learn fundamental skills when using a computer and accompanying technology. Complete the exercises and submit them to your instructor or teacher.

LEARN HOW TO 1:

Change a Web Browser's Home Page

When you start a Web browser, a Web page is displayed. You can change the page that appears when you start a Web browser or when you click the Home page button on the browser toolbar by completing the following steps.

a.   With the browser running, click tools on the
      menu bar and then click Internet Options on
      the tool menu. The Internet Options dialog box
      is displayed (Figure 2-26).
b.   If necessary, in the Home page area under the
      General tab, select the Web address in the Ad
      dress box.
c.   Type the Web address of the page you want
to   display for both when you start
the browser   and when you click the
Home button.
d.   Click the OK button in the Internet Options   dialog box.

When you start the browser or click the Home
button on the browser toolbar, the selected Web
page will be displayed.

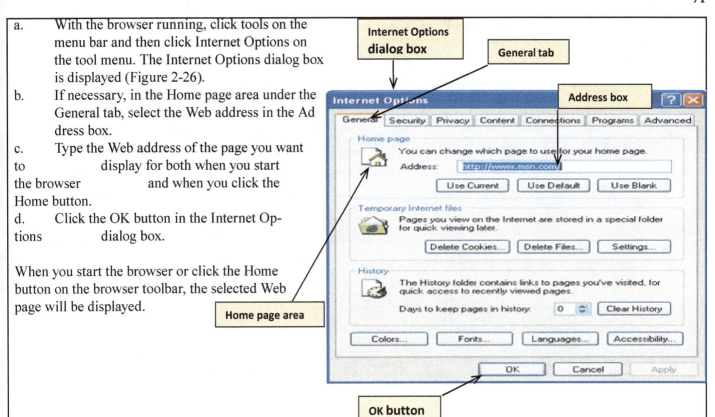

Exercise

1. Start your Web browser. Write down the address of the browser's current home page.

2. Then change the browser's home page to www.emmanuelclarke.com. Close the browser.

3. Start your Web browser. What are the main items on the page? Click the About button, when was Emmanuel Clarke born, and where did he grow up? Submit these answers to your Instructor or teacher. Change the browser's home page to your school's home page, if one exist. Click the home button on the browser toolbar. Click the Calendar or Events link, and then locate two campus events of which you were unaware of. Report these two campus events to your instructor or teacher.

4. Change the browser's home page back to the address you wrote down in step 1.

This Page Was Intentionally Left Blank

CHAPTER 3
APPLICATION SOFTWARE

3D-RA Before bleeding · 3D-RA After bleeding · Shear stress Before bleeding

OBJECTIVE

1. Identify the categories of application software
2. Explain how to work with application software
3. Identify the key features of widely used business programs
4. Identify the key features of widely used graphics and multimedia programs
5. Identify the key features of widely used home, personal, and educational programs
6. Identifying the different types of applications
7. Describe function of utility programs
8. Describe aids for software

OBJECTIVE

APPLICATION SOFTWARE

With the proper software, a computer is a valuable tool. Software allows user to create letters, reports, and other documents; design Web pages and diagrams; draw images; enhance audio and video clips; prepare taxes; play games; compose e-mail messages and instant messages; and much more. To accomplish these and many other tasks, users work with application software. **Application software** consists of programs designed to make users work more productive and to better assist them with personal tasks.

Application software has a variety of uses:

1. To make business activities more efficient.
2. To assist with graphics and multimedia projects.
3. To support home, personal, and educational tasks.
4. To facilitate communication.

The table in Figure 3-1 categorizes popular types of application software by their general use. Although many types of communication software exist, the ones listed in Figure 3-1 are application software oriented. Successful use of application software often requires the use of one or more utility programs identified in Figure 3-1. Application software is available in a variety of forms: packaged, custom, open source, shareware, freeware, and public domain. As computer savvy workers increase in Liberia, many are going to learn these application software.

CATEGORIES OF APPLICATION SOFTWARE

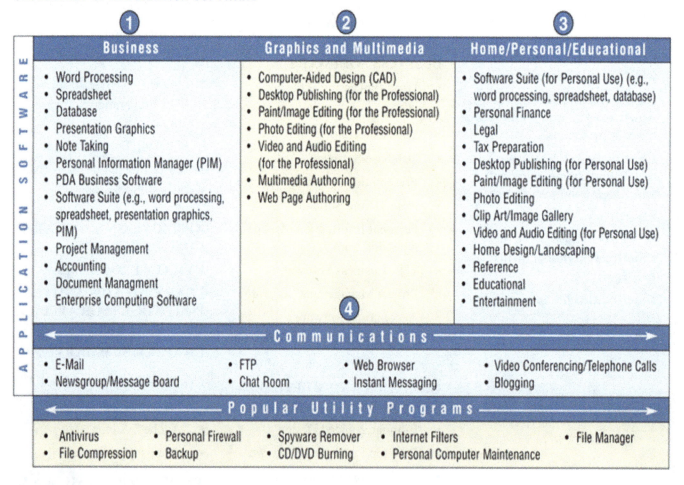

FIGURE 3-1 The four major categories of popular software are outlined in the table. Communications software is bundled with other application or system software. Also identified in the table are widely used utility programs. Which of these software have you use in your school or work here in Liberia and for what?

- **Package software** is mass-produced copyrighted retail software that meets the needs of a wide variety of users, not just a single user or company. Word processing and spreadsheet software are examples of packaged software. Packaged software is available in retail stores or on the Web.

- **Custom software** performs functions specifically for a business or industry. Sometimes a company cannot find packaged software that meets it unique requirements. In this case, the company may use programmers to develop tailor-made custom software.

- **Open source software** is software provided for use, modification, and redistribution. This software has no restrictions from the copyright holder regarding modification of the software's internal instructions and redistribution of the software. Open source software usually can be downloaded from the Internet, sometimes at no cost. Due to the free-of-charged nature of open source software, Liberian can benefit a lot from them.

- **Shareware** is copyrighted software that is distributed at no cost for a trial period. To use a shareware program beyond the trial period, then a payment must be made before you are able to continue usage of the program.

- **Freeware** is copyrighted software provided at no cost to a user by an individual or a company that retains all rights to the software. Like open source software, students in Liberia need to learn more it them.

- **Public-domain** software has been donated for public use and has no copyright restrictions. Anyone can copy or distribute public-domain software to others at no cost.

Thousands of shareware, freeware, and public-domain programs are available on the Internet for users to download. Examples include communications programs, graphics programs, and games.

The Role of System Software

System software serves as the interface between the user, the application software, and

the computer's hardware (Figure 3-1). To use application software, such as a word processing program, your computer must be running a system software – specifically, an operating system. Three popular personal computer operating systems are Windows XP, 7, and 8, Linux, and Mac OS X.

Each time you start a computer, the operating system is loaded (copied) from the computer's hard disk into memory. Once the operating system is loaded, it coordinating all the activities of the computer. This includes starting application software, transferring data among input and output devices and memory. While the computer is running, the operating system remains in memory.

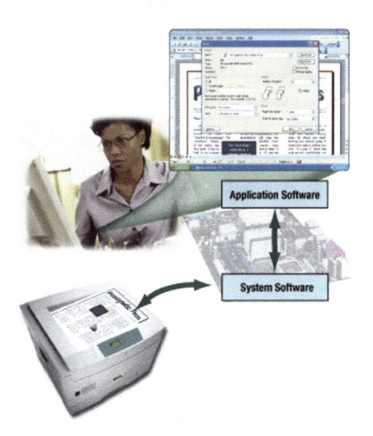

FIGURE 3-2 A user does not communicate directly with the computers hardware. Instead, system software is the interface between the user, the application software, and the hardware. For example, when a user instructs the application software to print, the application software sends the print instruction to the system software, which in turn sends the print instruction to the hardware.

Working with Application Software

To use application software, you must instruct the operating system to start the program. The steps in Figure 3-3 illustrate how to start and interact with the Paint program. The following paragraphs explain the steps in Figure 3-3. Personal computer operating systems often use the concept of a desktop to make the computer easier to use. The **desktop** is an on-screen work area that has a graphical user interface (read Looking Ahead 3-1 for a look at the next generation of user interfaces). Step 1 Figure 3-3 shows icons, a button, and a pointer on the Windows XP desktop. An icon is a small image displayed on the screen that represents a program, a document, or some other objects.

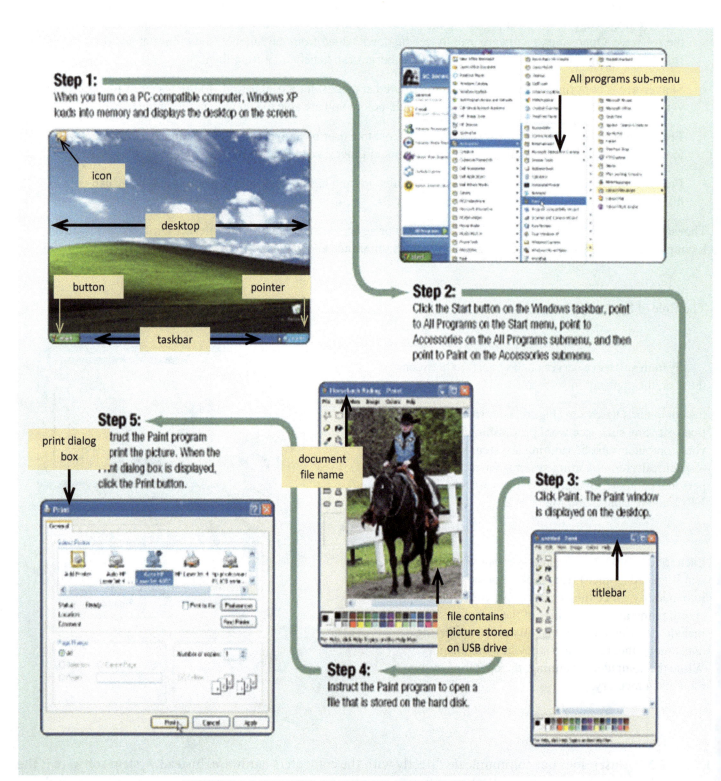

FIGURE 3-3 HOW TO START AN APPLICATION.

A **button** is a graphical element that you activate to cause a specific action to take place. One way to activate a button is to click it. To **click** a button on the screen requires moving the pointer to the help button and then pressing and releasing a button from the mouse (usually the left mouse button). The **pointer** is a small symbol displayed on the screen that moves when you move the mouse. Common pointer shapes are an I-beam (I), a block arrow, and a pointing hand.

The Window 8, 7, XP, or Windows Vista desktop contains a Start button on the lower-left corner of the taskbar. When you click the Start button, the Start menu is displayed on the desktop. A **menu** contains a list of commands from which you make selections. A **command** is an instruction that causes a program to perform a specific action. The arrowhead symbol at the right edge of some menu commands indicates a submenu of additional commands is available. A submenu is a menu that is displayed when you point to a command on a previous menu.

As illustrated in Step 2 of Figure 3-3, when you click the Start button and point to the All Programs command on the Start menu, the All Program submenu is displayed. Pointing to the Accessories command on the All Program submenu displays the Accessories submenu. To start a program, you click on its program name in a menu or submenu. This action instructs the operating system to start the application, in which the program's instructions load from a storage medium (such as a hard disk) into memory. For example, when you click Paint on the Accessories submenu, Windows loads the Paint program instructions from the computer's hard disk into memory.

> ### FAQ 3-1
>
> ### Will a document print like it looks on a screen?
>
> Yes, because most current application software is WYSWYG (what you see is what you get). The application software embeds invisible codes around the text and graphics, which instructs the computer how to present the information. For more info, visit www.clarkepublish.com or visit the Internet and then search Google for WYSIWYG.

Once loaded into memory, the program is displayed in a window on the desktop (Step 3 of Figure 3-3). A **window** is a rectangular area of the screen that displays data and information. The top of a window has a **title bar**, which is a horizontal space that contains the window's name.

With the program loaded, you can create a new file or open an existing one. A **file** is a named collection of stored data, instructions, or information. A file can contain text, images, audio, or video. To distinguish among various files, each file has a file name. The title bar of the document window usually displays a document's file name. Step 4 of Figure 3-3 shows the contents of the file, Horseback Riding, displaying in the Paint window.

In some cases, when you instruct a program to perform an activity such as printing, the program displays a dialog box. A dialogue box is a window that provides information, available options, or requests a response. Dialog boxes, like the one shown in Step 5 of Figure 3-3 often contains option buttons, text boxes, check boxes, and .command buttons

---

Looking Ahead 3-1

User Interface of the Future

Most computers today use a graphical user interface. Next-generation of user interfaces will be natural and human-centric, meaning they will enable people to interact with a computer using human-like communication methods.

Developments in this area include gesture recognition, 3-D interfaces, and Neutral interfaces. With gesture recognition, the computer will detect human motion. Computers with this interface will recognize sign language, reading lips, and eye gazes. All these scenarios will be possible with the upcoming 3-D user interfaces. These systems will use a tiny chip with sensors implanted in the brain as external computers can convert brainwaves into signals that

people can control. For more info, visit the Internet and then search Google for user Interfaces for more information. People in Liberia will also benefit from this next-generation of user interface in the not so far future.

Test your knowledge of pages 74 through 77 in Quiz Yourself 3-1

QUIZ YOURSELF 3-1

Instructions: Find the true statement below. Then rewrite the remaining false statement so they are true.

1. Application software is used to make business activities more efficient: assist with graphics and multimedia project; support home, personal, and educational tasks; and facilitate communication.

2. Public-domain software is mass-produce, copyrighted retail software that meets the needs of a wide variety of users, not just a single user or company.

3. To use system software, your computer must be running application software.

4. When an application is started, the program's instructions load from memory into a storage medium.

Quiz Yourself Online: To further test your knowledge of application software, categories and working with application software, visit www.clarkepublish.com or visit the Internet and then search www.google.com for more information.

BUSINESS SOFTWARE

Business software is application software that assists people in becoming more effective and efficient while performing their daily business activities. Business software includes programs such as word processing, spreadsheets, database, presentation graphics, note taking, and personal information manager software, PDA business software, software suites, project management, accounting, document management, and enterprise computing software. Figure 3-4 lists popular programs for each of these categories.

POPULAR BUSINESS PROGRAMS

Application Software	Manufacturer	Program Name
Word Processing	Microsoft	Word
	Sun	StarOffice Writer
	Corel	WordPerfect
Spreadsheet	Microsoft	Excel
	Sun	StarOffice Calc
	Corel	Quattro Pro
Database	Microsoft	Access
	Sun	StarOffice Base
	Corel	Paradox
	Microsoft	Visual FoxPro
	Oracle	Oracle Database
	MySQL AB	MySQL
Presentation Graphics	Microsoft	PowerPoint
	Sun	StarOffice Impress
	Corel	Presentations
Note Taking	Microsoft	OneNote
	Agilix	GoBinder
	Corel	Grafigo
Personal Information Manager (PIM)	Microsoft	Outlook
	IBM	Lotus Organizer
	Palm	Desktop
PDA Business Software	CNetX	Pocket SlideShow
	Microsoft	Pocket Word Pocket Excel Pocket Outlook
	PalmOne	VersaMail
	Ultrasoft	Money

Application Software	Manufacturer	Program Name
Software Suite (for the Professional)	Microsoft	Office Office for Mac
	Sun	StarOffice Office Suite
	Corel	WordPerfect Office
	IBM	Lotus SmartSuite
Project Management	Microsoft	Project
	Primavera	SureTrak Project Manager
Accounting	Intuit	QuickBooks
	Sage Software	Peachtree Accounting
Document Management	Adobe	Acrobat
	Enfocus	PitStop
	ScanSoft	PDF Converter PaperPort
Enterprise Computing Software	Oracle	PeopleSoft Enterprise Human Resources
	Best Software	Sage MAS 500
	MSC Software	MSC.SimManager
	Oracle	Oracle Manufacturing
	SAP	mySAP Customer Relationship Management
	NetSuite	NetERP
	Apropos Technology	Apropos Enterprise Edition

FIGURE 3-4 Popular Business Software that are Commonly Found in Offices Around the World.

Word Processing Software

Word processing, also known as a word processor, allows users to create and manipulate documents containing mostly text and sometimes graphics (Figure 3-5). Millions of people use word processing software everyday to develop documents such as letters, memos, reports, fax cover sheets, mailing labels, newsletters and Web pages. If you have used the computer to type your term paper at your local institution here in Liberia, then you have used this software. Do you think you can live without word processing software in modern Liberia?

Word processing software has many features to make documents look professional and visually appealing. Some of these features include the capability of changing the shape and size of characters, changing the color of characters, and organizing text in newspaper-columns. Most word processing software allows users to incorporate many types of graphical images in documents. One popular type of graphical image is clip art. **Clip art** is a collection of drawings, diagrams, maps, and photographs that you can insert in documents. In Figure 3-5, a user inserted a clip art image of an alarm clock in the document.

All word processing software provides at least some basic capabilities to help users create and modify documents. Defining the size of the paper on which to print and specifying the margins are examples of some of these capabilities. If you type text that extends beyond the right page margin, the word processing software automatically positions text at the beginning of the next line. This feature, called wordwrap, allows users to type words in a paragraph continually without pressing the ENTER key at the end of each line. As you type more lines of text they will be displayed on the screen as the top portion of the document will either move upwards or scroll off the screen.

A major advantage of using word processing software is that users can easily change what they have typed written. For example, a user can insert, delete, or rearrange words, sentences, paragraphs, or an entire section. Current word-processing programs also have features that automatically correct errors and make word substitutions as users type text. For instance, when you type the abbreviation ASAP, the word processing software replaces the abbreviation with as soon as possible.

Word processing software includes a spell checker, which reviews the spelling of individual words, through out the entire document. The spell check feature compares the words in the document with an electronic dictionary that is part of the word processing software.

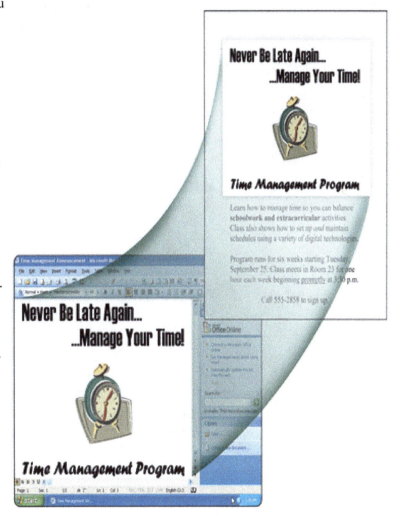

FIGURE 3-5 Word processing software enables users to create professional and visually appealing documents.

Developing a Document

With application software, such as word processing, users can create, edit, format, save, and print documents. When you **create** a document, you can either type text, numbers, insert graphical images, or perform other tasks using an input device such as a keyboard, mouse, microphone, or digital pen. Most programs support voice and handwriting recognition; as suppose to the computers spoken words and hand written text. If you are using Microsoft Word to design an announcement, for example, you create a document and then you need to go back and make changes to the document. In this program this is what we call editing. To **edit** a document means to make changes to its existing content. Common editing tasks include inserting, deleting, cutting, copying, and pasting. Inserting text involves adding text from a clipboard to a specific location in a document.

When users **format** a document, they change its appearance. Formatting is important because the overall look of a document significantly can affect its ability to communicate clearly. Examples of formatting tasks are changing the font, font size, and font style of text. A **font** is a name assigned to a specific design of characters. Time New Roman and Arial are examples of fonts. **Font size** indicates the size of the characters in a particular font. Font size is gauged by a measurement system called point. A single point is about 1/72 of an inch in height. The text you are reading in this book is 11 point. Thus, each characters is about 5/36 (10/72) of an inch in height. A **font style** adds emphasis to a font. Bold, italic, and underline are examples of font styles. Figure 3-6 illustrates fonts, font sizes, and font styles.

During the process of creating, editing, and formatting a document, the computer holds it in memory. To keep the document for future use requires that you save it. When you **save** a document, the computer transfers the document from memory to a storage medium such as a USB flash drive, hard disk, or CD. Once saved, a document is stored permanently as a file on the storage medium. When you **print** a document, the computer places the content of the document on paper or some other medium. Instead of printing a document and physically distributing it, some users e-mail documents to others on a network such as the Internet

FIGURE 3-6 The Times New Roman and Arial are shown in two font sizes and a variety of font styles. This book was actually written using 11-point Times New Roman

Spreadsheet Software

Spreadsheet software allows users to organize data in rows and columns and perform calculations on the data. These rows and columns collectively are called a **worksheet** (Figure 3-7). Most spreadsheet software has basic features to help users create, edit, and format worksheets. The following sections describe the features of most spreadsheet programs.

SPREADSHEET ORGANIZATION

Typically, a spreadsheet file is similar to a notebook with up to 255 related individual worksheets. Data is organized vertically in columns and horizontally in rows on each worksheet (Figure 3-7). Each worksheet typically has 256 columns and 65,536 rows. One or more letters identify each column, and a number identifies each row. Only a small fraction of these columns and rows are displayed on the screen at one time. Scrolling through the worksheet displays different parts of the worksheet on the screen.

A cell is the intersection of a column and row. The spreadsheet software identifies cells by the column and row in which they are located. For example, the intersecttion of column B and row 6 is referred to as cell B6, as shown in Figure 3-7, Cell B6 contains the number, $40,398.00 dollars which represents the store revenue for October.

Cells may contain three types of data: label, values, and formulas. The text or label, entered in a cell identifies the worksheet data and helps organize the worksheet. Using descriptive labels, such as Total Revenue and Total Expenses, helps make a worksheet more meaningful.

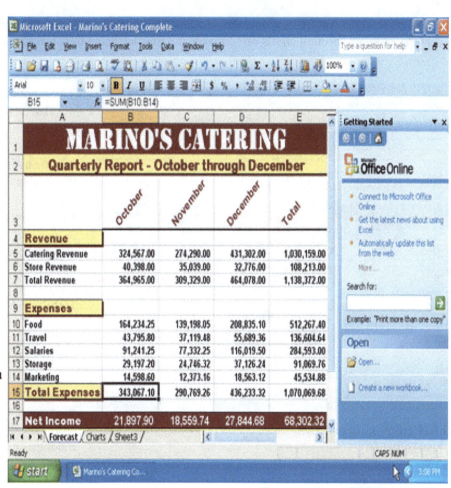

FIGURE 3-7 With spreadsheet software, you create worksheets that contain data arranged in rows and columns, and you can perform calculations on the data in the worksheet.

CALCULATION

Many of the worksheet cells shown in Figure 3-7 contains a number, called a value, that can be used in a calculation. Other cells, however, contain formulas that generate values. A formula performs calculations on the data in the worksheet and displays the resulting value in a cell, usually the cell containing the formula. When creating a worksheet, you can enter your own formulas.

In many spreadsheet programs, you begin a formula with an equal sign, a plus sign, or minus sign. Next you enter the formula, separating cell references (e.g., B10) with operators. Common operators are + for addition, - for subtraction, * for multiplication, and / for division. In Figure 3-7, for example, cell B15 could contain the formula =B10+B11+B12+B13+B14, which would add together (sum) the contents of cells B10, B11, B12, B13 and B14. That is, this formula calculated the total expenses for October.

A function is a predefined formula that performs common calculations such as adding the values in a group of cells or generating a value such as the time or date. For example, instead of using the formula, =B10+B11+B12+B13+B14 to calculate the total expenses for October, you could use the SUM function. This function requires you to identify the starting cell and the ending cell in a group to be summed, separating these two cells references with a colon. For example, the function =SUM(B10:B14) instructs the spreadsheet program to add all of the numbers in cell B10 through B14.

RECALCULATION

One of the more powerful features of spreadsheet software is its capability of recalculating the result of the worksheet when data in a worksheet changes. When you enter a new value to change data in a cell, any value affected by the change is updated automatically and instantaneously.

CHARTING

Another standard feature of spreadsheet software is charting, which depicts the data in a graphical form. A visual representation of data through charts often makes it easier for users to see at a glance the relationship among the numbers.

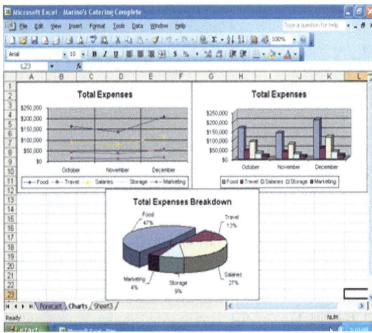

FIGURE 3-8 Three basic types of charts provided with spreadsheet software.

Three popular types are line charts, column charts, and pie charts. Figure 3-8 shows examples of these charts that were plotted from the data in Figure 3-7 on the previous page. A line chart shows a trend during a period of time as indicated by a rising or falling line. A column chart, also called a bar chart, displays bars of various lengths to show the relationship of data. The bars can be horizontal, vertical, or stacked on top of one another. A pie chart, which has a shape of a round pie cut into slices, shows the relationship of parts to a whole.

Database Software

A **database** is a collection of data organized in a manner that allows access, retrieval, and use of that data. In a manual database, you might record data on paper and store it in a filing cabinet. With a computerized database, such as the one shown in Figure 3-9, the computer stores the data in an electronic format on a storage medium such as a hard disk.

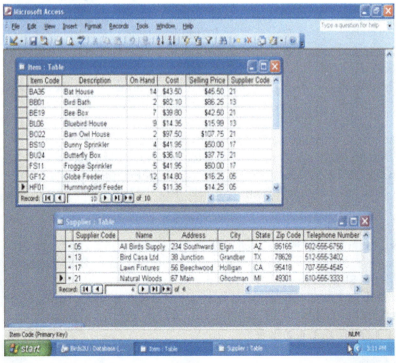

Database software is application software that allows users to create, access, and manage a database. Using database software, you can add, change, and delete data in a database; sort and retrieve data from the database; and create forms and reports using the data in the database.

FIGURE 3-9 This database contains two tables: one for items and one for suppliers.

With most popular personal computer database programs, a database consists of a collection of tables, organized in rows and columns. Each row, called a record, contains data about a given person, product, object, or event. Each column, called a field, contains a specific category of data within a record.

The store database shown in Figure 3-9 consists of two tables: an Item table contains 10 records (rows), each storing data about one item. The item data is grouped into six fields (columns): Item Code, Description, On Hand, Cost, Selling Price, and Supplier Code. The On Hand field, for instance, contains the quantity on hand. The Item and supplier tables relate to one another through a common field, the Supplier Code.

Users run queries to retrieve certain data information. A query is a request for specific data from the database. For example, a query might request a list of customers that have a balance due. Database software can take the results of a query and present it in a window on the screen or have it sent to the printer.

Presentation Graphics Software

Presentation graphics software is application software that allows users to create visual aids for presentation to communicate ideas, messages, and other information to a group. The presentations can be viewed as slides, sometimes called slide show, that are displayed on a large monitor or on projection screen (Figure 3-10).

Presentation graphics software typically provides a variety of predefined presentation formats that define complementary colors for backgrounds, text, and graphical accents to the slides. This software also provides a variety of layouts for each individual slide such a title slide, a two-column slide, a slide with clip art, a chart, a table, and animation. In addition, you can enhance any text, charts, and graphical images on a slide with 3-D or other special effects like shading, shadows, and textures.

When building a presentation, users can set the slide timing so the presentation automatically displays the next slide after preset delay. Presentation graphics software typically includes a clip gallery that provides images, pictures, video clips, and audio clips to enhance multimedia presentations. Some audio and video editing programs, such as producer, work with presentation graphics software, providing users with an easy means to record and insert video, music, and audio commentary in a presentation. Presentation graphics software incorporates features such as checking spelling, ink input, and converting an existing slide show into a format for the World Wide Web.

FIGURE 3-10 This presentation was created using presentation graphics software that consists of five slides.

Note Taking Software

Note taking software is application that enables users to enter typed text, handwritten comments, drawings, or sketches anywhere on a page as part of a notebook (Figure 3-11). Users also can include audio recordings as part of their notes. Once the notes are captured (entered and saved), users easily can organize them, reuse them, and share them. Clarke Publishing and Consulting Group, Inc. have several note taking software in its collection of software. The company also rents out these software to its education clients for a minimum fee.

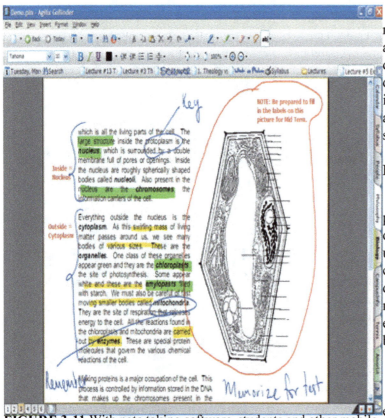

FIGURE 3-11 With note taking software, students and other mobile users can handwrite notes, draw sketches, and type text.

On a desktop or notebook computer, users enter notes primarily via the keyboard or microphone. On a Tablet PC, however, the primary input device is a digital pen. Users find note-taking software convenient during meetings, class lectures, conferences, in libraries, and other settings that previously required a pencil and tablet of paper for recording thoughts and discussions.

Personal Information Manager Software

A **personal information manager (PIM)** is application software that includes an appointment calendar, address book, note pad, and other features to help users organize personal information. The appointment calendar allows you to schedule activities for particular day and time. With the address book, you can enter and maintain names, addresses, telephone numbers, and e-mail address of customers, coworkers, family members, and friends.

You can use the notepad to record ideas, reminders, and other important information. Most PDAs and many smart phones today include, many other features with, PIM functionality. Using a PDA, you can synchronize, or coordinate, information so that both the PDA smart phone and the computer have the latest version of the information.

PDA iPad, eReader Business Software

In addition to PIM software, a huge variety of business software is available for PDAs, iPads and eReaders. Although some PDAs have software built in, most have the capability of accessing software on miniature storage media such as memory cards. Business software for PDAs allow users to create documents and worksheets, manage databases and lists, create slide shows, take notes, maintain budgets and finances, view and edit photographs, read electronic books, prepare travel routes, compose and read e-mail messages, send instant messages, and browse the Web. As the Web and other communication technologies improve in Liberia, consumers will greatly benefit from the use of PDAs, iPads, and eReaders. Like in many countries, the use of these portable computing devices is going to be a big part of everyday life in technology savvy Liberia

Software Suite

A **software suite is** a collection of individual programs sold as a single package. Business software suites typically include, at a minimum, the following programs: word processing, spreadsheet, e-mail, and presentation graphics. Two of the more widely used software suites are Microsoft Office and Sun StartOffice. Software suites offer two major advantages: lower cost and easy of use. Buying a collection of programs in a software suite usually cost significantly less than purchasing them individually. Software suites provide ease of use because the programs within a software suite normally use a similar interface and share features such as clip art and a spell check.

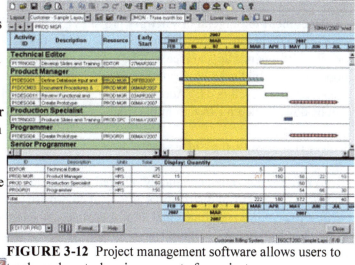

FIGURE 3-12 Project management software allows users to track, and control various aspect of a project.

Project Management Software

Project management software allows a user to plan, schedule, track, and analyze the events, resources, and costs of a project (Figure 3-12). Project management software helps users manage project variables, allowing them to complete a project on time and stay within a budget. An engineer, for example, might use project management software to manage new product development to schedule product screening, market evaluation, technical product evaluation, and manufacturing processes.

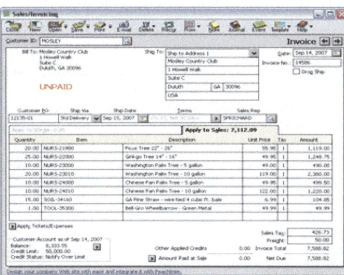

FIGURE 3-13 Accounting software help companies keep record transactions.

Accounting Software

Accounting software helps companies record and report their financial transactions (Figure 3-13). With accounting software, business users perform accounting activities related to general ledgers, accounts receivable, accounts payable, purchasing, invoicing, and payroll functions. Accounting software also enable users to write and print checks, track checking account activity, update and reconcile balances on demand. Newer accounting software support online credit checks, billing, direct deposit (this feature may not be available in Liberia), and payroll services.

Some accounting software offers more complex features such as job costing and estimating, time tracking, multiple company reporting, foreign currency reporting, and forecasting the amount of raw materials needed for products. The cost of accounting software for small businesses ranges from less than one hundred to several thousand dollars. Accounting software for large businesses can cost severely hundred thousand dollars.

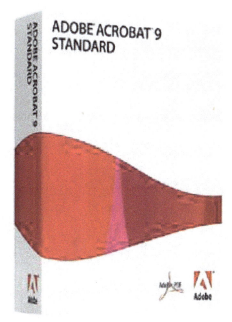

FIGURE 3-14 Adobe Acrobat allows users to create and edit PDF files.

Document Management Software

Document management software provides a means for sharing, distributing, and searching through documents by converting them into a format that can be viewed by the user (Figure 3-14). The converted document, which mirrors the original document's appearance, can be viewed and printed without the software that created the original document. A popular file format used by document management software to save converted documents is called **PDF** (Portable Document Format), developed by Adobe Systems. To view and print a PDF file, you will need Acrobat Reader software, which can be downloaded for free from the Adobe's Web site.

Enterprise Computing Software

A large organization commonly referred to as an enterprise, requires special computing solutions because of its size and large geographical distribution. A typical enterprise consists of a wide variety of departments, centers, and division – collectively known as functional units. Nearly every enterprise has the following functional units: human resources, accounting and finance, engineering or product development, manufacturing, marketing, sales, distribution, customer service, and information technology. Each of these functional units have specialized software requirements.

GRAPHICS AND MULTIMEDIA SOFTWARE

In addition to business software, many people work with software designed specifically for their field of work. Power users such as engineers, architects, desktop publishers, and graphic artists often use sophisticated software that allows them to work with graphics and multimedia. The software includes computer-aided design, desktop publishing, paint/image editing, photo editing, video and audio editing, multimedia authoring, and Web page authoring. Figure 3-15 lists the more popular programs for each of these categories, specifically designed for personal and professional or more technically astute users. Some of these programs incorporate user-friendly interfaces, or scaled-down version, making it possible for the home and small business users to crease documents using these programs. The program sections discuss the features and functions of graphic and multimedia software.

POPULAR GRAPHICS AND MULTIMEDIA SOFTWARE

Application Software	Manufacturer	Program Name
Computer-Aided Design (CAD)	Autodesk	AutoCAD
	Quality Plans	Chief Architect
	Microsoft	Visio
Desktop Publishing (for the Professional)	Adobe	InDesign
	Corel	Ventura
	Quark	QuarkXPress
Paint/Image Editing (for the Professional)	Adobe	Illustrator
	Corel	Painter
	Macromedia	FreeHand
Photo Editing (for the Professional)	Adobe	Photoshop
	Extensis	Photo Imaging Suite
Video and Audio Editing (for the Professional)	Adobe	Audition
		Encore DVD
		Premiere Pro
	Cakewalk	SONAR
	Sony	ACID Pro
	Ulead	MediaStudio Pro
		DVD Workshop
Multimedia Authoring	SumTotal Systems	ToolBook Instructor
	Macromedia	Authorware
		Director
Web Page Authoring	Adobe	GoLive
	Lotus	FastSite
	Macromedia	Dreamweaver
		Fireworks
		Flash
	Microsoft	FrontPage

FIGURE 3-15 Here are Some of the Most Popular Graphics and Multimedia Programs for the Professionals.

Computer-Aided Design

Computer-aided design (CAD) software is a sophisticated type of application software that assists professional users to development engineering, architectural, and scientific designs. For example, engineers create and design plans for airplanes and security systems. Architects design building structures and floor plans (Figure 3-16). Scientists design drawings of molecular structures.

Desktop Publishing Software (for the Professional)

Desktop publishing (DTP) software enables professional designers to create sophisticated documents that contain text, graphics, and many colors. Professional DTP software is ideal for the production of high-quality color documents such as textbooks, corporate newsletters, marketing literature (Figure 3-17), product catalogs, and annual reports. Today's DTP software also allows designers to convert a color document into a format for use on the World Wide Web.

Personal Paint/Image Editing Software (for the Professional)

Graphic artists, multimedia professionals, technical illustrators, and desktop publishers use paint software and image editing software to create and modify graphical images and Web pages. **Paint software,** also called illustration software, allows users to draw pictures, shapes, and other graphical images with various on-screen tools such as a pen, brush, eyedropper, and paint bucket (Figure 3-18). **Image editing software** provides the capabilities of paint software and also includes the capability to enhance and modify existing pictures and images. Modifications can include adjusting or enhancing image colors, and adding special effects such as shadows and glows.

FIGURE 3-16 DPT software for the professionals.

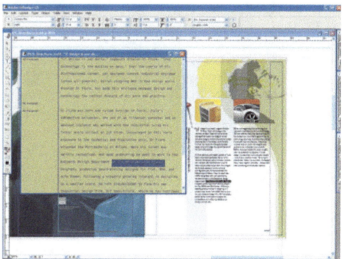

FIGURE 3-17 Architects use CAD to create building designs.

Professional photo editing software is a type of image editing software that allows photographers, videographers, engineers, scientists, and other high-volume digital photo users to edit and customize digital photographs. With this software, users can retouch photos, crop images, and much more.

FIGURE 3-18 Paint software helps arts do many creative things.

Video and Audio Editing Software
(for the Professional)

Video editing software (Figure 3-19) allows professionals to modify, a segment of a video, called a clip. For example, users can reduce the length of a video clip, reorder a series of clips, or add special effects such as words that move horizontally across the screen. Video editing software typically includes audio editing capabilities. **Audio editing software** lets users modify audio clips and produce studio-quality soundtracks. Read Discussion 3-1 for related discussion.

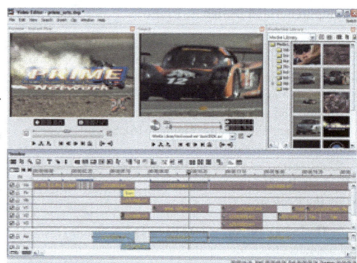

FIGURE 3-19 With video editing software, users modify video images.

DISCUSSION 3-1

What Should Be Done to Prevent Music and Video File Sharing In Liberia?

It is illegal to use networks or memory SD Card to share copyrighted music or video files. Despite the this, a number of street music venders all over Liberia participate in the illegal practice, and is estimated 1.5 million Liberians use SD Card or file-sharing network to locate and download copyrighted music and videos without paying. Much of this illegal activity that is killing the Liberian Music Industry takes place at in music stores, street corners, colleges and universities and even in government and private offices. To combat illegal file sharing, the Liberian Music Union, LIMU, and the Copyright Office of Liberia, COL have teamed up to fight Music Piracy throughout the country. The Copyright Office of Liberia (COL) and LIMU have been campaigning with government as well as other civil organizations to help educate people to stop this illegal act that is hurting the Liberian music industry and musicians throughout the country. The LIMU wants the government to put an anti piracy law that would protect the intellectual property of Liberian artists. The group wants those found guilty to be liable for hefty monetary fines for every stolen song. The COL and LIMU maintain that downloading or storing a copyrighted music on any portable mobile device or music player steals from both the recording artist and the recording industry. On the other hand, those that are involved in the selling and downloading of music do not think they're hurting the industry or the artists. Many of them think they are promoting the artists and not stealing from them. Should it be illegal to store copyrighted music or video files on SD Card or over a network? Why or Why not? Is it a good idea for schools in Liberia to subscribe to music collections? Why or Why not?

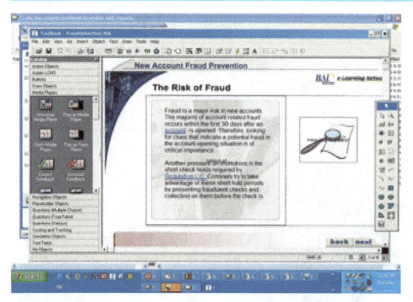

FIGURE 3-20 Multimedia Authoring Software allows users to create, edit or modify graphics, audio, video images, animation and other files.

Multimedia Authoring Software

Multimedia authoring software allows users to combine text, graphic, audio, video, and animation into an interactive application (Figure 3-19). With this software, users control the placement of text and images and the duration of sounds, video, and animation. Once created, a multimedia presentation often takes the form of interactive computer-based presentations or Web-based presentations designed to facilitated learning, demonstrate product functionality, and elicit direct-user participation. Training centers, educational institutions, and online magazine publishers all use multimedia authoring software to develop interactive applications. These applications may be available on a CD or DVD, over a local area network.

Web Page Authoring Software

Web page authoring software helps users of all skill levels create Web pages that include graphical images, video, audio, animation, and other special effects with interactive content. In addition, many Web page authoring programs allows users to organize, manage, and maintain Web sites. Application software, such as Word, and Excel, often includes Web page authoring features. This allows home users to create basic Web pages using application software they already own. For more sophisticated Web pages, users work with Web pages authoring the software.

Test your knowledge of pages 78 through 89 in Quiz Yourself 3-2

QUIZ YOURSELF 3-2

Instructions: Find the true statement below. Then rewrite the remaining false statement so they are true.

1. Enterprise computing software provides the capabilities of paint software and also includes the capability to modify existing images.
2. Millions of people use spreadsheet software every day to develop documents such as letters, memos, reports, fax cover sheets, mailing labels, newsletters, and Web pages.
3. Professionals accounting software is ideal for the production of high-quality color documents such as textbooks, corporate newsletters, marketing literature, product catalogs, and annual reports.
4. Spreadsheet software is application software that allows users to create visual aids for presentations to communicate ideas, messages, and other information to a group.
5. Two of the more widely used CAD programs are Microsoft Office and SunOffice.
6. Web page authoring software help users of all skill levels create Web pages.

Quiz Yourself Online: To further test your knowledge of types and feature of business programs and graphics/multi-media programs, visit www.clarkepublish.com or visit the Internet and then search www.google.com for more information.

SOFTWARE FOR HOME, PERSONAL AND EDUCATIONAL USE

A large amount of application software is designed specifically for home, personal, and educational used. Most of the programs in this category are relatively inexpensive, but often priced less than $100 dollars. Figure 3-21 lists popular programs for many of these categories. The following sections discuss the features and functions of these application software.

POPULAR SOFTWARE PROGRAMS FOR HOME/PERSONAL/EDUCATIONAL USE

Application Software	Manufacturer	Program Name	Application Software	Manufacturer	Program Name
Software Suite (for Personal Use)	Microsoft	Works	Photo Editing (for Personal Use)	Adobe	Photoshop Elements
	Sun	OpenOffice.org		Corel	Paint Shop Photo Album
Personal Finance	Intuit	Quicken		Dell	Picture Studio
	Microsoft	Money		Microsoft	Digital Image Photo Story
Legal	Broderbund	Family Lawyer		Roxio	PhotoSuite
	Cosmi	Perfect Attorney		Ulead	PhotoImpact Photo Express
	H&R Block	Kiplinger's Home & Business Attorney Kiplinger's WILLPower	Clip Art/Image Gallery	Broderbund	ClickArt
	Nolo	Quicken Legal Business Quicken WillMaker		Nova Development	Art Explosion
Tax Preparation	2nd Story Software	TaxACT	Video and Audio Editing (for Personal Use)	Microsoft	Movie Maker Producer for PowerPoint
	H&R Block	TaxCut		Pinnacle Systems	Studio MovieBox
	Intuit	TurboTax		Roxio	VideoWave
Desktop Publishing (for Personal Use)	Broderbund	The Print Shop PrintMaster		Ulead	VideoStudio
	Microsoft	Publisher	Home Design/ Landscaping	Broderbund	3D Home Architect
Paint/Image Editing (for Personal Use)	Corel	CorelDRAW Paint Shop Pro		Quality Plans	Home Designer
				ValuSoft	LandDesigner
	Sun	StarOffice Draw	Reference	Learning Company	American Heritage Talking Dictionary
	The GIMP Team	The Gimp		Microsoft	Encarta Streets & Trips
				Rand McNally	StreetFinder TripMaker

FIGURE 3-21 Many popular software programs are available for home, personal, and educational use.

Software Suite (for Professional Use)

A software suite (for personal use) combines application software such as word processing, spreadsheet, database, and other programs in a single, easy-to-use package. Many computer vendors install a software suite for personal use, such as Microsoft Works, on new computers sold to home users. As mentioned earlier, the programs in a software suite use a similar interface and share some common features. For many home users, the capabilities of software suites for personal use, meets more than their needs.

Personal Finance Software

Personal finance software is a simplified accounting program that helps home users and small office/home office users balance their checkbook, pay bills (like they do in the U.S.), track personal income and expenses, and evaluate financial plans (Figure 3-22). Most personal finance software includes financial planning features, such as analyzing home and personal loans, preparing income tax, and managing retirement savings, (this is done in the U.S. and other Western countries). Other features include managing home inventory and setting up budgets. Most of these programs also offer a variety of online services, such as online banking, which require access to the Internet.

FIGURE 3-22 Personal finance software assist home users with tracking personal income and expenses.

Legal Software

Legal software assist in the preparation of legal documents and provides legal information to individuals and small businesses (Figure 3-23). Legal software provides standard contracts and documentations associated with buying, selling, and renting property; estate planning; marriage and divorce; and preparing a will or living trust. By answering a series of questions and completing some forms, the legal software can tailor the legal document to one specific needs.

Tax Preparation Software

Tax preparation software can guide individuals, families or small businesses through the process of filing taxes in the U.S.(Figure 3-24). These programs forecasts tax liability and offer money-saving tax tips, designed to lower your tax bill. After you answer a series of questions and complete basic forms, the software creates and analyzes your tax forms to search for missed potential errors and deduction opportunities.

Once the forms are completed, you can print any of the necessary paperwork, and then they are ready for filing. Some tax preparation programs also allows you to file your tax forms electronically.

Desktop Publishing Software (for Personal Use)

Personal DTP software (Figures 3-24) helps home and small business users create newsletters, brochures, advertisements, postcards, greeting cards, letterhead, business cards, banners, calendars, logos, and Web sites. Personal DTP programs provide hundreds of thousands of graphical images. You can also import (upload) your own digital photographs into the documents. These programs typically guide you through the development of a document by asking you a series of questions. You can then print a finished publication on a color printer or post it on the Web. Many personal DTP programs also include paint/image editing software and photo editing software.

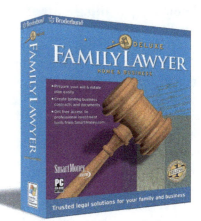

FIGURE 3-24 software provides legal information to individuals, families, and small businesses.

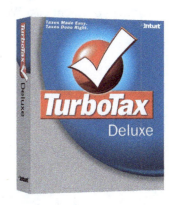

FIGURE 3-25 Tax preparation software guides individuals, families, or small businesses (this is mainly used in the U.S.).

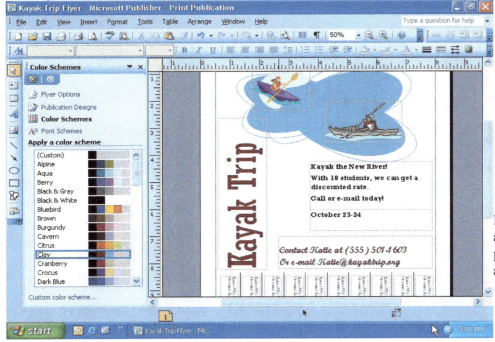

FIGURE 3-26 With Publisher, home and small business users can create professional-looking publications such as this flyer with tear-offs..

Paint/Image Editing Software
(for Personal Use)

Personal paint/image editing software provides an easy-to-use interface including various simplified tools that allows you to draw pictures, shapes, and other images; and provides the capability of modifying existing graphics and photos. These products also include many templates to assist
you in adding an image to documents such as greeting cards, banners, calendar, signs, labels, business cards, and letterhead.

Personal photo editing software, a popular type of image editing software, allows users to edit digital photographs by removing red-eye, erasing blemishes, restoring aged photos, and adding special effects (Figure 3-26), or creating electronic photo albums. When you purchase a digital camera, it usually includes photo editing software. You can print edited photographs on labels, calendars, business cards, and banners; or post them on a Web page

FAQ 3-2

How do pictures get in the computer from a digital camera?

Most digital cameras save pictures on miniature storage media, such as a memory card. By inserting the memory card in a card reader/writer in or attached to the computer or printer, users can access images the same way they access files on a disk drive. With some cameras, pictures also can transfer along a cable that connects the camera to the computer or printer. For more info, visit www.clarke-publish.com or visit the Internet and then search Google for WYSIWYG.

FIGURE 3-27 Personal photo editing software enables home users to edit digital photographs.

Clip Art/Image Gallery

Application software often includes a **clip art/image gallery,** which is a collection of clip art and photographs. Some applications have links to additional clips available on the Web. You can also purchase clip art/image gallery software that contains hundreds of thousands of images (Figure 3-27).

In addition to clip art, many clip art/image galleries provide fonts, animations, sounds, video clips, and audio clips.
You can use the images, font, and other items from the clip art/image gallery in all types of documents, including word processing, desktop publishing, spreadsheet, and presentation graphics.

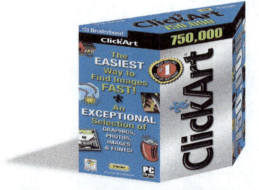

FIGURE 3-28 Clip art/image gallery software contains hundreds of thousands of images.

Video and Audio Editing Software (for professional Use)

Many home users work with easy-to-user video and audio editing software, which is much simpler to use than its professional counterparts, for small-scale movie making projects (Figure 3-28). With these programs, home users can edit home movies, add music or other sounds to the video, and share their movies on the Web. Some operating systems include video editing and audio editing software.

FIGURE 3-29 With personal video and audio editing software, home users can edit their home movies.

Home Design/Landscaping Software

Homeowners or potential home owners can use home design/landscaping software to assist them with the design, remodeling, or improvement of a home, deck, or landscape (Figure 3-29). This software includes hundreds of pre-drawn plans that you can customize to meet your needs. Once designed, many print out materials list outlining cost and quantities for the entire project. People in Liberia will soon gegin using home design software instead of going to local architects.

FIGURE 3-30 Home design/landscaping software can help you design or remodel a home, deck, or landscape.

Educational and Reference Software

Educational software is software that teaches a particular skill. Educational software exists for just about any subject, from learning how to type to learning how to cook. Preschool to high school learners use educational software to assist them with subjects such as reading and math or to prepare them for class or college entry exams. Educational software often includes games and other content to make the learning experience more fun.

Many educational programs use a computer-based training approach. Computer-base training (CBT) is a type of education in which students learn by using and completing exercises with instructional software. CBT typically consist of self-paced instruction about a topic. The military and airlines use CBT simulations to train pilots to fly in various conditions and environments. Some schools use CBT to help teach students' math, language, and other software skills.

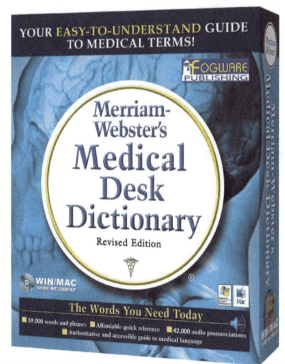

FIGURE 3-31 This reference dictionary gives text definitions and audio pronunciation of medical terms.

Reference software provides valuable and thorough information for all individuals (Figure 3-30). Popular reference software includes encyclopedias, dictionaries, health/medical guides, and travel directories.

Entertainment Software

Entertainment software for personal computers includes interactive games, videos, and other programs designed to support a hobby or provide amusement and enjoyment. For example, you might use entertainment software to play games, (Figure 3-31), make a family tree, listen to music, or fly an aircraft.

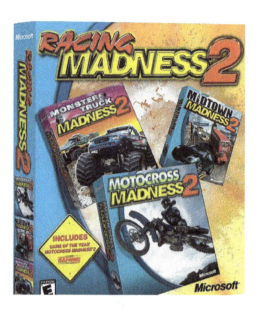

FIGURE 3-32 Entertainment software can provide hours of recreation.

APPLICATION SOFTWARE FOR COMMUNICATION

One of the main reasons people use computers is to communicate and share information with others. Some communications software is considered system software because it works with hardware and transmission media. Other communication software performs specific task for users, and thus, is considered application software. Chapter 2 presented a variety of application software for communications, which summarized in the table in Figure 3-32. Read Discussion 3-2 for a related discussion. Read Looking Ahead 3-2 for a look at the next generation of Web access.

DISCUSSION 3-2

Should Companies Monitor Employee's E-mail?

According to one survey, more than 42 percent of all companies monitor (after transmission) or intercept (during transmission) employees' e-mail. Employers can use software to find automatically personal or offensive e-mail message that have been sent or received, and intercept and filter messages while they are being sent or received. Companies monitor e-mail to improved productivity, increase security, reduce misconduct, and control liability risks. In the U.S. few laws regulate employee monitoring, and the courts have given employers a great deal of leeway in watching emails on company-owned computers. Presently in Liberia, there is no law against or in favor of companies monitoring employee's e-mail. Mean while, in one case, in the U.S., an employee's termination for using her office e-mail system to complain about her boss was upheld, even though the company allowed e-mail use for personal communications. The court decreed that the employee's messages were inappropriate for work place communications. Executives have not escaped scrutiny, either. Prominent leaders, such as Bill Gates, have had his e-mail messages used against him in court. Many employees believe that monitoring software violates their privacy rights, but employers believe that it helps employees become productive. Should companies monitor or intercept employees' e-mail? Why or Why not? How can a company balance workplace security and productivity with employee privacy? If a company monitors e-mail use, what guidelines should be followed to maintain worker morale? Why? Is intercepting and filtering e-mail more offensive than monitoring e-mail? Why?

APPLICATION SOFTWARE FOR COMMUNICATIONS

E-Mail
- Messages and files sent via a network such as the Internet
- Requires an e-mail program
  - Integrated in many software suites and operating systems
  - Available free at portals on the Web
  - Included with paid Internet access service
  - Can be purchased separately from retailers

FTP
- Method of uploading and downloading files with other computers on the Internet
- Download may require an FTP program; upload usually requires an FTP program
  - Integrated in some operating systems
  - Available for download on the Web for a small fee
  - Can be purchased separately from retailers

Web Browser
- Allows users to access and view Web pages on the Internet
- Requires a Web browser program
  - Integrated in some operating systems
  - Available for download on the Web free or for a fee

Video Conferencing/Telephone Calls
- Meeting/conversation between geographically separated people who use a network such as the Internet to transmit video/audio
- Requires a microphone, speakers, and sometimes a video camera attached to your computer
- Requires video conferencing software

Newsgroup/Message Board
- Online area where users have written discussions
- Newsgroup may require a newsreader program
  - Integrated in some operating systems, e-mail programs, and Web browsers
  - Available for download on the Web, usually at no cost
  - Included with some paid Internet access services

Chat Room
- Real-time, online typed conversation
- Requires chat client software
  - Integrated in some operating systems, e-mail programs, and Web browsers
  - Available for download on the Web, usually at no cost
  - Included with some paid Internet access services
  - Built into some Web sites

Instant Messaging
- Real-time exchange of messages, files, audio, and/or video with another online user
- Requires instant messenger software
  - Integrated in some operating systems
  - Available for download on the Web, usually at no cost
  - Included with some paid Internet access services

Blogging
- Time-stamped articles, or posts, in a diary or journal format, usually listed in reverse chronological order
- Blogger needs blog software, or blogware, to create and maintain a blog
  - Some Web sites are hosting services that do not require installation of blog software

FIGURE 3-32 A summary of application software for home and business communication.

Looking Ahead 3-2
Driving Down the Web Highway

M Analyst predict you will access the Internet from practically every where: home, office, airport, grocery store, and local coffee shops. Why not from your car? As it sits in your garage, your car's computer could connect to your home computer and then relay information about fluid levels and amount of gas in the tank. It could notify you when the oil needs to be changed and when the tire should be rotated. You even could start the car remotely on chilly days by pressing a button on your notebook computer as you eat your breakfast at the kitchen table. Automobile manufacturers are touting their cyber cars of the future to be equipped with Internet access. They are planning in-dash screens with continuous information about traffic, weather forecasts, and restaurant guides. Their plans also call for having the Internet access disconnected when the vehicle is in motion so the drivers do not attempt to drive and surf the Web simultaneously. For more info, visit the Internet and then search Google for Cyber Cars.

POPULAR UTILITY PROGRAMS

Utility programs are considered system software because they assist a user with controlling or maintaining the operation of a computer, its devices, or its software. Utility programs typically offer features that provide an environment conducive to successful use of application software. One of the more important utility programs should protect a computer against viruses. A computer virus is a potentially damaging program that affects, or infects, a computer negatively by altering the way a computer works without the user's knowledge or permission.

Other features of utility programs include protecting a computer against unauthorized intrusions, removing spyware, filtering e-mail and Web content, managing files, disks, compressing files, backing up drives, burning (recording on) a CD or DVD, and maintaining a personal computer. The table in Figure 3-33 briefly describes several types of utility programs.

WIDELY USED UTILITY PROGRAMS

Utility Program	Description
Antivirus Program	An antivirus program protects a computer against viruses by identifying and removing any computer viruses found in memory, on storage media, or in incoming files.
Personal Firewall	A personal firewall detects and protects a personal computer from unauthorized intrusions.
Spyware Remover	A spyware remover detects and deletes spyware on your computer.
Internet Filters • Anti-Spam Program • Web Filter • Pop-up Blocker	 An anti-spam program attempts to remove spam (Internet junk mail) before it reaches your e-mail inbox. A Web filter restricts access to specified Web sites. A pop-up blocker stops advertisements from displaying on Web pages and disables pop-up windows.
File Manager	A file manager provides functions related to file and disk management.
File Compression	A file compression utility shrinks the size of a file(s), so the file takes up less storage space than the original file.
Backup	A backup utility allows users to copy selected files or an entire hard disk to another storage medium.
CD/DVD Burning	A CD/DVD burner writes text, graphics, audio, and video files on a recordable or rewritable CD or DVD.
Personal Computer Maintenance	A personal computer maintenance utility identifies and fixes operating system problems, detects and repairs disk problems, and includes the capability of improving a computer's performance.

FIGURE 3-33 A summary of widely used utility.

FIGURE 3-34 Many programs include online Help.

LEARNING AIDS AND SUPPORT TOOLS FOR APPLICATION SOFTWARE

Learning how to use application software effectively involves time and practice. To assist in the learning process, many programs provide online Help (Figure 3-34) and Web-based Help.

Online Help is the electronic equivalent of a user manual. It usually is integrated in a program. In most programs, a function key or a button on the screen starts the Help feature. When using a program, you can use the Help feature to ask a question or access the Help topic in subject or alphabetical order.

Most online Help also link to Web sites that offer Web-based help, which provides updates and more comprehensive resources to respond to technical issues about software. Some Web sites contain chat rooms, in which a user can talk directly with a technical support person or join in on a conversation with other users who may be able to answer questions or solve problems. If you want to learn more about a particular program from a printed manual, many books are available to help you learn to use the many features of personal computer programs. These books typically are available in bookstores and software stores (Figure 3-35).

Web-Based Training

Web-base training (WBT) is a type of CBT (computer-based training) that uses Internet technology and consists of application software on the Web. Similar to CBT, WBT typically consists of self-directed, self-paced instruction about a topic. WBT is popular in business, industry, and schools for teaching new skills or enhancing existing skills of employees, teacher, or students.

Many Web sites offer WBT to the general public (Figure 3-36). Such training covers a wide range of topics, from how to change a flat tire to creating documents in Word. Many of these Web sites are free, but there are others that require registration and payment to take a complete Web-based course.

WBT often is combined with other materials for distance learning courses. **Distance learning** is the delivery of education at one location while the learning takes place at other locations.

FIGURE 3-35 Bookstores often sell trade books to help you learn to use features of personal computer applications software.

Seeing in the Dark
How Night Vision Works
Most of us instinctively think of darkness as a "cloak," a way to hide. Night vision has changed all that. So, how can you see someone standing over 200 yards away on a pitch-black night? It's pretty amazing.

Learn how various night-vision technologies let you see in the dark.

ing Soon: Costumes 101

How Zombies Work
Did you know that zombies ha folklore and -- according to so real events in Haiti?

How Lock Picking Works
In movies, burglars can open clip. Is it really so easy? Explo technology of locks and keys.

How Google Earth Works
Online mapping programs ca way, and they're just plain fun no ordinary mapping applicat

How Rail Guns Work
Using a magnetic field power electromagnetic rail gun can away in six minutes.

FIGURE 3-35 At the HowStuff-Works Web-based training site, you can learn how computers, autos, electronics, and many other products work.

Test your knowledge of pages 89 through 97 in Quiz Yourself 3-3

QUIZ YOURSELF 3-3

Instructions: Find the true statement below. Then rewrite the remaining false statement so they are true.

1. An anti-spam program protects a computer against viruses by identifying and removing and computer viruses found in memory, on storage media, or incoming files.

2. Computer-based training is a type of Web-based training that uses Internet technology and consists of application software on the Web.

3. E-mail and Web browsers are examples of communications software that are considered application software.

4. Legal software is a simplified accounting program that helps home users and small office/home office users balance their checkbooks, pay bills, track investments, and evaluate financial plans.

5. Personal DTP software is a popular type of image editing software that allows users to edit digital photographs.

Quiz Yourself Online: To further check your knowledge of types and feature of home, personal, educational, and communication programs, utility programs, and software learning aids visit www.clarkepublish.com or visit the Internet and then search www.google.com for more information.

CHAPTER SUMMARY

This chapter illustrated how to start and use application software. Then it presents an overview of a variety of business software, graphics and multimedia software, home/personal/educational software, and communication software. Finally, utility programs and learning aids for application software were presented, as they are widely used.

Help Desk Specialist

CAREER CORNER

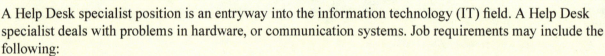

A Help Desk specialist position is an entryway into the information technology (IT) field. A Help Desk specialist deals with problems in hardware, or communication systems. Job requirements may include the following:

*   Solve procedural and software questions both in person and over the telephone
*   Develop and maintain Help Desk operations manuals
*   Assist in training new Help Desk personnel

Usually, a Help Desk specialist must be knowledgeable about major programs in being used. Entry-level positions primary involve answering calls from people with questions. Other position provide additional assistance and assume further responsibilities, often demanding greater knowledge and problem-solving skills that can lead to a more advanced position in the IT field. Help Desk specialist is an ideal position for people who must work irregular hours, because many companies need to support people who work evenings and weekends. Part-time Educational requirements are less stringent than they are for other positions in the computer field. In some cases, a high school diploma is sufficient enough. Advancement requires a minimum of a two-year degree, while management generally requires a bachelor's degree in IT or a related field. Certification is another why Help Desk specialist can increase their attractiveness in the marketplace. Entry-level salaries range from $37,000 to $60,000 per year. Manager's range from $49,500 to $90,000, but these salaries may not be the same for Help Desk Specialist in Liberia and other countries. For more info, visit the Internet and then search Google for Help Desk Specialist.

COMPANIES ON THE CUTTING EDGE

Adobe System

Digital Imaging Leader

Practically every image seen on a computer and in print has been shaped by software developed by Adobe Systems, Inc. The company, based in San Jose, California, is one of the World's largest application software corporations and is committed to helping people communicate effectively.

Adobe Photoshop and Portable Album have set the industry standard for digital imaging and digital video software, while creative Suite is used for design and publishing. The company's Portable Document Format (PDF) and Adobe Reader are used to share documents among users electronically. More than 600 million copies of the free Adobe Reader have been downloaded in 26 languages.

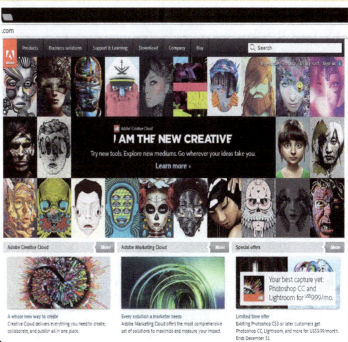

In 2005, Adobe entered into an agreement to acquire Macromedia, which develops such Web page authoring software as Flash MX and Dreamweaver MX. For more info, visit www.clarkepublish.com or visit Google and then search for Adobe.

Microsoft

Realizing Potential with Business Software

Microsoft mission is "to enable people and businesses throughout the world to realize their potential." As the largest software company in the world, Microsoft has indeed helped computer users in every field reach their goals.

When Microsoft was incorporated in 1975, the company had three programmers, one product and revenues of $16,000. Thirty years later, the company employs more that 57,000 people, produces numerous of software, naming Office and Windows leading the industry, and has annual revenue of more than $36 billion.

The company's recent efforts have focused on security issues, with it being to 35 percent of the research and development, budget being spent on preventing malicious software from getting onto computers, and promoting its Media Center, an entertainment hub designed for the living room. For more info, visit www.clarkepublish.com or Google and then search Microsoft.

TECHNOLOGY TRAILBLAZER

Dan Bricklin

VisiCalc Developer

When Dan Bricklin was enrolled at the Harvard Business School in the 1970s, he often used his calculator to determine the effect of changing one value on a balance sheet. He recognized the need to develop a program that would perform a series of calculations automatically when the first number is entered.

He named his creation VisiCalc, short for Visible Calculator. He and a friend formed a company called Software Arts and programmed the VisiCalc prototype using Apple Basic on an Apple II computer. The small program was the first piece of application software that provided a reason for businesses to buy Apple Computers. It laid the foundation for the development of other spreadsheets and included many of the features found in today's Spreadsheets and included many of the features found in 1985, where he started this type of software. He currently is president of Software Garden, Inc., a company he founded in 1985, where he does software product development and consulting. For more info, visit www.clarkebuplish.com or Google then search for Dan Bricklin.

Masayoshi Son

Softbank President and CEO

Many students carry photographs of family and friends in their wallets and book bags. As a 16-year-old student in the 1970s, Masayoshi Son carried a picture of a microchip. He predicted that the microchip was going to change people's lives, and he wanted to be a part of the trend.

While majoring in economics, at the University of California, Berkeley, he earned his first million dollars by importing arcade games from Japan to the campus, developing new computer games, and selling a patent for multilingual pocket translator to Sharp Corporation.

At age 23 he founded Softbank, which is Japan's second-largest broadband Internet service and telephone provider. He also is chairman of Yahoo! Japan. Today, he's one of the world's wealthiest entrepreneurs. For more info, visit www.clarkepublish.com or Google and then search for Masayoshi Son.

Chapter Review

The Chapter Review section summarizes the concepts presented in this chapter. To obtain help from other students regarding any subject in this chapter, visit the book's Web site.

1. **What Are the Categories of Application Software??**

   Application software consists of programs designed to make users more productive and/or assist them with personal tasks. The major categories of application software are business software; graphics and multimedia software; home, personal, and educational software; and communications software.

2. **How Do You Work with Application Software?**

   Personal computer operating systems often use the concept of a **desktop**, which is an on-screen work area that has a graphical user interface. To start an application in Windows XP or Vista, move the pointer to the Start button in the corner of the desktop and click the Start button by pressing and releasing a button on the mouse. Then, click the program name on the Start menu or on the submenu that displays when you point to a command. Once loaded in memory, the program is displayed in a window on the desktop.

3. **What Are the Key Features of Widely Used Business Programs?**

   Business software is application that assists people in becoming more effective while performing daily business activities. Business software includes the following programs Word processing software allows users to create a document by entering text or number and inserting graphical images, editing the document by making changes to its existing content, and format the document by altering its appearance. Spreadsheet software allows users to organize data in rows and columns, perform calculations, recalculate when data changes, and chart the data in graphical form. Database software allows users to create a database, which is a collection of data organized in a manner that allow access, retrieval, and use of that data. Presentation graphics software allows users to create slides that are displayed on a monitor or on a projection screen. Note taking software enables users to enter text, handwritten comments, drawings, and sketches. A personal information manager (PIM) is software that includes an appointment calendar, address book, notepad, and other features to help users organize personal information. Project management software allows users to plan, schedule, track, and analyze the events, resources, and costs of a project. Accounting software helps companies record and report their financial transactions. Document management software provides a means for sharing, distributing, and searching through documents by converting them into a format that can be viewed by any user.

4. **What Are the Key Features of Widely Used Graphics and Multimedia Programs?**

   Graphics and multimedia software includes the following. Computer-aided design (CAD) software assist a professional user in creating engineering, architectural, and scientific design. Desktop publishing (DTP) software enables professional designers to create sophisticated documents that contain text, graphics, and colors. Paint software allows users to draw pictures, shapes, and other graphical images with various on-screen tools. Image editing software provides the capabilities of paint software and also includes the capability to modify existing images. Professional photo editing software is a type of image editing software that allows photographers, videographers, engineers, scientist, and other high-volume digital photo users to edit and customize digital photographs. Video editing software allows professionals to modify a segment of a video, called a clip. Audio editing software lets users modify audio clips and produce studio-quality soundtracks. Multimedia authoring software allows users to combine text, graphics, audio, video, and animation into an interactive application.

5. **What Are the Key Features of Widely Used Home, Personal, and Educational Programs?**

   Software for home, personal, and educational use includes the following. A software suite (for personal use) combines application software such as word processing, spreadsheet, and database into a single, easy-to-use package. Personal finance software is a simplified accounting program that helps users balance their checkbooks, pay bills (this is done in the U.S. and other western countries), track personal income and expenses, track investments, and evaluate financial plans. Personal DTP software helps home and small business users create newsletters, brochures, advertisements, postcards, greeting cards, letterhead, business cards, banners, calendars, logos, and Web pages.

Paint/image editing software for personal use provides an easy-to-use interface, and includes various simplified tools that allow users to draw pictures, shapes, and other image and modify existing graphics and photos. Application software often includes a clip art/image gallery, which is a collection of clip art and photographs. Home design/landscaping software assists users with the design, remodeling, or improvement of a home, deck, or landscape. Educational software teaches a particular skill. Reference software provides valuable and thorough information for all individuals.

6. **What Are the Types of Application Software Used in Communications?**

Application software for communications includes e-mail programs to transmit messages via a network, FTP program to upload and download files on the Internet, Web browser programs to access and view Web pages, video conferencing/telephone call software for meeting or conversations on a network between geographically separated people, newsreader/message board programs that allow online written discussions with other users, chat room software to have real-time, online typed conversations, instant messaging software for real-time exchange of message or files, and blog software, or blogware, to create and maintain a blog.

7. **What Are the Functions of Utility programs?**

Utility programs support the successful use of application software. An antivirus program protects a computer against a computer virus, which is a potentially damaging computer program. A personal firewall detects and protects a personal computer from unauthorized intrusions. A spyware remover detects and deletes spyware. An anti-spam program removes spam (Internet junk mail). A Web filter restricts access to specified Web sites. A pop-up blocker disables pop-up windows on a Web page. A file manager provides functions related to file and disk management. A backup utility allows users to copy selected files or an entire hard disk to another storage medium. A CD/DVD burner writes files to a recordable CD or DVD. A personal computer maintenance utility fixes operating system and disk problems.

8. **What Learning Aids Are Available for Application Software?**

To assist in the learning process, many programs provide a variety of Help features. Online Help is the electronic equivalent of a user manual. Most online Help also links to Web-based help, which provides updates and more comprehensive resources to respond to technical issues about software.

Key Terms

You should know the Key Terms. Use the list below to help focus your study. To further enhance your understanding of the Key Terms in this chapter, visit www.clarkepublish.com and click the chapter 1 link.

accounting software (85)
application software (74)
audio editing software (88)
business software (78)
button (76)
click (76)
clip art (83)
clip art/image gallery (92)
command (77)
computer-aided design
(CAD) software (87)
computer-based training
(93)
create (80)
custom software (75)
database (82)
database software (82)
desktop (76)
desktop publishing (DTP)
software (87)

distance learning (97)
document management
software (86)
edit (80)
educational software (93)
entertainment software (95)
file (77)
font (80)
font size (80)
font style (80)
format (80)
freeware (75)
Help Desk specialist (98)
home design/landscaping
software (93)
icon (76)
image editing software (87)
legal software (91)
menu (77)
multimedia authoring

software (88)
note taking software (84)
online Help (96)
open source software (75)
package software (75)
paint software (87)
PDF (84)
personal DTP software (91)
personal finance
software (90)
personal information
manager (PIM) (84)
personal paint/image
editing software (92)
personal photo editing
software (87)
pointer (76)
presentation graphics
software (83)
print (80)

public-domain software (75)
reference software (94)
save (80)
shareware (75)
software suite (85)
spreadsheet software (80)
system software (75)
tax preparation
software (91)
title bar (77)
video editing software (88)
Web page authoring
software (89)
window (77)
word processing
software (79)
Worksheet (80)

Checkpoint

Use the Checkpoint exercises to check your knowledge level of the chapter.

True/False	Mark T for True and F for False. (see page numbers in parentheses.)

_____ 1. Open source software has restrictions for the copyright holder regarding modification of the software's internal instructions and redistribution of the software.

_____ 2. Shareware, freeware, and public-domain programs usually are available on the Web for download.

_____ 3. The desktop is an on-screen work area that has a graphical user interface.

_____ 4. A menu contains a list of commands from which you make selections.

_____ 5. Business software includes programs such as word processing, spreadsheet, and presentation graphics.

_____ 6. A font is a name assigned to a specific design of characters.

_____ 7. The programs in a software suite use a similar interface and share some common features.

_____ 8. Legal software assists in the preparation of legal documents and provides legal information to individuals, families, and small businesses.

_____ 9. Not all communications software is considered to be application software.

_____ 10. When using a program, you can use the Help feature to ask a question or access the Help topics in subject or alphabetical order.

104

Multiple Choice **Select the best answer (see page numbers in parentheses.)**

1. The title bar of a document window usually displays the document's _____.
   a. file name
   b. file size
   c. file path
   d. all of the above

2. A feature, called _____, allows users of word processing software to type words continually without pressing the ENTER key at the end of each line.
   a. wordwrap
   b. autocorrect
   c. auto format
   d. clipboard

3. When using spreadsheet software, a function _____.
   a. depicts data in graphical form
   b. changes certain values to reveal the effects of the changes
   c. is a predefined formula that performs common calculation
   d. contains the formation necessary for a specific worksheet type

4. With database software, users can run a _____ to request specific data from the database.
   a. query
   b. record
   c. field
   d. form

1. _____ software provides a means for sharing, distributing, and searching through documents by converting them into a format that can be viewed by any user.
   a. Database
   b. Document management
   c. Portable Document Format
   d. Word processing

2. Training center, educational institutions, and online magazines publishers all use _____ software to develop interactive applications.
   a. Image editing
   b. desktop publishing
   c. computer-aided design
   d. multimedia authoring

3. _____ provides valuable and thorough information for all individuals.
   a. computer-based training (CBT)
   b. Reference software
   c. Online Help
   d. Web-base training

4. A (n) _____, which can be used to upload and download files with other computers and on the Internet, is integrated in some operating systems.
   a. FTP program
   b. e-mail program
   c. Web browser
   d. chat client

Matching **Match the terms with their definitions. (see page numbers in parentheses.)**

_____ 1. clip art

_____ 2. clipboard

_____ 3. font

_____ 4. communication management software

_____ 5. PDF

a. popular file format used by document management software to save converted documents

b. provides a means for sharing, distributing, and searching through documents

c. collection of drawings, diagrams, maps, and photographs

d. name assigned to a specific design of characters

e. temporary storage location that contains items cut from a document

f. delivers applications to meet a specific business need

Write a brief answer to each of the following questions.

1.   What is charting? _____ How are line charts, column charts, and pie charts, different? _____

2.   What are the features of personal information manager software? _____ Where might you find personal informa tion manger software? _____

3.   What are the benefits of document software? _____ Why do businesses use document management software? _____

4.   What is computer-based training CBT? _____ How is CBT used? _____

5.   What is online Help? _____ How can Web-based Help assist software users? _____

Working Together   **Working in a group of your classmates, complete the following team exercise.**

1.   In any software application, each program is not exactly the same. Different spreadsheet program, for example, may have different methods to enter formulas, use functions, and draw charts. Have each member of your team interview someone who works with an application described in this chapter: What specific program is used? Why for what purpose is the program used? What does the interviewee like, or dislike about the program? Would the interviewee recommend this program? Why? Meet with your team to discuss the result of you interviews. Then, use PowerPoint to create a group presentation and share your findings with the class.

Web Research

Use the Internet-based Web Research exercises to broaden your understand of the concepts presented in this chapter. Visit book's Web site to obtain more information pertaining to each exercise. To discuss any of the Web Research exercises in this chapter with other students, post your thoughts or questions at the forum.

1.   Journaling Respond to your readings in this chapter by writing at least one page about your reactions, evaluations, and reflections about the first time you used home, personal, and educational software. For example, have you en-hanced or modified digital photos with paint/image editing software? What video games have you played on a home computer? You also can writhe about the new terms you learned by reading this chapter. If required, submit your journal to your instructor or teacher.

2.   Scavenger Hunt Use one of the search engines listed in Figure 2-8 in chapter 2 on page 46 or your own favorite search engine to find the answer to the question below. Copy and paste the Web address from the Web page where you found the answer. Some question may have more than one answer. If required, submit your answer to your in-struction or teacher.

   (1) What is the name of the latest Boeing flight deck added to Microsoft Flight Simulator?

   (2) What video game did Atari begin selling at Sears under the label telegames in 1975?

   (3) What inventor designed one of the first mechanical calculating devices, called the Codex?

   (4) What Web site features software that creates a game requiring a player to put number in nine rows of nine boxes?

   (5) What is the name of the first successful word processing program?

   (6) How many schools and colleges in Liberia have their own Web site?

3.   Search Sleuth A virus is a potentially damaging computer program that can harm files and the

   operating system. The National Institute of Standard and Technology Computer Security Resource Center (csrc.nist.gov/virus) is one of the more comprehensive Web sites discussing viruses. Visit this Web site and then use your word processing program to answer the following questions. Then, if required, submit your answer to you instructor or teacher.

(1) The virus information page provides general information about viruses and links to various resources that provides more specific details. What two steps does the National Institute recommend to detect and prevent viruses from spreading?

(2) Click the Symantec link in the Virus Resources & Other Areas of Interest section. What viruses are the latest threats, and when were they discovered?

(3) Click Search at the top of the page and then type "Sasser worm" as the keyword in the Search text box. How man articles discuss the Sasser worm on the Symantec Web site? What three functions does the Sasser Removal Tools perform?

(4) Click your browser's Back button or press the BACKSPACE key to return to the National Institute of Standard and Technology Virus Information page. Click the F-Secure link in the Virus Resources & Other Areas of Interest section.

(5) What are three viruses listed in the Latest Threats section?

(6) Click one of the Latest News links and review the material. Summarize the information you read and then write a 50-word summary.

Learn How To

Use the Learn How To activities to learn fundamental skills when using a computer and accompanying technology. Complete the exercises and submit them to your instructor or teacher.

LEARN HOW TO 1:

Saving a File in Application Software

When you use application software, most of the time you either will be creating a new file or modifying an exiting file. For example, if you are using a word processor, when you create a new document, the document is a file. When you create or modify a file, it is contained in RAM. If you turn off you computer or lose electrical power, the file will not be retained. In order to retain the file, you must save it on disk or other permanent storage, such as a USB drive, CD R/RW. As you create the file, you should save the file often.

To save a new file, you must complete several tasks:
1. Initiate an action indicating you want to save the file, such as clicking the save button on the standard toolbar.
2. Designate where the file should be stored. This includes identifying both the device (such as drive C) and the folder (such as Desktop).
3. Specify the name of the file, using the file name rules as specified by the application or operating system.
4. Click the Save button to save the file.

Task 2 through 4 normally can be completed using a dialog box such as shown in Figure 3-37. If you use application software to create or modify a file and attempt to close the program prior to saving the new or modified file, the program will display a dialog box that asks if you want to save the file. If you click the Yes button, a modified file will be saved using the same file name in the location from which it was retrieved. Saving a new file requires that you complete task 2 through 4.

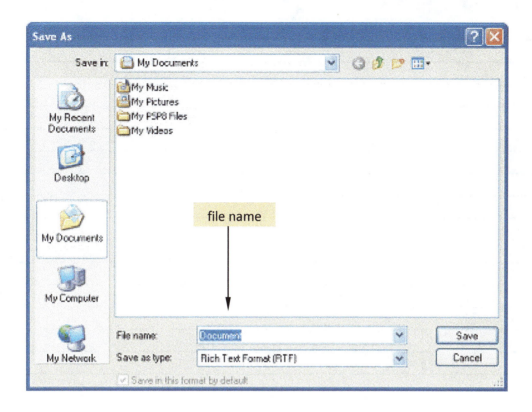

file name

Exercise

1. Start the WordPad program from the Accessories submenu on the all programs submenu.

2. Type Saving a file is the best insurances against losing work.

3. Click the Save button on the WordPad toolbar. What dialog box is displayed? Where will the file be saved? What is the default file name? If you wanted to save the file in My Documents, what would you do? (Hint: Look in the left margin of the dialog box.) Click the cancel button in the dialog box. Submit the answer to your instructor or teacher.

4. Click the Close button in the upper-right corner of the WordPad window. What happened? Click the Yes button in the WordPad dialog box. What happened? Place either a floppy disk in drive A or a USB in a USB port. Select either the floppy disk or the USB drive as the location for saving the file. Name the file, Chapter 3 How To 1. Save the file. What happened when you clicked the Save button? Submit your answer to your instructor or instructor.

This Page Was Intentionally Left Blank

CHAPTER 4
THE COMPONENTS OF THE SYSTEM UNIT

power supply
drive bays
intel pentium 4
processor
ports
memory
sound card
network card
modem card
video card

OBJECTIVES

After completing this chapter you will be able to:

1. Differentiate among various styles of system units
2. Describe the components of a processor and how they complete a machine cycle
3. Define a bit and describe how a series of bits represents data
4. Differentiate among the various types of memory
5. Describe the types of expansion slots and adapter card
6. Explain the differences among a serial port, a parallel port, a USB port, and other ports
7. Describe how buses contribute to a computer's processing speed
8. Identify components in mobile computers and mobile devices
9. Understand how to clean a system unit

CONTENTS

Whether you are a home user or a business user in Liberia or wherever you travel, you most likely will make the decision to purchase a new computer or upgrade an existing computer within the next several years. Thus, you should understand the purpose of each component in a computer. As Chapter 1 discussed, a computer includes devices used for input, processing, output, storage, and communications. Many of these components are part of the system unit. Due to the scarcity of financial resources in Liberia, many people often hold onto their computers longer than recommended by experts. Usually, the lifespan of a laptop computer is three years.

The **system unit** is a case that contains electronic components of the computer used to process data. System units are available in a variety of shapes and sizes. The case of the system unit is made of metal or plastic and protects the internal electronic components from damage. All computers have a system unit (Figure 4-1).

On desktop personal computer, the electronic components and most storage devices are part of the system unit. Other devices, such as the keyboard, mouse, microphone, monitor, printer, scanner, PC video camera, and speakers, normally occupy space outside the system unit. On notebook computers, the keyboard and pointing devices often occupy the area on the top of the system unit, and the display attaches to the system unit by hinges. The location of the system unit…

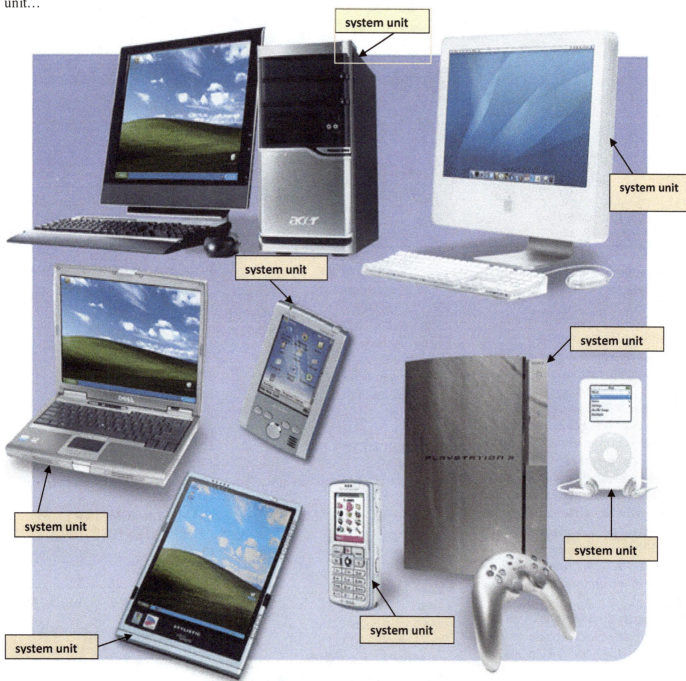

FIGURE 4-1 All sizes of computers have a system unit.

on a Tablet PC varies, depending on the design of the Tablet PC. Some models build the system unit behind the display (as shown in Figure 4-1), while others position the system unit below the keyboard (shown later in the chapter). The system unit on a PDA or iPad and smart phone usually consumes the entire device. On these mobile devices, the display often is built into the system unit. With game consoles, the input devices, such as controllers and televisions, reside outside the system unit. On handheld game consoles and digital audio players, by contrast, the packaging around the system unit houses the input devices and display.

At some point, you might have to open the system unit on a desktop personal computer to replace or install a new electronic component. For this reason, you should be familiar with the electronic components of a system unit. Figure 4-2 identifies some of these components, which include the processor, memory, adapter cards, ports, drive bays, and the power supply. Computer technicians in Liberia need to get familiar with these components that are found in modern computing devices.

The processor interprets and carries out the basic instructions that operate a computer. Memory typically holds data waiting to be processed and instructions waiting to be executed. The electronic components and circuitry of the system unit, such as the processor and memory, usually are part of or are connected to a circuit board called the motherboard. Many motherboards also integrate modem and network capabilities.

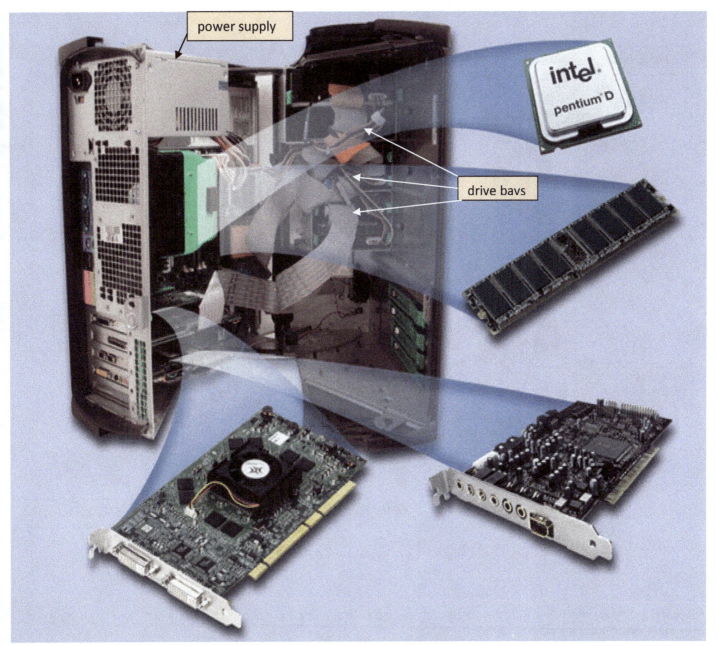

FIGURE 4-2 The system unit on a typical personal computer consist of numerous electronic components. Some of which are shown in this figure. The sound card and video card are two types of adapter cards.

Adapter cards are circuit boards that provide connections and functions not built into the motherboard. Two adapter cards found in some desktop personal computers today are a sound card and a video card.

Devices outside the system unit often attached to ports on the system unit by a connector on a cable. These devices may include a keyboard, mouse, microphone, monitor, printer, scanner, card reader/writer, digital camera, PC video camera, and speakers. A drive bay holds one or more disk drives. The power supply allows electricity to travel through a power cord for a wall outlet into a computer

The Motherboard

The **motherboard,** sometimes called a system board, is the main circuit board of the system unit. Many electronic components attach to the motherboard; others are built into it. Figure 4-3 shows a photograph of a current desktop personal computer motherboard and identifies some components that attach to it, including adapter cards, a processor chip, and memory module. Memory chips are installed on memory cards (modules) that fit in a slot on the motherboard.

A computer **chip** is a small piece of semiconducting material, usually silicon, on which integrated circuits are etched. An integrated circuit contains many microscopic pathways capable of carrying electrical current. Each integrated circuit can contain millions of elements such as resistors, capacitors, and transistors.

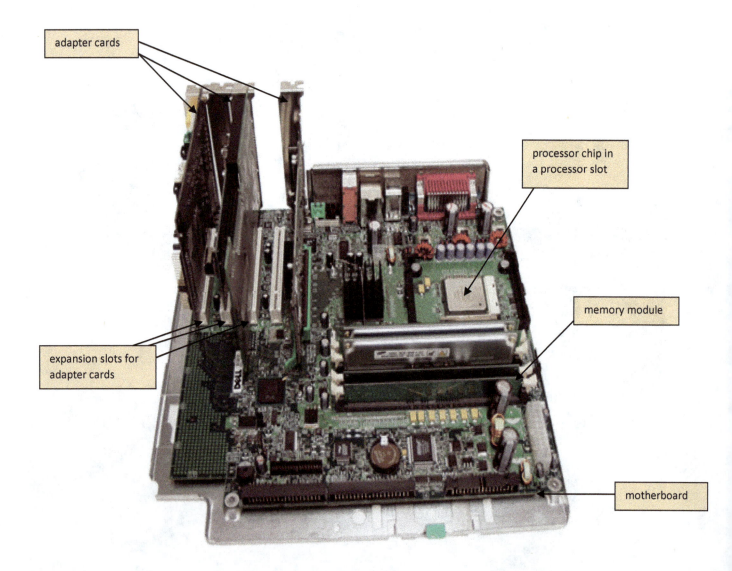

FIGURE 4-3 Many electronic components attach to the motherboard in a desktop personal computer, including a processor chip, memory module, and adapter cards.

PROCESSOR

The **processor**, also called the **central processing unit (CPU),** interprets and carries out the basic instructions that operate a computer. The processor significantly impacts overall computing power and manages most of a computer's operations. On a personal computer, all functions of the processor usually are on a single chip. Some computer and chip manufactures use the term **microprocessor** to refer to a personal computer processor chip.

Processors contain a control unit and an arithmetic logic unit (ALU). These two components work together to perform processing operations. Figure 4-4 illustrates how other devices that are connected to the computer communicate with the processor to carry out a task.

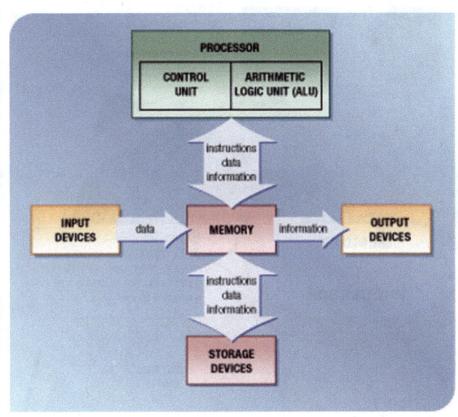

FIGURE 4-4 Most devices connected to the computer communicate with the processor to carry out a task. When a user starts a program, for example, its instructions transfer from a storage device to memory from either an input device or a storage device. The control unit interprets and executes instructions in memory, and the ALU performs calculations on the data in memory, from which it can be sent to an output device or a storage device for future access, as needed.

The Control Unit

The **control unit** is the component of the processor that directs and coordinates most of the operations in the computer. The control unit has a role much like a traffic cop: it interprets each instruction issued by a program and then initiates the appropriate action to carry out the instruction.

The Arithmetic Logic Unit

The **arithmetic logic unit (ALU),** another component of the processor, performs arithmetic, comparison, and other operations. Arithmetic operations include basic calculation such as addition, subtraction, multiplication, and division. Comparison operations involve comparing one data item with another to determine whether the first item is greater than, equal to, or less than the other item. Depending on the result of the comparison, different actions may occur.

Machine Cycle

For every instruction, a processor repeats a set of four basic operations, which comprise a machine cycle (Figure 4-5): (1) fetching, (2) decoding, (3) executing, and, if necessary, (4) storing. Fetching is the process of obtaining a program instruction or data item from memory. The term decoding refers to the process of translating the instruction into signals the computer can execute. Executing is the process of carrying out the commands. Storing, in this context, means writing the result to memory (not to a storage medium).

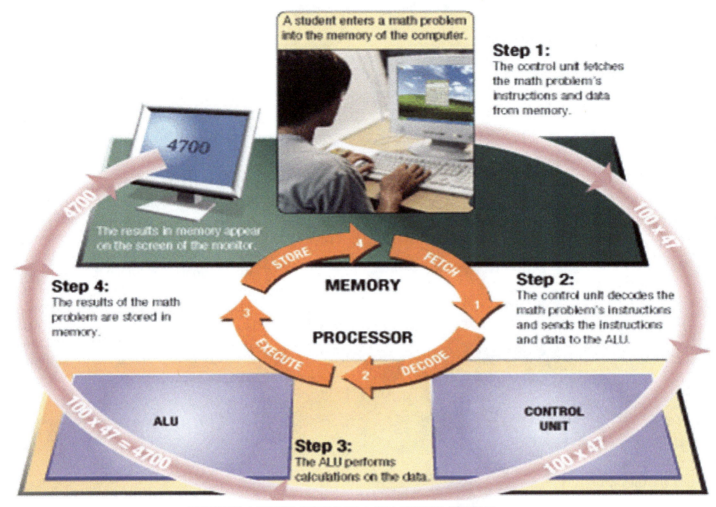

FIGURE 4-5 THE STEPS IN A MACHINE CYCLE

The System Clock

The processor relies on a small quartz crystal circuit called the **system clock** to control the timing of all computer operations. Just as your heart beats at a regular rate to keep your body functioning, the system clock generates regular electronic pulses, or ticks, that set the operating pace of components of the system unit.

The pace of the system clock, called the **clock speed,** is measured by the number of ticks per second. Current personal computer processors have clock speeds in the gigahertz range. **Gig** is a prefix that stands for billion, and a hertz is one cycle per second. Thus, one **gigahertz (GHz)** equals one billion ticks of the system clock per second. A computer that operates at 3.8 GHz has 3.8 billion (giga) clock cycles in one second (hertz). The faster the clock speed, the more instructions the processor can execute per second. The speed of the system clock is just one factor that influences a computer's performance. Other factors, such as the type of processor chip, amount of cache, memory access time, bus width, and bus clock speed, are discussed later in this chapter. Read Looking Ahead 4-1 for a look at the next generation of processing speeds.

Comparison of Personal Computer Processors

The leading processor chip manufactures for personal computers are Intel, AMD (Advanced Micro Devices), Transmeta, IBM, and Motorola. These manufactures often identify their processor chips by a model name or model number.

With its earlier processors, Intel used a model number to identify the various chips. After learning that processor model numbers could not be trademarked and protected from use by competitors, Intel began identifying its processor with name–thus emerged the series of processors know as the Pentium. Most high-performance desktop PCs use some type of Pentium processor. Many notebook computers and Tablet PCs use a Pentium M processor. Less expensive, basic PC use a brand of Intel processor called the Celeron. Two more brands, called the Xeon and Itanium processors, are ideal for workstations and low-end servers.

AMD is the leading manufacture of Intel-compatible processors, which have an internal design similar to Intel processor, perform the same functions, and can be as powerful, but often are less expensive. Transmeta, also a manufacturer on Intel-compatible processors, specializes in processors for mobile computers and devices. Intel and Intel-compatible processors are used in PCs.

Until recently, Apple computers used only an IBM processor or a Motorola processor, which had a design different from the Intel-style processor. Today's Apple computers, however, use Intel processors.

In the past, chip manufactures listed a processor's clock speed in marketing literature and advertisements. As previously mentioned, though, clock speed is only one factor that impacts processing speed in today's computers. To help consumers evaluate various processors, manufacturers such as Intel and AMD now use a numbering scheme that more accurately reflects the processing speed of their chips

Buying a Personal Computer

If you are ready to buy a new computer, the processor you select should depend on how you plan to use the computer. If you purchase an IBM-compatible PC or Apple computer, you will choose an Intel processor or an Intel-compatible processor.

Most users will realize greater processing performance with a dual-core/multicore processor.

A **dual-core processor** is a chip that has two separate processors, and a **multicore processor** has two or more separate processors. Each processor on a dual-core/multicore chip generally runs at a slower clock speed than a single-core processor, but dual-core/multicore chips typically reduce the power consumption and heat output, while increasing overall performance. There are newer processors available on the market, such as quad-core from AMD and Intel.

If you plan to purchase an entertainment desktop computer, you will want it to use Intel's Viiv technology, which is designed enhance digital entertainment through the home computer.

For detailed computer purchasing guidelines, read Discussion 4-1 on the previous page for related discussion.

Test your knowledge of pages 110 through 116 in Quiz Yourself 4-1.

QUIZ YOURSELF 4-1

Instructions: Find the true statement below. Then rewrite the remaining false statement so they are true.

1. A computer chip is a small piece of semiconducting material, usually silicon, on which integrated circuits are etched.

2. four basic operations in a machine cycle are: (1) comparing, (2) decoding, (3) executing, and if necessary, (4) pipelining.

3. Processors contain a motherboard and an arithmetic logic unit (ALU).

4. The central processing unit, sometimes called a system board, is the main circuit board of the system unit.

5. The leading processor chip manufacturers for personal computers are Microsoft, AMD, IBM, Motorola, and Transmeta.

6. The system unit is a case that contains mechanical components of the computer used to process data

Quiz Yourself Online: To further check your knowledge of system unit style, processor components, and machine cycles, visit www.clarkepublish.com or visit the Internet and then search www.google.com for more information.

DATA REPRESENTATION

To understand fully the way a computer processes data, you should know how a computer represents data. Most computers are **digital**. They recognize only two discrete states: on and off. The two digits, 0 and 1, easily can represent these two states (Figure 4-6). The digit 0 represents the electronic state of off (absence of an electronic charge). The digit 1 represents the electronic state of on (presence of an electronic charge).

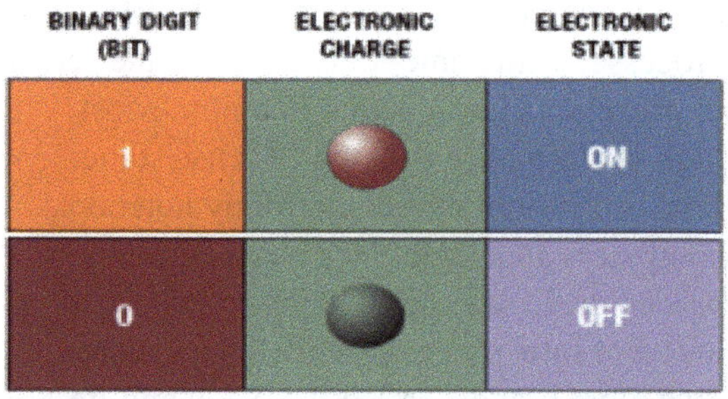

FIGURE 4-6 A shows how computer represent data.

The computer uses a binary system because it recognizes only two states. The **binary system** is a number system that has just two unique digits, 0 and 1, called bits. A **bit** (short for binary digit) is the smaller unit of data the computer can process. By itself, a bit is not very informative.

When 8 bits are grouped together as a unit, they form a **byte**. A byte provides enough different combinations of 0s and 1s to represent 256 individual characters. These characters include numbers, uppercase and lowercase letters of the alphabet, punctuation marks, and others, such as the letters of the Greek alphabet.

The combinations of 0s and 1s that represent characters are defined by patterns called a coding scheme. In one coding scheme, the number 4 is represented as 00110100, the number 6 as 00110110, and the capital letter E as 010001010 (figure 4-7). Two popular coding schemes

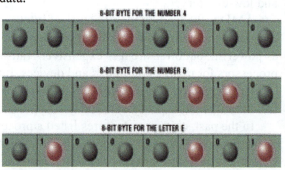

FIGURE 4-7 Eight bits grouped together as a unit are called a byte. A byte represents a single character in the computer.

are ASCII and EBCDIC (Figure 4-8). The American Standard Code for Information Interchange (ASCII pronounced ASK-ee) scheme is the most widely   used coding system to represent data. Most personal computers and servers use the ASCII coding scheme. The Extended Binary Coded Decimal Interchange Code (EBCDIC pronounced EB-see-dik) scheme is used primarily on mainframe computers and high-end servers.

Coding schemes such as ASCII makes it possible for human to interact with a digital computer that processes only bits. When you press a key on a keyboard, a chip in the keyboard converts the key's electronic signal into a scan code that is sent to the system unit. Then, the system unit converts the scan code into a binary form the computer can process and is stored in memory. Every character is converted to its corresponding byte. The computer then processes the data as bytes, which actually is a series of on/off electronic states. When processing is finished, software converts the byte into a human-recognizable number, letter of the alphabet, or special character that is displayed on a screen or is printed (Figure 4-9). All of these conversions take place so quickly that you do not realize they are occurring.

Standards, such as those define by ASCII and EBCDIC, also make it possible for components in computers to communicate successfully with each other.

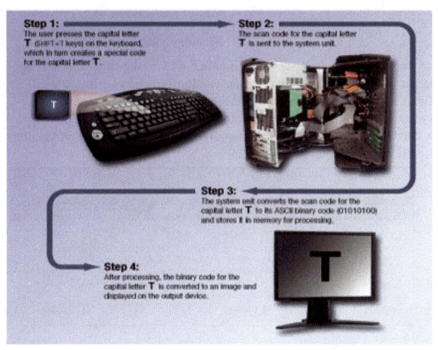

FIGURE 4-9 HOW A LETTER IS CONVERTED TO BINARY FORM AND BACK

ASCII	SYMBOL	EBCDIC
00110000	0	11110000
00110001	1	11110001
00110010	2	11110010
00110011	3	11110011
00110100	4	11110100
00110101	5	11110101
00110110	6	11110110
00110111	7	11110111
00111000	8	11111000
00111001	9	11111001
01000001	A	11000001
01000010	B	11000010
01000011	C	11000011
01000100	D	11000100
01000101	E	11000101
01000110	F	11000110
01000111	G	11000111
01001000	H	11001000
01001001	I	11001001
01001010	J	11010001
01001011	K	11010010
01001100	L	11010011
01001101	M	11010100
01001110	N	11010101
01001111	O	11010110
01010000	P	11010111
01010001	Q	11011000
01010010	R	11011001
01010011	S	11100010
01010100	T	11100011
01010101	U	11100100
01010110	V	11100101
01010111	W	11100110
01011000	X	11100111
01011001	Y	11101000
01011010	Z	11101001
00100001	!	01011010
00100010	"	01111111
00100011	#	01111011
00100100	$	01011011
00100101	%	01101100
00100110	&	01010000
00101000	(	01001101
00101001	)	01011101
00101010	*	01011100
00101011	+	01001110

FIGURE 4-8 Two popular coding schemes are ASCII and EBCDIC.

MEMORY

Memory consists of electronic components that store instructions waiting to be executed by the processor, data needed by those instructions, and the results of processed data (information). Memory usually consists of one or more chips on the motherboard or some other circuit board in the computer.

Memory stores three basic categories of items: (1) the operating system and other system software that control or maintain the computer and its devices; (2) application programs that carry out a specific task such as word processing; and (3) the data being processed by the application programs and resulting information. This role of memory to store both data and programs is known as the stored program concept..

Bytes and Addressable Memory

A **byte** (character) is the basic storage unit in memory. When application program instructions and data are transferred to memory from storage devices, the instructions and data exist as bytes. Each byte resides temporarily in a location in memory that has an address. An address simply is a unique number that identifies the locations of the byte in memory. The illustration in Figure 4-10 shows how seats in a concert hall are similar to addresses in memory: (1) a seat, which is identified by a unique seat number, holds one person at a time, and location in memory, which is identified by a unique address, holds single byte; and (2) both a seat, identified by a seat number, and a byte, identified by an address, can be empty. To access data or instructions in memory, the computer references the addresses that contain bytes of data.

FIGURE 4-10 Seats in a concert hall are similar to addresses in memory: seat holds one person at a time, and location in memory holds a single byte; and both a seat and a byte can be empty.

Memory Sizes

Manufactures state that size of memory chips and storage devices in terms of the number of bytes the chip or device has available for storage (Figure 4-11). Recall that storage devices hold data, instructions, and information for future use, while most memory holds these items temporarily. A **kilobyte (KB or K)** is equal to exactly 1,024 bytes. To simplify memory and storage definitions, computer users often round a kilobyte down to 1,000 bytes. For example, if a memory chip can store 100 KB, it can hold approximately 100,000 bytes (characters). A **megabyte (MB)** is equal to approximately 1 million bytes. A **gigabyte (GB)** equals approximately 1 billion bytes. A **terabyte (TB)** is equal to approximately 1 trillion bytes.

FIGURE 4-11 Seats in a concert hall are similar to addresses in memory: seat holds one person at a time, and location in memory holds a single byte; and both a seat and a byte can be empty.

MEMORY AND STORAGE SIZES

Term	Abbreviation	Approximate Number of Bytes	Exact Amount of Bytes	Approximate Number of Pages of Text
Kilobyte	KB or K	1 thousand	1,024	1/2
Megabyte	MB	1 million	1,048,576	500
Gigabyte	GB	1 billion	1,073,741,824	500,000
Terabyte	TB	1 trillion	1,099,511,627,776	500,000,000

Types of Memory

The system unit contains two types of memory: volatile and nonvolatile. When the computer's power is turned off, **volatile memory** loses its contents. Nonvolatile memory, by contrast, does not lose its contents when power is removed from the computer. Thus, **volatile memory** is temporary and nonvolatile memory is permanent. RAM is the most common type of volatile memory. Examples of nonvolatile memory include ROM, flash memory, and CMOS. The following sections discuss these types of memory.

RAM

Users typically are referring to **RAM** when discussing computer memory. RAM (random access memory), also called main memory, consists of memory chips that can be read from and written to by the processor and other devices. When you turn on power to a computer, certain operating system files (such as the files that determine how the Windows Vista desktop appears) load into RAM from a storage device such as hard disk. These files remain in RAM as long as the computer has continuous power. As additional programs and data are requested, they also load into RAM from storage.

The processor interprets and executes a program's instructions while the program is in RAM. During this time, the contents of RAM may change (Figure 4-12). RAM can hold multiple programs simultaneously, provided the computer has enough RAM to accommodate all the programs.

Most RAM is volatile, which means it loses its contents when the power is removed from the computer. For this reason, you must save any items you may need in the future. Saving is the process of copying items from RAM to a storage device such as a hard disk.

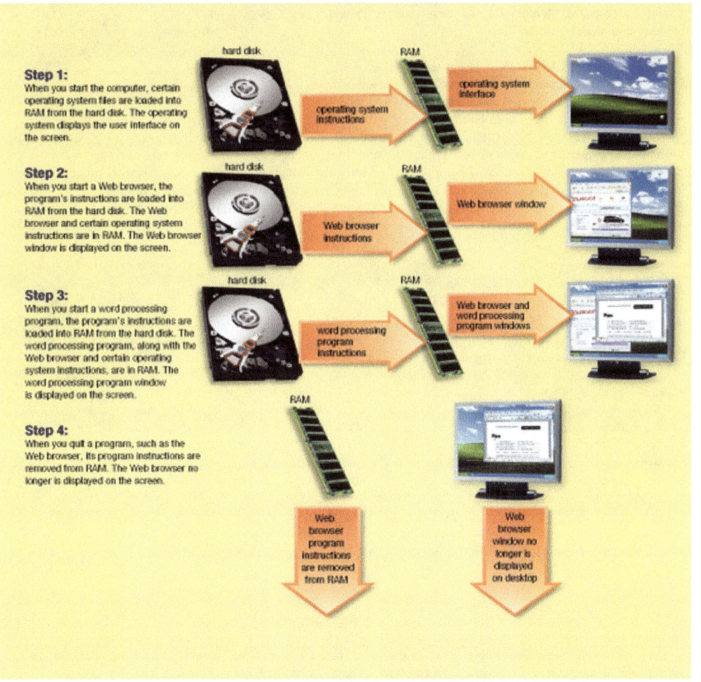

FIGURE 4-12 HOW PROGRAM INSTRUCTION TRANSFER IN AND OUT OF RAM

Three basic types of RAM chips exist: dynamic RAM, static RAM, and magnetoresistive RAM.

- Dynamic RAM (DRAM pronounced DEE-ram) chips must be re-energized constantly or they lose their contents.
- Static RAM (SRAM pronounced ESS-ram) chips are faster and more reliable than any variation of DRAM chips. These chips do not have to be re-energized as often as DRAM chips, thus, the term static.
- A newer type of RAM, called magnetoresistive RAM (MRAM pronounced EM-ram), stores data using magnetic charges instead of electrical charges. Manufacturers claim that MRAM has greater storage capacity, consumes less power, and has faster access times than electronic RAM.

RAM chips usually reside on a **memory module,** which is a small circuit board. **Memory slots** on the motherboard hold memory modules (Figure 4-13).

RAM CONFIGURATION The amount RAM necessary in a computer often depends on the types of software you plan to use. A computer executes programs that are in RAM. The more RAM a computer has, the faster the computer will respond.

FIGURE 4-13 This photo shows a memory module being inserted in a motherboard.

A software package typically indicates the minimum amount of RAM it requires. If you want the application to perform optimally, usually you need more than the minimum speed specifications on the software package.

Generally, home users running Windows Vista and using basic application software such as word processing should have a least 256 MB of RAM. Most business requiring multimedia capabilities should have a minimum of 512 MB or RAM. Users creating professional Web sites or using graphics intensive applications will want at least 2 GB of RAM. The amount of RAM in computers purchased today ranges from 256 MB to 16 GB. Read discussion 4-2 for related discussion.

DISCUSSION 4-2

How Much Should You Pay for a Computer?

Ex Today, you can buy a personal computer for less than $500 that can do more than one sold at nearly twice its cost three years ago. Some manufacturers even are offering basic computers for less than $300. Part of the plunge in prices is lower-cost components, but another factor is a growing demand for cheaper machine.

Many of the new buyers are from families earning less than $40,000, far below the $50,000 average that once characterized typical computer buyers. These consumers are looking for inexpensive computer that are adequate for the most popular task. Spending more money on a computer means faster processor, more memory, 3-D graphics cards, higher-quality sound cards, more hard drive space, and other extras that some consider to be unnecessary, frivolous expenses. As one industry analyst asks, "Why by a Porsche when you are going to only drive 55 mile per hour?" But others point out that perhaps you should spend more money and buy for the future in anticipation of more robust software and peripherals that can take advantage of more computing power. How might greater availability of lower costing personal computers change the way people, schools, and businesses buy and use them? With respect to computers, does a higher price always mean greater usefulness? Why or Why not? Who might be satisfied with less than the latest and greatest computer technology? Why? What is the average price for computer in Liberia? Do you think computer price will fall in Liberia? Why or Why not?

Cache

Most of today's computers improve processing times with **cache** (pronounced cash). Two types of cache are memory cache and disk cache. This chapter discusses memory cache.

Memory cache helps speed the processes of the computer because it stores frequently used instructions and data. Most personal computers today have at least two types of memory cache: L1 cache and L2 cache.

- **L1** cache is built directly in the processor chip. L1 cache usually has a very small capacity, ranging from 8 KB to 128 KB.
- **L2** cache is slightly slower than L1 cache but has a much larger capacity, ranging from 64 KB to 16 MB. Current processors include advanced transfer cache, a type of L2 cache built directly on the processor chip. Processors that use **advanced transfer cache** perform at much faster rate than those that do not use it. Personal computers today typically have from 512 KB to 2 MB of advanced transfer cache.

Cache speeds up processing time because it store frequently used instructions and data. When the processor needs an instruction or data, it searches memory in this order: L1 cache, then L2 cache, then RAM – with a greater delay in processing for each level of memory it must search. If the instruction or data is not found in memory, then it must search a slower speed storage medium such as a hard disk, CD, or DVD.

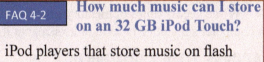

FAQ 4-1 **Can I add more RAM to my computer?**

Check you computer documentation to see how much RAM you can add. RAM modules are relatively expensive and usually include easy-to-follow installation instructions. Be sure to purchase RAM compatible with your brand and model of computer. For more info, visit Internet and the search www.google.com for Upgrading RAM.

ROM

Read-only memory (ROM pronounced rahm) refers to memory chips storing permanent data and instructions. The data on most ROM chips cannot be modified – hence, the name read-only. ROM is nonvolatile, which means its contents are not lost when power is removed from the computer.

Manufacturers of ROM chips often record data, instructions, or information on the chips when they manufacture the chips. These ROM chips, called firmware, contain permanently written data, instructions, or information.

FAQ 4-2 **How much music can I store on an 32 GB iPod Touch?**

iPod players that store music on flash memory chips can hold up to 240, 500, 1000 songs. A 32 GG iPod player with built-in hard disks have a much greater storage capacity–can store 1750, 7000, 14,000 songs. Visit the Internet and the search www.google.com for iPod.

Flash Memory

Flash memory is a type of nonvolatile memory that can be erased electronically and rewritten. Most computers use flash memory to hold their startup instructions because it allows the computer easily to update its contents. For example, when the computer changes from standard time to daylight saving time, the contents of a flash memory chip (and the real-time clock chip) change to reflect the new time.

Flash memory chips also store data and programs on many mobile computers and devices, such as PDAs, smart phones, printers, digital cameras, automotive devices, audio players, digital voice recorders, and pagers. Some MP3 players store music on flash memory chips (Figure 4-14). Others store music on tiny hard disk or flash memory cards. a later section in this chapter discusses flash memory cards, which contain flash memory on a removable device instead of a chip.

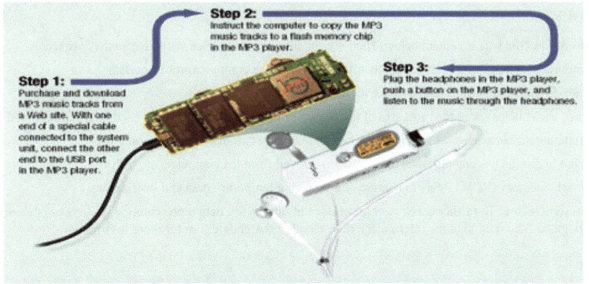

FIGURE 4-14 HOW AN MP3 MUSIC PLAYER STORE MUSIC IN FLASH MEMORY

CMOS

Some RAM chips, flash memory chips, and other types of memory chips use complementary metal-oxide semiconductor (CMOS pronounced SEE-moss) technology because it provides high speeds and consumes little power. CMOS technology uses battery power to retain information even when the power to the computer is off. Battery-backed CMOS memory chips, for example, can keep the calendar, date, and time current even when the computer is off. The flash memory chips that store a computer's startup information often use CMOS technology.

Memory Access Times

Access time is the amount of time it takes the processor to read data, instructions, and information from memory. A computer's access time directly affects how fast the computer processes data. Accessing data in memory can be more than 200,000 times faster than accessing data on a hard disk because of the mechanical motion of the hard disk.

Today's manufacturers use a variety of terminology to state access time (Figure 4-15). Some use fractions of a second, which for memory occurs in nanoseconds. A **nanosecond** (abbreviated ns) is one billion of a second. A nanosecond is extremely fast (Figure 4-16). Other manufacturers state access times in MHz; for example 533 MHz RAM.

While access times of memory greatly affect overall computer performance, manufacturers and retailers usually list a computer's memory in term of its size, not its access time.

FAQ 4-3

What should I do if my computer's date and time are wrong?

First, try resetting the date and time. To do this in Window Vista, double-click the time on the taskbar. If the computer continues to lose time or display an incorrect date, you may need to replace the CMOS battery on the motherboard that powers the system clock. For more info, visit the Internet and then search www.google.com for CMOS Battery.

ACCESS TIME TERMINOLOGY

Term	Abbreviation	Speed
Millisecond	ms	One-thousandth of a second
Microsecond	µs	One-millionth of a second
Nanosecond	ns	One-billionth of a second
Picosecond	ps	One-trillionth of a second

FIGURE 4-15 Access times are measured in fractions of a second. This table lists the terms used to define access times.

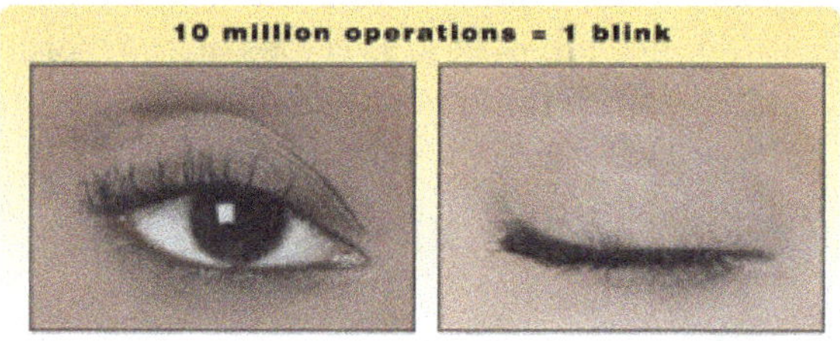

10 million operations = 1 blink

FIGURE 4-16 It takes about one-tenth of a second to blink your eye, which is the equivalent of 100 million nanoseconds. In the time it takes to blink your eye, a computer can perform some operations 10 million times.

Test your knowledge of pages 116 through 122 in Quiz Yourself 4-2

QUIZ YOURSELF 4-2

Instructions: Find the true statement below. Then rewrite the remaining false statement so they are true.

1. A computer's memory access time directly affects how fast the computer processes data.

2. A gigabyte (GB) equals approximately 1 trillion bytes.

3. Memory cache helps speed the processes of the computer because it stores seldom used instructions and data.

4. Most computers are analog, which means they recognize only two discrete states: on and off.

5. Most RAM retains its contents when the power is removed from the computer.

6. Read-only memory (ROM) refers to memory chips storing temporary data and instructions.

Quiz Yourself Online: To further check your knowledge of bits, bytes, data representation, and types of memory, visit www.clarkepublish.com or visit the Internet and then search www.google.com for more information.

EXPANSION SLOTS AND ADAPTER CARDS

An **expansion slot** is a socket on the motherboard that can hold an adapter card. An **adapter card**, sometimes called an expansion card, is a circuit board that enhances functions of a component of the system unit and/or provides connections to peripherals. A **peripheral** is a device that connects to the system unit and is controlled by the processor in the computer. Examples of peripherals are modems, disk drive, printers, scanners, and keyboards.

Figure 4-17 lists a variety of types of adapter cards. Sometimes, all functionality is built into the adapter card. With others, a cable connects the adapter card to a device, such as a digital video camera, outside the system unit. Figure 4-18 shows an adapter card being inserted in an expansion slot on a personal computer motherboard.

Some motherboards include all necessary capabilities and do not require adapter cards. Other motherboards may require adapter cards to provide capabilities such as sound and video. A **sound card** enhances the sound-generating capabilities of a personal computer by allowing sound to be input through a microphone and output through external speakers or headphones. A **video card,** also called a graphics card connects to the motherboard of a computer system and generates output images to display.

TYPES OF ADAPTER CARDS

Adapter Card	Purpose
Disk controller	Connects disk drives
FireWire	Connects to FireWire devices
Graphics accelerator	Increases the speed at which graphics are displayed
MIDI	Connects musical instruments
Modem	Connects other computers through telephone or cable television lines
Network	Connects other computers and peripherals
PC-to-TV converter	Connects a television
Sound	Connects speakers or a microphone
TV tuner	Allows viewing of television channels on the monitor
USB 2.0	Connects to USB 2.0 devices
Video	Connects a monitor
Video capture	Connects a camcorder

FIGURE 4-17 Currently used adapter cards and their functions.

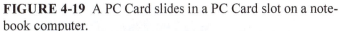

FIGURE 4-18 An adapter card being inserted in an expansion slot on the motherboard of a personal computer.

FIGURE 4-19 A PC Card slides in a PC Card slot on a notebook computer.

PC Cards, Flash Memory Card, and USB Flash Drives

Notebook and other mobile computers have at least one PC Card slot, which is a special type of expansion slot that holds a PC Card. A PC Card is a thin, credit card-sized device that adds memory, storage, sound fax/modem, network, and other capabilities to mobile computers (Figure 4-19). Most computers manufactured after 2008 were made with PC Card Slot. Instead, computers made from 2008 onward come equipped with internal wireless card and onboard RJ 45 connection for fax, modem and other interfaces.

All PC Cards conform to standard developed by the Personal Computer Memory Card International Association (these cards originally were called PCMCIA cards). These standards help to ensure the interchangeability of PC among mobile computers. Although some PC Cards contain tiny hard disk, many PC Cards are type of flash memory card.

A flash memory card is a removable flash memory device that allows users to transfer data and information conveniently from mobile devices to their desktop computers. Many mobile and consumer devices, such as PDAs, smart phones, digital cameras, and digital audio players use these memory cards. Some printers and computers have built-in card readers/writers or slots that read flash memory cards. In addition, you can purchase and external card reader/writer that attaches to any computer. The type of flash memory card you have will determine the type of card reader/writer you need. Storage capacities of flash memory cards range from 64 MB to 5 GB.

Another widely used type of removable flash memory is the USB flash drive. A **USB flash** drive is a flash memory storage device that plugs in a USB port on a computer or portable device. (The next section discusses USB ports.) Storage capacities of USB flash drives range from 64 MB to 5 GB.

Figure 4-20 shows a variety of removable flash memory devices.

FIGURE 4-20 Removable flash memory devices are available in a range of sizes.

PORTS AND CONNECTORS

A **port** is the point at which a peripheral attaches to or communicates with a system unit so the peripheral can send data to or retrieve information from the computers. An external device, such as a keyboard, monitor, printer, mouse, and microphone, often attaches by a cable to a port on the system unit. Instead of port, the term jack sometimes is used to identify audio ports. The back of the system unit contains many ports; newer personal computers also have ports on the front of the system unit (Figure 4-21).

FIGURE 4-21 The back of a system unit has many ports. Most computers have ports on the front of the system unit, also.

Ports have different types of connectors. A **connector** joins a cable to a peripheral. One end of a cable attaches to the connector on the system unit, and the other end of the cable attaches to a connector on the peripheral.

Desktop personal computers may have a serial port, a parallel port, several USB ports, and a FireWire port. The next section discusses these and other ports.

Serial Ports

A **serial port** is a type of interface that connects a device to the system unit by transmitting data one bit at a time (Figure 4-22). Serial ports usually connect devices that do not require fast data transmission rates, such as a mouse, keyboard, or modem. The COM port (short for communications port) on the system unit is one type of serial port.

Parallel Ports

Unlike a serial port, a **parallel port** is an interface that connects devices by transferring more than one bit at a time (Figure 4-23). Parallel ports originally where developed as an alternative to the slower speed serial ports. Some printers can connect to the system unit using a parallel port. This parallel port can transfer eight bits of data (one byte) simultaneously through eight separate line in a single cable.

USB Ports

A **USB port,** short for universal serial bus port, can connect up to 127 different peripheral together with a single connector. Devices that connect to a USB port include The following: mouse, printer, digital camera, scanner, speakers, iPod, MP3 music player, CD, DVD, and removable hard disk. Personal computers typically have six to eight USB ports either on the front or back of the system unit (Figure 4-21). The latest version of USB, called USB 2.0, is a more advanced and faster USB, with speeds 40 times higher than that of its predecessor.

To attach multiple peripherals using a single port, you can use a USB hub. A **USB hub** is a device that plugs in a USB port on the system unit and contains multiple USB ports in which you plug cables from USB devices. Some newer peripherals may attach only to a USB port. Others attach either a serial or parallel ports, as well as USB port.

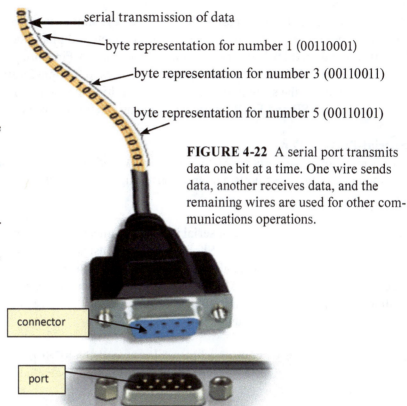

serial transmission of data

byte representation for number 1 (00110001)

byte representation for number 3 (00110011)

byte representation for number 5 (00110101)

connector

port

FIGURE 4-22 A serial port transmits data one bit at a time. One wire sends data, another receives data, and the remaining wires are used for other communications operations.

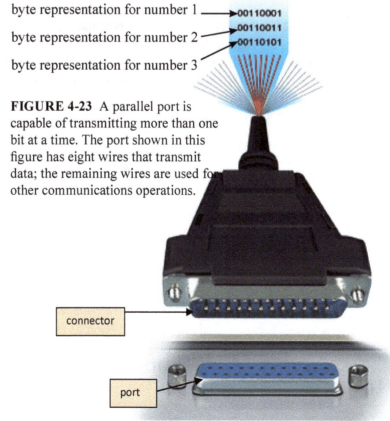

byte representation for number 1 ——▶ 00110001

byte representation for number 2 —— 00110011

byte representation for number 3 —— 00110101

FIGURE 4-23 A parallel port is capable of transmitting more than one bit at a time. The port shown in this figure has eight wires that transmit data; the remaining wires are used for other communications operations.

connector

port

FireWire Ports
Previously called IEEE 1394 port, a **FireWire port** is similar to a USB port in that it can connect multiple types of devices that require faster data transmission speeds, such as digital video cameras, digital VCRs, color printers, scanners, digital cameras, and DVD drives, to a single connector. A FireWire port allows you to connect up to 63 devices together. You can use a FireWire hub to attach multiple devices to a single FireWire port. A **FireWire hub** is a device that plugs in a FireWire port on the system unit and contains multiple FireWire ports in which you plug cables from FireWire devices. Ports such as a USB and FireWire are replacing all other types of ports.

Special-Purpose Ports
Four special-purpose ports are MIDI, SCSI, IrDA, and Bluetooth. These ports are not included in typical computers. For a computer to have these ports, you must customize the computer purchase order. The following sections discuss each of these ports.

MIDI PORT   A special type of serial port that connects the system unit to a musical instrument, such as an electronic keyboard, is called a **MIDI port**. Short for Musical Instrument Device Interface, MIDI (pronounced MID-dee) is the electronic music industry's standard that defines how devices, such as sound cards and synthesizers, represent sounds electronically. A synthesizer, which can be a peripheral or a chip, creates sound from digital instructions. A system unit with a MIDI port has the capability of recording sounds that have been created by a synthesizer and then processing the sounds (the data) to create sounds.

SCSI PORT   A special high-speed parallel port, called a **SCSI port,** allows you to attach SCSI (pronounced skuzzy) peripherals such as disk drives and printers. Some computers include a SCSI port. Others have a slot that supports a SCSI card.

IRDA PORT   Some devices can transmit data via infrared light waves. For these wireless devices to transmit signals to a computer, both the computer and the device must have an IrDA port.
To ensure nothing obstructs the path of the infrared light wave, you must align the IrDA port on the device with the IrDA port on the computer, similarly to the way you operate a television remote control. Devices that use IrDA ports include a PDA, smart phone, keyboard, mouse, printer, and pager.

BLUETOOTH PORT   An alternative to IrDA, **Bluetooth** technology uses radio waves to transmit data between two devices. Unlike IrDA, the Bluetooth devices do not have to be aligned with each other. Many computers, peripherals, PDAs, smart phones, cars, and other consumer electronics are Bluetooth-enabled, which means they contain a small chip that allows them to communicate with other Bluetooth-enabled computers and devices. If you have a computer that is not Bluetooth enabled, you can purchase a Bluetooth wireless port adapter that will convert an existing USB port or serial port into a Bluetooth port. Also available are Bluetooth PC Cards for notebook computers and Bluetooth cards for PDAs and smart phones.

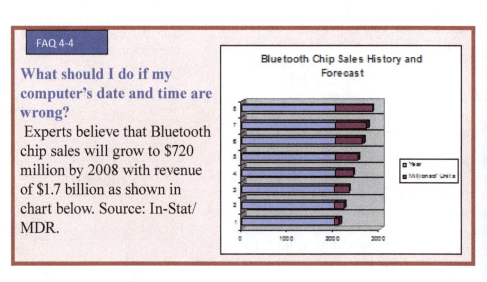

FAQ 4-4

What should I do if my computer's date and time are wrong?
Experts believe that Bluetooth chip sales will grow to $720 million by 2008 with revenue of $1.7 billion as shown in chart below. Source: In-Stat/MDR.

BUSES

As explained earlier in this chapter, a computer processes and store data as a series of electronic bits. These bits transfer internally within the circuitry of the computer along electrical channels. Each channel, called a bus, allows the various devices both inside and attached to the system unit to communicate with each other. Just as vehicles travel on a highway to move from one destination to another, bits travel on a bus (Figure 4-29).

Buses transfer bits from input devices to memory, from memory to the processor, from the processor to memory, and from memory to output or storage devices. Buses consist of two parts: a data bus and an address bus. The data bus transfers actual data and the address bus transfers information about where the data should reside in memory.

The size of a bus, called the bus width, determines the number of bits that the computer can transmit at one time. For example, a 32-bit bus can transmit 32 bits (4 bytes) at a time. On a 64-bit bus, bits transmit from one location to another 64 bits (8 bytes) at a time. The larger the number of bits handled by the bus

Every bus also has a clock speed. Just like the processor, manufactures state the clock speed for a bus in hertz. Recall that one megahertz (MHz) is equal to one million ticks per second. Most of today's processors have a bus clock speed of 400,533 or 800 MHz. the higher the bus clock speed, the faster the transmission of data, which results in applications running faster.

A computer has two basic types of buses: a system bus and an expansion bus. A **system bus** is part of the motherboard and connects the processor to main memory. When computer professionals use the term bus by itself, they usually are referring to the system bus.

An **expansion bus** allows the processor to communicate with peripherals. Some peripherals outside the system unit connect to a port on an adapter card,

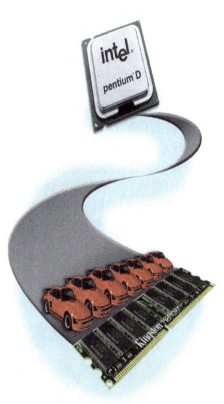

FIGURE 4-24 Just as vehicle travel on a highway, bits travels on a bus.

which is inserted in an expansion slot on the motherboard. This expansion slot connects to the expansion bus, which allows the processor to communicate with the peripheral attached to the adapter card.

BAYS

After you purchase a computer, you may want to install an additional storage devices such as a disk drive in the system unit. A **bay** is an opening inside the system unit in which you can install additional equipment. A bay is different for a slot, which is used for the installation of adapter cards. Rectangular openings, called drive bays, typically holds drives.

Two types of drive bays exist: external and internal. An **external drive bay** allows a user to access the drive from outside the system unit (Figure 4-25). CD drives, DVD drives, Zip drives, floppy disk drives, and tape drives are examples of devices installed in external drive bays. An **internal drive bay** is concealed entirely within the system unit. Hard disk drives are installed in internal bays.

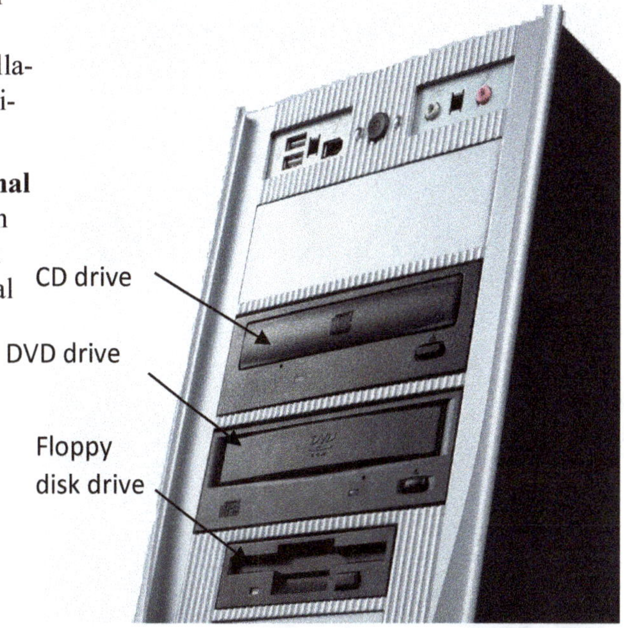

CD drive

DVD drive

Floppy disk drive

FIGURE 4-25 External drive bays usually are located beside or on top of one another.

POWER SUPPLY

Many personal computers plug in standard wall outlets, which supply an alternating current (AC) of 115 to 120 volts. This type of power is unsuitable for use with a computer, which requires a direct current (DC) ranging from 5 to 12 volts. The **power supply** is the component of the system unit that converts the wall outlet AC power into DC power.

Some external peripherals such as an external modem, speakers, or a tape have an **AC adapter,** which is an external power supply. One end of the AC adapter plugs in the wall outlet and the other end attaches to the peripheral. The AC adapter converts the AC current into the DC power that the peripheral requires.

MOBILE COMPUTERS AND DEVICES

As businesses and schools expand to serve people across the country and around the world, increasingly more people need to use a computer while traveling to and from a main office or school to conduct business, communicate, or do homework. Users with such mobile computing needs often have a mobile computer, such as a notebook computer or Tablet PC, or a mobile device such as a iPad, smart phone or PDA (Figure 4-26).

Weighting on average between 2.5 and 9 pounds, notebook computers can run either using batteries or using a standard power supply. Smaller PDAs and smart phones run straightly on batteries. Like their desktop computers, mobile computers and devices have a motherboard that contains electronic components that process data.

PC Card in PC Card slot

FIGURE 4-26 Users with mobile computing needs often have a notebook computer, PDA, and/or smart phone.

A **notebook computer** usually is more expensive than a desktop computer with the same capabilities because it is more costly to miniaturize the components. Notebook computers may have video, serial, parallel, modem, network, FireWire, USB, headphones, and microphone ports (Figure 4-27).

Two basic designs of Tablet PC are available: slate and convertible. With the slate Table PC (shown in Figure 4-27 on page 105), all hardware is behind the display – much like a PDA. Users can attach a removable keyboard to the slate Tablet PC. The display on the convertible Tablet PC, which attached to a keyboard, can be rotated 180 degrees and folded down over the keyboard. Thus, the convertible Tablet PC can be repositioned to look like either a notebook computer or a slate Tablet PC. Tablet PCs usually include several slots and ports (Figure 4-28).

PDAs and smart phones are quite affordable, usually priced at a few hundred dollars or less. These mobile devices often have an IrDA port or are Bluetooth enabled so users can communicate wirelessly with other computers or devices such as a printer. Read Looking Ahead 4-2 for a look at the next generation of mobile computer.

Looking Ahead 4-2

DNA Computer Work to Fight Cancer

One of the newest computers is so tiny that one trillion of them can fit inside a drop of water. The hardware of this biological invention is composed of enzymes that manipulate DNA, and the software is composed of actual DNA   The concept for this computer had been proposed in 1936, but the actual computer was developed at the Weizmann Institute in Israel in 2001. Today, researchers at the Weizmann Institute are developing applications that process biological information. Their most current success is being able to program the computer to diagnose and treat cancer.

The researchers are hopeful they will be able to have the medical computer function inside a human cell. For more info, visit www.clarke-publish.com or visit www.google.com and search for DNA Computer.

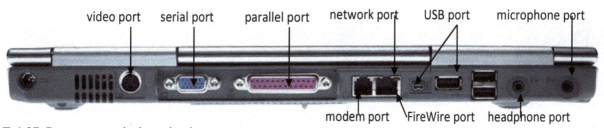

FIGURE 4-27 Ports on a typical notebook computer.

FIGURE 4-28 Ports and slots on a Tablet PC.

PUTTING IT ALL TOGETHER

When you purchase a computer, it is important to understand how the components of the system unit work. Many components of the system unit influence the speed and power of a computer. These include the type of processor, the clock speed of the processor, the amount of RAM, bus width, and the clock speed of the bus. The configuration you require depends on your intended use.

The table in Figure 4-29 lists the suggested minimum processor and RAM requirements base on the needs of a various types of computer users.

SUGGESTED MINIMUM CONFIGURATIONS BY USER

User	Processor and RAM
HOME 	Intel Celeron D or AMD Sempron or Intel Pentium 4 or AMD Athlon 64 Minimum RAM: 256 MB
SMALL OFFICE/HOME OFFICE 	Intel Pentium D or AMD Athlon 64 FX Minimum RAM: 512 MB
MOBILE 	Intel Celeron M or Intel Pentium M or AMD Turion 64 Minimum RAM: 512 MB
POWER 	Intel Itanium 2 or AMD Opteron or Intel Pentium Extreme Edition or Intel Xeon MP or AMD Athlon MP or AMD Athlon 64 X2 Minimum RAM: 2 GB
LARGE BUSINESS 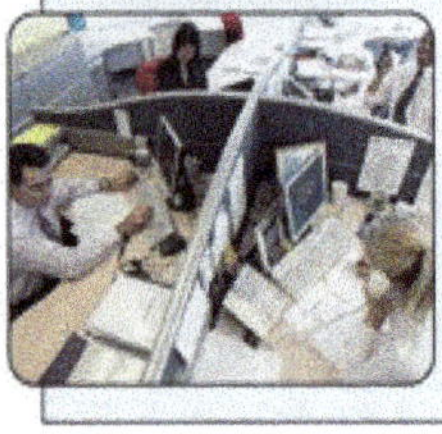	Intel Pentium D or AMD Athlon 64 FX Minimum RAM: 1 GB

FIGURE 4-29 Suggested processor and RAM configuration by user.

KEEPING YOUR COMPUTER CLEAN

Over time, the system unit collects dust–even in a clean environment, let alone you as a computer user living Liberia where there is dust everywhere. Built up dust can block airflow in the computer, which can cause it to overheat, corrode, or even stop working. By cleaning your computer once or twice a year, you can help extend its life. This preventive maintenance requires a few basic products (Figure 4-30):

*   can of compressed air–(removes dust and lint from difficult-to-reach areas
*   lint-free antistatic wipes and swabs
*   bottle of rubbing alcohol
*   small computer vacuum (or small attachment on your house vacuum)
*   antistatic wristband–to avoid damaging internal components with static electricity
*   small screwdriver (may be required to open the case or remove adapter cards)

Before cleaning the computer, turn it off, unplug it from the electrical outlet, and unplug all cables from the ports. Blow away any dust from all openings on the computer case, such as drives, slots, and ports. Vacuum the power supply fan on the back of the computer case to remove any dust that has accumulated on it. Next, release short blasts of compressed air on the power supply fan. Use and antistatic wipe to clean the exterior of the case.

If you need assistance opening the computer case, refer to the instructions that came with the computer. Once the case is open, put the antistatic wristband on your wrist and attach its clip to the case of the computer. Use the antistatic wipe to clean dust and grime inside the walls of the computer case. Vacuum as much dust as possible from the interior of the case, including the wires, chips, adapter cards, and fan blades. Next, release short blast of compressed air in areas the vacuum cannot reach. If the motherboard and adapter cards still look dirty, gently clean them with lint-free wipes or swabs lightly dampened with alcohol.

When finished, be sure all adapter cards are tightly in their expansion slots. Then close the case, plug in all cables, and attach the power cord. Write down the date you cleaned the computer so you have a record for you next cleaning.

If you don not feel comfortable cleaning the system unit yourself, have a local computer company or technician clean it for you. There are many small businesses operating in Liberia that have qualified computer technicians. Whether you live in Pleebo in Maryland County or in Voinjama, Lofa County, ore even in Gbondoi, Bong County, you can find a technician within your community to help you clearn your system unit.

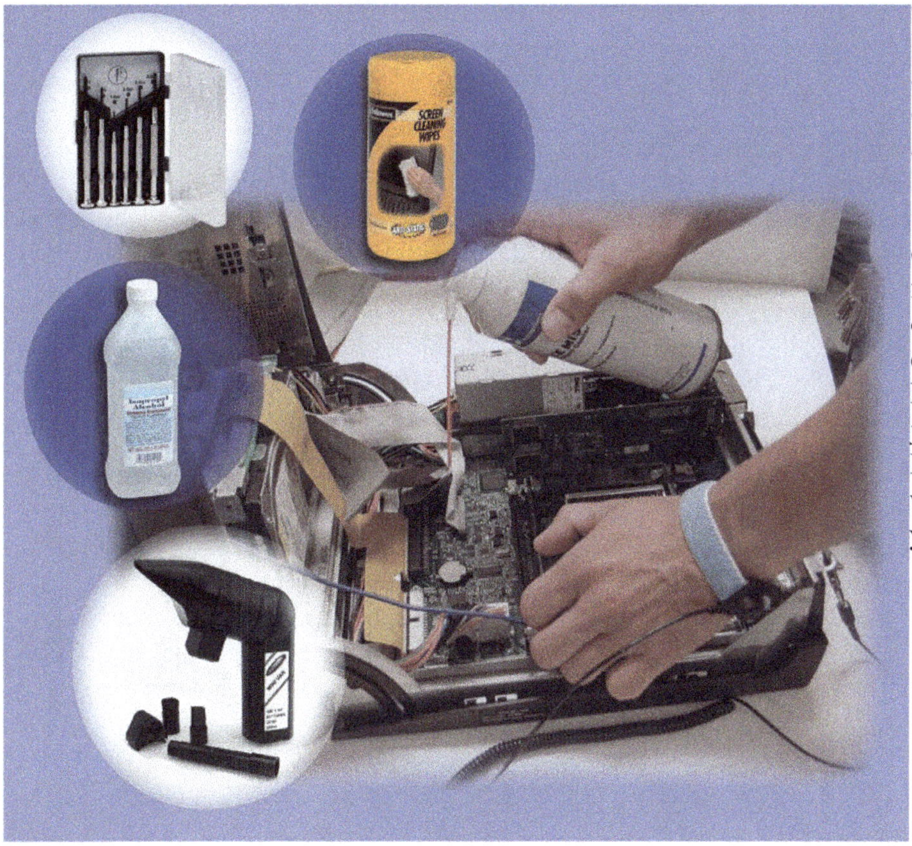

FIGURE 4-30 With a few products, this computer users keeps his computer clean. As a savvy computer user in Liberia, how do you keep your computer clean? Do you do it yourself or give it to a local technician to clean it.

Test your knowledge of pages 123 through 131 in Quiz Yourself 4-3

QUIZ YOURSELF 4-3

Instructions: Find the true statement below. Then rewrite the remaining false statement so they are true.

1. A bus is the point at which a peripheral attaches to or communicates with a system unit so the peripheral can send data to or receive information from the computer.

2. An AC adapter is a socket on the motherboard that can hold an adapter card.

3. Serial ports can connect up to 127 different peripherals together with a single connector.

4. The higher the bus clock speed, the slower the transmission of data.

5. when cleaning the insider of the system unit, wear an antistatic wristband to avoid damaging internal components with static electricity

Quiz Yourself Online: To further check your knowledge of expansion slots, adapter cards, ports, buses, components of mobile computers and devices, and cleaning a computer, visit www.clarkepublish.com or visit the Internet and then search www.google.com for more information.

CHAPTER SUMMARY

Chapter 4 presented the components of the system unit; described how memory stores data, instructions, and information; and discussed the sequence of operations that occur when a computer executes and instruction. The chapter included a comparison of various personal computer processors on the market today. It also discussed how to clean a system unit.

Computer Engineer

A computer engineer designs and develops the electronic components found in computers and peripheral devices. They also work as researchers, theorist, and inventors. Companies may hire computer engineers for permanent positions or as consultants, with jobs that extend from a few months to a few years, depending on the project. Engineers in research and development often work on projects that will not be released to the general public for two years.

Responsibilities vary from company to company. All computer engineering work, however, demands problem-solving skills and ability to create and use new technologies. The ability to handle multiple tasks and concentrate on detail is a key component. Assignments often are taken on as part of a team. Therefore, computer engineers must be able to communicate clearly with both computer personnel and computer users, who may have little technical knowledge.

Before taking in-depth computer engineering design and development classes, students usually take mathematics, physics, and basic engineering. Computer engineering degrees include B.S., M.S., and Ph.D. because computer engineers employed in private industry often advance into managerial positions, many computer engineering graduates obtain a master's degree in business administration (M.B.A) most computer engineers earn between $63,500 and $106,500 annually, depending on their experience and employer, but salaries can exceed $125,000 but these salaries may not be the same for computer engineers in Liberia and countries. For more info, visit the Internet and then search www.google.com for Computer Engineer.

AMD

PC Processor Supplier

Customer needs influence the integrated circuits Advanced Micro Devices (AMD) develops for the computing, communications, and consumer electronic industries. AMD calls this philosophy "customer-centric innovation."

As a global supplier of PC processors, AMD engineers its technologies at its Submicron Development Center (SDC) in Sunnyvale, California. The technologies are put into production at manufacturing facilities in the United States, Europe, Asia, and Japan.

Among the company's more successful line of processors is the AMD 64 family, which is composed of the AMD Athlon 64 processor for desktop and personal computers, the AMD Opteron processor for servers and workstations, and the AMD Turion mobile technology for notebook computers. The company is partnering with portable multimedia manufacturers, including TiVo, to use it Alchemy processor in providing high-performance video entertainment products. For more info, visit book's Web site.

Intel

Chip Maker Dominates the Computer Market

When Gordon Moore and Robert Noyce started Intel in 1968, their goal was to replace magnetic core memory with semiconductor memory. Noyce and Moore, together with Andy Grove, refined the process of placing thousands of tiny electric devices on a silicon chip. In 1971, the company introduced the Intel 4004, the first single-chip microprocessor.

When IBM chose the Intel 8008 chip for its new personal computer in 1980, Intel chips became standard for all IBM-compatible personal computers. Today, Intel's microprocessors are the building blocks in countless personal computers, servers, networks, and communications devices. In 2006, Intel introduced its Viiv technology, which is designed to enhance the entertainment experience in the digital home. For more info, visit www.google.com.

Jack Kilby

Integrated Circuit Inventor

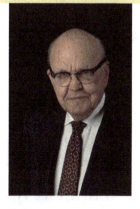

Jack Kilby was awarded more than 60 patents during his lifetime, but one has changed the world. His integrated circuit, or microchip, invention made microprocessors possible.

Kilby started his work with miniature electrical components at Centralab, where he developed transistors for hearing aids. He then took a research position with Texas Instruments and developed a working model of the first integrated circuit, which was patented in 1959. Kilby applied this invention to various industrial, military, and commercial applications, including the first pocket calculator, called the Pocketronic.

Kilby is considered one of the more influential people in the world who has had the greatest impact on business computing in the past 50 years. He was awarded the Nobel Prize in physics in 2000 for his part in the invention of the integrated circuit, a product he believed will continued to change the world. For more info, visit www.google.com and search for Jack Kilby.

Gordon Moore

Intel Cofounder

More 40 years ago, Gordon Moore predicted that the number of transistors and resistors place on computer chips would double every year, with a proportional increase in computing power and decrease in cost. This bold forecast, now know as Moore's Law, proved amazingly accurate for 10 years. Then, Moore revised the estimate to doubling every two years.

Convinced of the future of silicon chips, Moore cofounded Intel in 1968. Moore's lifelong interest in technology was kindled at an early age when he experimented with a neighbor's chemistry set. Even then, he displayed the passion for practical outcomes that has typified his work as a scientist and engineer.

Moore says that the semiconductor industry's progress will far surpass that of nearly all other industries. For more info, visit www.google.com and then search for Gordon Moore.

Chapter Review

The Chapter Review section summarizes the concepts presented in this chapter. To obtain help from other students regarding any subject in this chapter, visit book's Web site.

(1) How Are Various Styles of System Units Different?

The **system unit** is a case that contains electronic components of the computer used to process data. On desktop personal computers, most storage devices also are part of the system unit. On notebook computers, the keyboard and pointing devices often occupy the area on top of the system unit, and the display attaches to the system unit by hinges. On mobile devices, the display frequently is built into the system unit. Whit game console, the input and output devices such as controllers and a television, resides outside the system unit. On handheld game consoles and digital music players, by contrast, the packaging around the system unit also houses the input devices and display.

(2) What Are the Components of a Processor, and How Do They Complete a Machine Cycle?

The **processor** interprets and carries out the basic instructions that operate a computer. Processors contain a **control unit** that directs and coordinates most of the operations in the computer and an **arithmetic logic unit (ALU)** that performs arithmetic, comparison, and other operations. The machine cycle is a set of four basic operations – fetching, decoding, executing, and storing – that the processor repeats for every instruction. The control unit fetches program instructions and data from memory and decodes the instructions into commands the computer can execute. The ALU executes the commands, and the results are stored in memory.

(3) What Is a Bit, and How Does a Series of Bits Represent Data?

Most computers are **digital** and recognize only two discrete states: off and on. To represent these two states, computers use the **binary system,** which is a number system that has just two unique digits – 0 (for off) and 1 (for on) – called bits. A **bit** is the smallest unit of data a computer can process. Grouped together as a unit, 8 bits form a byte, which provides enough different combinations of 0s and 1s to represent 256 individual characters. The combinations are defined by patters, called coding schemes, such as ASCII and EBCDIC.

(4) What Are the Various Types of Memory?

The system unit contains volatile and nonvolatile memory. **Volatile memory** loses it contents when the computer's power is turned off. **Nonvolatile memory** does not lose its contents when the computer's power is turned off. **RAM** is the most common type of volatile memory. ROM, flash memory, and CMOS are examples of nonvolatile memory. RAM consists of memory chips that can be read from and written to by the processor and other devices. **ROM** refers to memory chips storing permanent data and instructions that usually cannot be modified. Flash memory can be erased electronically and rewritten. **CMOS** technology uses battery power to retain information even when the power to the computer is turned off.

(5) What Are the Types of Expansion Slots and Adapter Cards?

An **expansion slot** is a socket on the motherboard that can hold an adapter card. An **adapter card** is a circuit board that enhances functions of a component of the system unit and/or provides a connection to a **peripheral** such as modem, disk drive, printer, scanner, or keyboard. Several types of adapter cards exist. A **sound card** enhances the sound-generating capabilities of a personal computer. A **video card** converts computer output into a video signal that displays an image on the screen.

(6) How Are a Serial Port, a Parallel Port, a USB Port, and Other Different?

A **port** is the point at which a peripheral attaches to or communicates with a system unit so the peripheral can send data to or receive information from the computer. A **serial port,** which transmits data one bit at a time, usually connects devices that do not require fast data transmission, such as a mouse, keyboard, or modem. A **parallel port**, which transfers more than one bit at a time, sometimes connects a printer to the system unit. A **USB port** can connect up to 127 different peripherals together with a single connector. A **FireWire port** can connect multiple types of devices that require faster data transmission speeds. Four special-purpose ports are MIDI, SCSI, IrDA, and Bluetooth. A **MIDI port** connects the system unit to a musical instrument. A **SCSI port** attaches the system unit to SCSI peripherals, such as disk drives. An **IrDA port** and Bluetooth technology allow wireless devices to transmit signals to a computer via infrared light waves or radio waves.

(7) How Do Buses Contribute to a Computer's Processing Speed?

A **bus** is an electrical channel along which bits transfer within the circuitry of a computer, allowing devices both inside and attached to the system unit to communicate. The size of a bus, called the bus width, determines the number of bits that the computer can transmit at one time. The larger the bus width, the faster the computer transfers data.

(8) What Are the Components in Mobile Computers and Mobile Devices?

Mobile computers and devices have a motherboard that contains electronic components that process data. The system unit for a typical notebook computer often has video, serial, parallel, modem, network, FireWire, USB, headphones, and microphone ports. Tablet PCs usually include several slots and ports. PDAs and smart phones often have an IrDA or are Bluetooth enabled so users can communicate wirelessly.

(9) How Do You Clean a System Unit?

Before cleaning a system unit, turn off the computer and unplug it from the wall. Use a small vacuum and a can of compressed air to remove external dust. After opening the case, wear an antistatic wristband and vacuum the interior. Wipe away dust and grime using lint-free antistatic wipes and rubbing alcohol.

Key Terms

You should know the Key Terms. Use the list below to help focus your study. To further enhance your understanding of the Key Terms in this chapter, visit book's Web site and click the chapter 1 link.

AC adapter (128)	connector (125)	L1 cache (121)	power supply (128)
access time (122)	control unit (113)	L2 cache (121)	processor (113)
adapter card (112)	digital (116)	megabyte (MB) (118)	RAM (119)
advanced transfer cache (121)	drive bay (127)	memory (118)	read-only memory (ROM) (121)
arithmetic logic unit (113)	dual-core processor (116)	memory cache (120)	SCSI port (126)
bay (127)	expansion bus (127)	memory module (120)	serial port (125)
binary system (116)	expansion card (123)	memory slots (120)	sound card (123)
bit (115)	expansion slot (123)	microprocessor (113)	system bus (127)
Bluetooth (126)	FireWire hub (126)	MIDI port (126)	system clock (114)
bus (127)	FireWire port (126)	Motherboard (112)	system unit (110)
byte (116)	firmware (121)	multicore processor (116)	terabyte (TB) (118)
cache (120)	flash memory (121)	nanosecond (122)	USB flash drive (124)
central processing unit (CPU) (113)	flash memory card (124)	nonvolatile memory (118)	USB hub (125)
chip (112)	gigabyte (GB) (118)	parallel port (125)	USB port (125)
clock speed (114)	gigahertz (114)	PC Card (123)	Video card (123)
CMOS (122)	graphics card (123)	PC Card slot (123)	Volatile memory (118)
	IrDA port (126)	peripheral (123)	
	kilobyte (KB or K) (118)	port (124)	

Checkpoint

Use the Checkpoint exercises to check your knowledge level of the chapter.

True/False	Mark T for True and F for False. (see page numbers in parentheses.)

_____ 1. On desktop personal computers, the electronic components and most of the storage devices normally occupy space inside of the system unit.

_____ 2. The motherboard is the main circuit board of the system unit.

_____ 3. The arithmetic logic unit directs and coordinates most of the operations in the computer.

_____ 4. The speed of the system clock is just one factor that influences a computer's performance.

_____ 5. A bit is the smallest unit of data that the computer can process.

_____ 6. A gigabyte equals approximately 1 millions bytes.

_____ 7. RAM can hold only one program at a time.

_____ 8. Read-only memory (ROM) refers to memory chips storing data and instructions temporarily.

_____ 9. Access time is the amount of time it takes the processor to read data, instructions, and information from memory.

_____ 10. Serial ports usually connect devices that require fast transmission rates, such as printers.

_____ 11. The power supply is the component of the system unit that converts the wall outlet AC power into DC power.

Multiple Choice	Select the best answer (see page numbers in parentheses.)

1. On _____, the display is built into the system unit.
a. desktop personal computer
b. notebook computers
c. mobile devices
d. all of the above

2. Processor contain _____.
a. a chip
b. a motherboard
c. an adapter card
d. a control unit

3. The term decoding refers to the process of _____.
a. obtaining a program instruction or data item from memory
b. translating an instruction into signals a computer can execute
c. carrying out commands
d. writing a result to memory

4. Less expensive, basic PCs use a band of Intel processor called the _____.
a. Pentium
b. Xeon
c. Celeron
d. Itanium

5. _____ is the most widely used coding scheme and is used by most personal computers and servers.
a. EBCDIC
b. Unicode
c. ASCII
d. Microcode

6. Memory stores _____.
a. the operating system and other system software
b. application programs that carry out specific tasks
c. the data being processed by the application program
d. all of the above

7. A(n) _____ is part of the motherboard and connects the processor to the main memory.
a. expansion bus
b. system clock
c. system bus
d. memory module

8. _____ usually are installed in internal bays.
a. Floppy disk drive
b. Hard disk drives
c. Zip drive
d. DVD drives

Matching   Match the terms with their definitions. (see page numbers in parentheses.)

_____ 1. processor

_____ 2. memory module

_____ 3. USB flash drive

_____ 4. MIDI port

_____ 5. bay

a. small ceramic or metal component that absorbs and ventilates heat

b. interprets and carries out the basic instructions that operate a computer

c. allows the processor to communicate with peripherals

d. small circuit board on which RAM chips usually reside

e. opening inside the system unit in which additional equipment can be installed

f. special type of serial port that connects the system unit to a musical instrument

g. memory storage device that plugs in a port on a computer or portable device

Short Answer   Write a brief answer to each of the following questions.

1. What is clock? _____ How does speed affect a computer's speed? _____

2. What is the binary system? _____ What is the difference between a bit and a byte? _____

3. What is memory cache? _____ How are the two types of cache (L1 cache and L2 cache) difference? _____

4. What is a port? _____ How are a serial port, a parallel port, USB port, and a FireWire port different? ___

5. What are the two basic types of buses in a computer? _____ What are their purposes? _____

Working Together   Working in a group of your classmates, complete the following team exercise.

1. Prepare a report on the different types of ports and the way you connect peripheral devices to a computer. As part of your report, include the following subheadings and an overview of each of each subheading topic: (2) What is a connector? (3) What is a serial port and how does it work? (4) What is a parallel port and how does it work? (5) What is a USB port and how does it work? Expand your report so that it includes information beyond that in your textbook. Create a PowerPoint presentation from your report. Share your presentation with you class.

Web Research

Use the Internet-based Web Research exercises to broaden your understand of the concepts presented in this chapter. Visit book's Web site to obtain more information pertaining to each exercise. To discuss any of the Web Research exercises in this chapter with other students, post your thoughts or questions at the forum.

1. Journaling Respond to your readings in this chapter by writing at least one page containing your reactions, evaluations, and reflections about cleaning your computer. For example, have you tried cleaning a computer with the basic products recommended in this chapter? When? Where is the cleanest environment in your home to use the computer? If you do not feel comfortable cleaning the system unit yourself, where would you take it for this preventive maintenance? You also can write about the new terms you learned by reading this chapter. If required, submit your journal to your instructor.

2. Scavenger Hunt   Use one of the search engines listed in Figure 2-8 in chapter 2 on page 46 or your own favorite search engine to find the answer to the question below. Copy and paste the Web address from the Web page where you found the answer. Some question may have more than one answer. If required, submit your answer to your instruction or teacher. (1) Which Microsoft Windows operating system USB? (2) The USB port supports hot plug-

ging or hot swapping. What is "hot plugging"? (3) What is the name of the suit that people wear when they work in chip manufacturing clean room? (4) What is CASH Latency? (5) What are rune stones and their connection to Danish King Harald Blatand (Bluetooth)? (6) What is the name of the type of memory that retains its contents until it is exposed to ultraviolet light?

3. Search Sleuth   Ask Jeeves (ask.com) is one of the faster growing research Web sites. The search engine uses natural language, which allows researchers to type millions of questions each day using words human would use rather than words a computer understands. This enables you to ask a question just like you would ask your instructor a question during class. Visit this Web site and then use your word processing program to answer the following question. Then, if required, submit your answer to your instructor or teacher. (1) Click the P.G. Wodehouse link at the bottom of the home page. Who are P.G. Wodehouse and Bertie Wooster? (2) Click your browser's Back button or press the BACKSPACE key to return to the Ask Jeeves home page. Click the Search textbox and then type what were the tip selling DVD this week? as the keywords in the Search textbook. (3) Scroll through the links Ask Jeeves returns and then click one that provides the information requested. What three DVDs generated the best sales this past week? (4) Click your browser's Back button or press the BACKSPACE key to return to the Ask Jeeves home page. Click the Bloglines link at the bottom of the page. (5) Click the Today's hot topics link and review the material. Review the information you read and then write a 50-word summary.

Learn How To

Use the Learn How To activities to learn fundamental skills when using a computer and accompanying technology. Complete the exercises and submit them to your instructor or teacher.

LEARN HOW TO 1: Purchase and Install Memory in a Computer

One of the less expensive and more effective ways to speed up a computer, make it capable of processing more programs at the same time, and enable it to handle graphics, gaming, and other high-level programs is to increase the amount of memory. The process of increasing memory is accomplished in two phases – purchasing the memory and installing the memory. To purchase memory for a computer, complete the following steps:

1. Determine the amount of memory currently in your computer. Before beginning these steps, find out about the computer you're using by clicking the Start button, point to All Programs menu, point to Accessories, and then point to System Tools.

2. Determine the maximum amount of memory your computer can contain. This value can be change for different computers, based primarily on the number of slots on the motherboard available for memory and the size of the memory modules you can place in each slot. On most computers, different size memory modules can be inserted in slots. A computer, therefore, might allow a 128 MB, 256 MB, or 512 MB memory module to be inserted in each slot. To determine the maximum memory for a compute, in many cases you can multiply the number of memory slots on the computer by the maximum size memory module that can be inserted in each slot.

   For example, if a computer contains four memory slots and is able to accept memory modules of 128 MB, 256 MB, or 512 MB in each of its memory slots, the maximum amount of memory the computer can contain is 2 GB (4x 512 MB).

   You can find the number of slots and the allowable size of each memory module by contacting the computer manufacturer, looking in the computer's documentation, or contacting sellers of memory such as Kingston (www.kingston.com) or Crucial (www.crucial.com) on the Web. These sellers have documentation for most computers, and even programs you can download to run on your computer that will specify how much memory your computer currently has and how much you can add.

3. Determine how much memory you want to add, which will be somewhere between the current memory and the Maximum memory allowed on the computer.

4. Determine the current configuration of memory on the computer. For example, if a computer with four memory slots contains 512 MB of memory, it could be using one memory module of 512 MB in a single slot and the other three slots would be empty; two memory modules of 256 MB each in two slots with two slots empty; one memory module of 256 MB and two memory modules of 128 MB each in three slots with one slot empty; or four memory modules of 128 MB each in four slots with no slots empty. You may be required to look inside the system unit to make the determination. The current memory configuration on a computer will determine what new memory modules you should buy to

increase the memory to the amount determine in step 3.

You also should be aware that a few computers require memory to be installed in the computer in matching pairs. This means that a computer with four slots could obtain 512 MB of memory with two memory modules of 256 MB each in two slots, or four memory modules of 128 MB each in four slots.

5.   Determine the number of available memory slots on your computer and the number and size of memory

   modules you must buy to fulfill your requirement. Several scenarios can occur (in the following examples, assume you can install memory one module at a time).n

a.   Scenario 1: The computer has one or more open slots. In this case, you might be able to purchase a memory module that matches the amount of memory increase you desire. For example, if you want to increase memory by 256 MB, you should purchase a 256 MB memory module for insertion in the open slot. Generally, you should buy the maximum size module you can for an open slot. So, if you find two empty slots and wish to increase memory by 256 MB, it is smarter to buy one 256 MB module and leave one empty slot rather than buy 128 MB memory modules and use both slots. This allows you to increase memory again without removing currently used modules.

b.   Scenario 2: The computer has no open slots. For example, a computer containing 512 MB of memory could have four slots each containing 128 MB memory modules. If you want to increase the memory on the computer to 1 GB, you will have to remove some of the 128 MB memory modules and replace them with the new memory modules you purchase. In this example, you want to increase the memory by 512 MB. You would have several options: (1) You could replace all four 128 MB memory modules with 256 MB memory modules; (2) You could replace all four 128 MB memory modules with two 512 MB memory modules; (3) You could replace one 128 MB memory module with a 512 MB of memory module, and replace a second 128 MB memory module with a 256 MB memory module. Each of these options results in a total memory of 1 GB. The best option will depend on the price of memory and whether you anticipate increasing the memory size at a later time. The least expensive option probably would be number 3. For computer users in Africa, I would recommend option number 3; since cash is a problem for must of us around here.

c.   Scenario 3: Many other combinations can occur. You may have to perform arithmetic calculations to decide the combination of memory module that will work for the number of slots on the computer and the desired additional memory.

6.   Determine the type of memory to buy for the computer. Computer memory has many types and configurations,

   and it is critical that you buy the kind of memory for which the computer was designed. It is preferable to buy the same type of memory that currently is found in the computer. That is, if the memory is DDR SDRAM with a certain clock speed, then that is the type of additional memory you should place in the computer. The documentation for the computer should specify the memory type. In addition, the Web sites cited on the previous page, and others as well, will present a list of memory modules that will work with your computer. Enough emphasis cannot be placed on the fact that the memory you buy must be compatible with the type of memory usable on your computer. Because there are so many types and configurations, you must be especially diligent to ensure you purchase the proper memory for your computer.

7.   Once you have determined the type and size of memory to purchase, buy it from a reputable dealer. Buying

   poor or mismatched memory is a reason for a computer's erratic performance and is one the more difficult problems to troubleshoot.

   After purchasing the memory, you must install it on your computer. Complete the following steps to install memory on a computer.

1.   Unplug the computer, and remove all electrical cords and device cables from the ports on the compute. Open

   the case of the system unit. You may want to consult the computer's documentation to determine the exact   procedure for opening the system unit

2.   Ground yourself so you do not generate static electricity that can cause memory or other components in the

   system unit to be damage. To do this, wear an antistatic wristband you can purchase inexpensively in a computer or electronic store; or, before you touch any component within the system unit, touch an unpainted metal surface such as the metal on the back of the computer. If you are not wearing an antistatic wristband, periodically touch an unpainted metal surface to dissipate any static electricity.

3.   Within the system unit, fid the memory slots on the motherboard. The easiest way to look for memory modules

That are similar to those you purchase. The memory slots often are located near the processor. If you cannot find the slot, consult the documentation. A diagram often is available to help you spot the memory slots.

4.   Insert the memory module in the next empty slot. Orient the memory module in the slot to match the modules currently installed. A notch or notches on the memory module will ensure you do not install the module backwards. If your memory module is a DIMM, insert that module straight down into grooves on the clips and then apply gentle pressure to seat the module properly (see Figure 4-13 on page 109). If your memory is SIMM, which used on older computers, insert the module at a 45 degree angel and then rotate it to vertical position until the module snaps into place.

5.   If you must remove one or more memory modules before inserting the new memory, carefully release the clips before lifting the memory module out of the memory slot.

6.   Plug in the machine and replace all the device cables without replacing the cover.

7.   Start the computer. In most cases, the new memory will be recognized and the computer will run normally. If an error message appears, determine the cause of the error. In most cases, if you turn off the computer, remove the cords and cables, ground yourself, and then reinstall the memory, everything will be fine

8.   Replace the computer cover.

Adding memory to a computer can extend its usefulness and increase its processing power.

Exercise

1.   Assume you have a computer that contains 256 MB of memory. It contains four memory slots. Each slot can contain 128 MB or 256 MB memory modules. Two of the slots contain 128 MB memory modules. What memory chip(s) would you buy to increase the memory on the computer to 512 MB? What is the maximum memory on the computer? Submit your answer to your instructor or teacher.

2.   Assume you have a computer that contains 1 GB of memory. It contains four memory slots. Each slot can contain 128 MB, 256 MB, 512 MB or 1 GB memory modules. Currently, the four slots each contain a 256 MB memory module. What combinations of memory modules will satisfy your memory upgrade to 2 GB? Visit an appropriate Web site to determine which of these combinations is the least expensive. What is your recommendation? Submit your answer to your instructor or teacher.

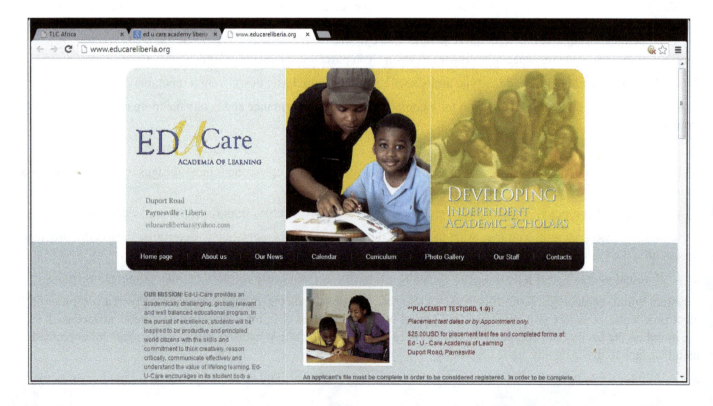

CHAPTER 5
INPUT AND OUTPUT

input

WHAT IS INPUT?

Input is any data and instructions entered into the memory of a computer. As show in Figure 5-1, people have a variety of options for entering input into a computer. Most computer users living in Liberia use the keyboard and the mouse to enter data into the computer.

     An **input device** is any hardware component that allows users to enter data and instructions into a computer. The following pages discuss a variety of input devices.

FIGURE 5-1 Users can enter data and instructions into a computer in a variety of ways.

KEYBOARD AND POINTING DEVICES

Two of the more widely used input devices are the keyboard and the mouse. Most computers include a keyboard and or keyboard compatibilities.

The mouse is a **pointing device** because it allows user to control a pointer on the screen. In a graphical user interface, a **pointer** is a small symbol on the screen whose location and shape change as a user moves a pointing device. A pointing device can select text, graphics, and other objects, and click buttons, icons, links, and menu commands.

The following pages discuss the keyboard and a variety of pointing devices.

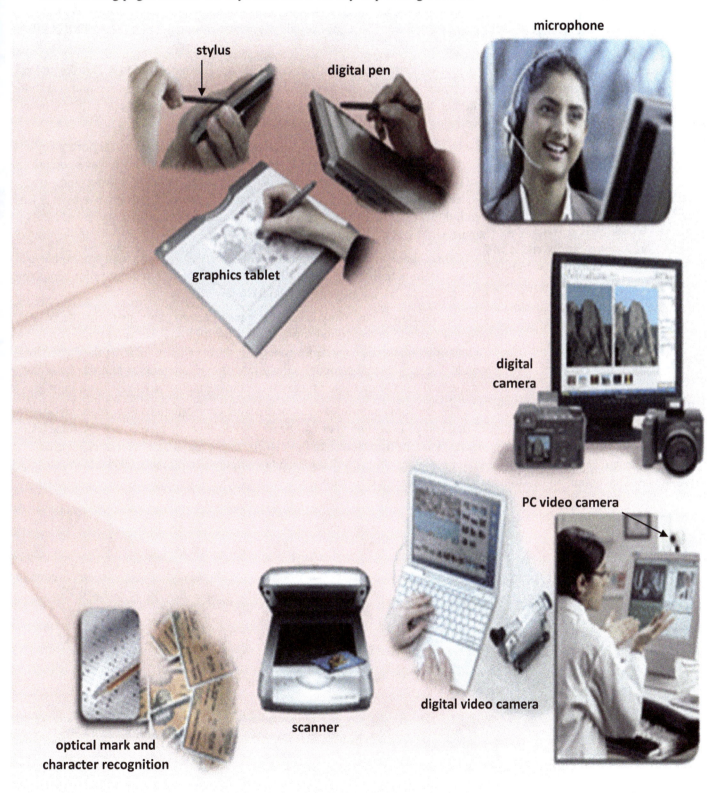

FIGURE 5-1a Users can enter data and instructions into a computer in a variety of ways.

The Keyboard

Many people use a keyboard as one of their input devices. A **keyboard** is an input device that contains keys users press to enter data and instructions into a computer (Figure 5-2).

All computer keyboards have a typing area that includes the letters of the alphabet, numbers, punctuation marks, and other basic keys. Many desktop computer keyboards also have a numeric keypad on the right side of the keyboard.

Most of today's desktop computer keyboards are enhanced keyboards. An enhanced keyboard has twelve function keys along the top and a set of arrow and additional keys between the typing area and the numeric keypad (Figure 5-2). Function keys are special keys programmed to issue commands to a computer. Many keyboards also have a WINDOWS key(s) and an APPLICATION key. When pressed, the WINDOWS key displays the Start menu, and the APPLICATION key displays an item's shortcut menu.

Newer keyboards also include media control buttons that allow you to access the computer's CD/DVD drive and adjust speaker volume, and Internet controls that allow you to open an e-mail program, start a Web browser, and search the Internet. Some keyboards include buttons and other features specifically for users that enjoy playing games on the computer.

Desktop computer keyboards often attach via a cable to a serial port, a keyboard port, or a USB port on the system unit. Some keyboards, however, do not use wires at all. A wireless keyboard, or cordless keyboard, is a battery-powered device that transmits data using wireless technology, such as radio waves or infrared light waves. Wireless keyboards often communicate with a receiver attached to a port on the system unit.

On notebook and some handheld computers, iPads, PDAs, and smart phones, the keyboard is built in the top of the system unit. To fit in these smaller computers, the keyboards usually are smaller and have fewer keys.

Regardless of size, many keyboards have a rectangular shape with the keys aligned in straight, horizontal rows. Users who spend a lot of time typing on these keyboards sometimes experience repetitive strain injuries (RSI) of their wrist and hands. For this reason, some manufactures offer ergonomic keyboards. An ergonomic keyboard has a design that reduces the chance of wrist and hand injuries.

The goal of **ergonomics** is to incorporate comfort, and safety in the design of the workplace. Employees can be injured or develop disorders of the muscles, nerves, tendons, ligaments, and joints from working in an area that is not ergonomically designed. Right now in Liberia, people are at health risk for using computers and other electronic devices the wrong way. Discussion on this topic is discussed later in this textbook.

> **FAQ 5-1**
> **What can I do to reduce chances of experiencing repetitive strain injuries?**
> Do not rest your wrist on the edge of a desk; use a wrist rest. Keep you forearm and wrist level so your does not bend. Do hand exercises every fifteen minutes. Keep you shoulders, arms, hands, and wrists relaxed while you work. Maintain good posture. Keep feet flat on the floor, with one foot slightly in front of the other. For more info, visit www.clarkepublish.com.

FIGURE 5-2 On a desktop computer keyboard, you type using keys in the typing area and on the numeric keyboard.

Mouse

A **mouse** is a pointing device that fits comfortably under the palm of your hand with a mouse, users control the movement of the pointer. As you move a mouse, the pointer on the screen also moves. Generally, you use the mouse to move the pointer on the screen to an object such as a button, a menu, an icon, a link, or text. Then, you press a mouse button to perform a certain action association with that object.

A **mechanical mouse** has a rubber or metal ball on its underside (Figure 5-3a). When the rolls in a certain direction, electronic circuits in the mouse translate the movement of the mouse into signals the computer can process. You should place a mechanical mouse on a mouse pad. A **mouse pad** is a rectangular rubber or foam pad that provides better traction than the top of a desk.

An optical mouse, by contrast, has no moving mechanical parts inside. Instead, an **optical mouse** uses devices that emit and sense light to detect the mouse's movement. Some use optical sensors (Figure 5-3b); others use laser (Figure 5-3c). An optical mouse is more precise than a mechanical mouse and does not require cleaning as does a mechanical mouse, but it also is more expensive.

A mouse connects to a computer in several ways. Many types connect with a cable that attaches to a serial port, mouse port, or USB port on the system unit. A wireless mouse, or cordless mouse, is a battery-powered device that transmits data using wireless technology, such as radio waves or infrared light waves. Read Discussion 5-1 for related discussion.

FIGURE 5-3a (mechanical mouse)   **FIGURE 5-3b** (optical mouse that uses optical sensor)   **FIGURE 5-3c** (optical mouse that uses laser)

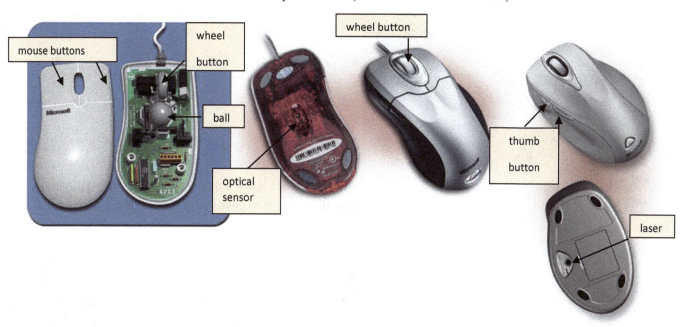

FIGURE 5-3 A mechanical mouse contains a small ball. An optical mouse uses an optical sensor or a laser. Many include buttons to push with your thumb and index finger.

DISCUSSION 5-1
Should the Government Set Computer Use Standard?

When you consider the cause of workplace injuries, you might not put clicking a mouse in the same category with lifting a bag of concrete, but perhaps you should. According to the chairman of a U.S. National Academy of Science panel that investigated workplace injuries, every year one million Americans lose workdays because of repetitive strain injuries. The same things are happening right here in Liberia but these incidences are not being reported. The reason being is sample—there is not legislation on the book that protects victims of workplace computer related injuries. Repetitive strain injuries are caused when muscle groups perform the same actions over and over again. In the U.S., repetitive strain injuries were once common among factory workers who performed the same task on an assembly line for hours a day. Today, these injuries, which often result from prolonged use of a computer mouse and keyboard, are the largest job-related injury and illness problem in the United States as well as Liberia. Should the government establish laws regarding computer use? Why or Why not? Who is responsible for this type of workplace injury? Why? not?

Trackball

Similar to a mechanical mouse that has a ball on the bottom, a **trackball** is a stationary pointing device with a ball on its top or side (Figure 5-4).

To move the pointer using a trackball, you rotate the ball with your thumb, fingers, or the palm of your hand. In addition to the ball, a trackball usually has one or more buttons that work just like mouse buttons.

FIGURE 5-4 A trackball is like an upside-down.

Touchpad

A **touchpad** is a small, flat, rectangular pointing device that is sensitive to pressure and motion (Figure 5-5). To move the pointer using a touchpad, slide your fingertip across the surface of the pad. Some touchpads have one or more buttons around the edge of the pad that work like a mouse buttons. On most touchpads, you also can tap the pad's surface to imitate mouse operations such as clicking. Touchpads are found most often on notebook computers. Most laptops and notebooks that are currently in Liberia have touchpad.

FIGURE 5-5 Most notebook computers have a touchpad that allows users to control the movement of the pointer.

Pointing Stick

A pointing stick is a pressure-sensitive pointing device shaped like a pencil eraser that is position between keys on a keyboard (Figure 5-6). To move the pointer using a pointing stick, you push the pointing stick with a finger. The pointer on the screen moves in the direction you push the pointing stick. By pressing buttons below the keyboard, users can click and perform other mouse-type operations with a pointing stick. IBM developed the pointing stick for its notebook computers

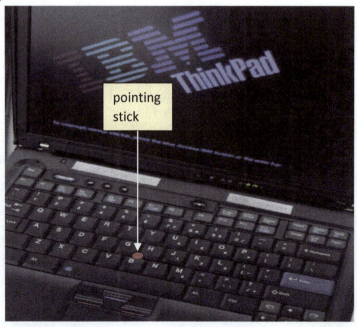

pointing stick

FIGURE 5-6 Some notebook computers include a pointing stick to allow a user to control the movement of the pointer.

Joystick and Wheel

User running game software or flight and driving simulation software often use a joystick or wheel as a pointing device (Figure 5-7). A **joystick** is a vertical level mounted on a base. You move the lever in different directions to control the actions of the simulated vehicle or player. The lever usually includes buttons called triggers that you press to activate certain events.

A **wheel** is a steering-wheel-type input device. Users turn the wheel to simulate driving a car, truck, or other vehicle. Most wheels also include foot pedals for breaking and acceleration actions.

Audio Player Control Pad

The **control pad** on an audio player is a pointing device that enables users to scroll through and play music, adjust volume, and customize settings. Control pads typically contain buttons or wheels that are operated with a thumb or finger. For example, users rotate the iPod's **Click Wheel** to browse through its song lists and press the Click Wheel's buttons to play or pause a song, display a menu, and other actions (Figure 5-8).

Gamepad

A **gamepad**, sometimes called a game controller, is a pointing device that controls the movement and action of players or objects in video games or computer games. On the gamepad, users press buttons or move sticks in various directions to activate events. Gamepads communicate with a game console or a personal computer via wired or wireless technology.

Light Pen

A **light pen** is a handheld input device that can detect the presence of light. To select objects on the screen, a user presses the pen against the surface of the screen or points the light pen at the screen and then presses a button on the pen.

Touch Screen

A **touch screen** is a touch-sensitive display device. Users can interact with these devices by touching areas of the screen. Because touch screens require a lot of arm movements, you do not enter large amounts of data using a touch screen. Instead, users touch words, pictures, numbers, letters, or locations identified on the screen. Kiosks, which are freestanding computers, often have touch screens (Figure 5-9). Many handheld games consoles also have touch screens.

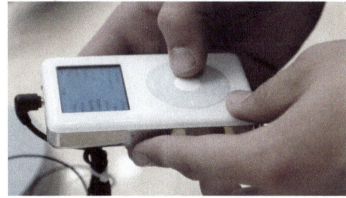

FIGURE 5-7 Joysticks and wheels help a user control the action of players and vehicles in game and simulation software.

FIGURE 5-8 You rotate the wheel or press button on the iPod's Click Wheel to select and play songs.

FIGURE 5-9 A desktop user using a touch screen computer to perform a task in his home office.

FIGURE 5-10 Tablet PCs use a pressure-sensitive pen.

Pen Input

Mobile users often enter data and instructions with a pen-type device. With **pen input**, users write, draw, and tap on a flat surface to enter input. The surface may be a monitor, a screen, a special type of paper, or a graphics tablet. Two devices used for pen input are the stylus and digital pen. A **stylus** is a small metal or plastic device that looks like a tiny ink pen but uses pressure instead of ink. A **digital pen**, which is slightly larger than a stylus, is available in two forms, some are pressure-sensitive; others have built-in digital cameras.

Some mobile computers and nearly all mobile devices have touch screens. Instead using a finger to enter data and instructions, most of these devices include a pressure-sensitive digital pen or stylus. You write, draw, or make selections on the computer screen by touching the screen with the pen

or stylus. For example, Tablet PCs use a pressure-sensitive digital pen (Figure 5-10) and PDAs use a stylus. Pressure-sensitive digital pens, often simply called pens, typically provide more functionality than a stylus, featuring electronic erasers and programmable buttons.

Pen input is possible on computers without touch screen by attaching a graphics tablet to the computers. A **graphics tablet** is a flat, rectangular, electronic, plastic board. Architects, mapmakers, designers, artists, and home users create drawings and sketches by using a pressure-sensitive pen on a graphics tablet (Figure 5-11).

FIGURE 5-11 An Artist using a pen and a Graphics Tablet pad or graphics pad.

Digital pens that have built-in digital cameras work differently from pressure-sensitive digital pens. These pens look very much like a ballpoint pen and typically do not contain any additional buttons. As you write or draw on special digital paper with the pen, it captures every handwritten mark and then stores the images in the pen's memory. You then can transfer the images from the pen to a computer (Figure 5-12) or mobile device, such as a iPad or smart phone.

FIGURE 5-12 Some digital pens have built-in digital cameras that store handwritten marks and allow you to transfer your handwriting to a computer.

Test your knowledge of pages 142 through 148 in Quiz Yourself 5-1

QUIZ YOURSELF 5-1

Instructions: Find the true statement below. Then rewrite the remaining false statement so they are true.

1. A keyboard is an output device that contains keys users press to enter data and instructions into a computer.

2. A trackball is a small, flat, rectangular pointing device commonly found on notebook computers.

3. Input is any data and instructions entered into the memory of a computer.

4. An optical mouse has moving mechanical parts inside.

5. PDAs use a pressure-sensitive digital pen, and Tablet PCs use a stylus.

Quiz Yourself Online: To further check your knowledge of the keyboard, mouse, and other pointing devices, visit www.clarkepublish.com or visit the Internet and then search www.google.com for more information.

OTHER TYPES OF INPUT

In addition to the keyboard, mouse, and pointing devices just discussed, users have a variety of other options available to enter data and instructions into a computer. These include voice input; input for the iPads, eReaders, PDAs, smart phones, and Tablet PCs; digital cameras; video input; scanners and reading devices; terminals; and biometric input. Read Looking Ahead 5-1 for a look at the next generation of input devices.

Voice Input

Voice input is the process of entering input by speaking into a microphone. **Voice recognition,** also called **speech recognition,** is the computer capability of distinguishing spoken words. Voice recognition programs recognize a vocabulary of preprogrammed words. The vocabulary of voice recognition programs can range from two words to millions of words. Some business software, such as word processing and spreadsheet, includes voice recognition as part of the program. For example, users can dictate memos and letters into word processing program instead of typing them.

Looking Ahead 5-1

Wearable Computers Makes Performance Statement

Frodo, the hero in *Lord of the Rings* trilogy, wears a durable, inconspicuous tunic that saves his life. You, too, may one day wear a garment with biosensors that may save your life by detecting health problems and summoning emergency help.

While this clothing is practical, other researchers are creating the newest fashions and accessories outfitted with computers. For example, reporters may one day wear trench coats equipped with 10 cameras to gave a 360-degree panoramic view of the scene. Children wearing the Dog@watch jacket and watch might transmit their location via a GPS unit and wireless computer. Buttons on your jacket also may serve as cameras, sunglasses may have a built-in audio player and smart phone, and your shirt might display text messages from a friend. For more info, visit www.google.com and search forclick Wearable Computers.

AUDIO INPUT Voice input is part of a larger category of input called audio input. **Audio input** is the process of entering any sound into the computer such as speech, music, and sound effects. To enter high-quality sound into a personal computer, the computer must have a sound card. Users enter sound into a computer via devices such as microphones, tape players, CD/DVD players, or radios, each of which plugs in a port on the sound card.

FIGURE 5-13 An electronic piano keyboard is an external MIDI device that allows users to record music, which can be store in the computer.

Some users also enter music and other sound effects using external MIDI devices such as an electronic piano keyboard (Figure 5-13). MIDI (musical instrument digital interface) is electronic music industry's standard that defines how digital musical devices represent sounds electronically. Software that conforms to the MIDI standard allows users to compose and edit music and many other sounds.

Input for iPod, iPads, eReaders, PDAs, Smart Phones, and Tablet PCs

Mobile devices, such as the PDA and smart phone, and mobile computers such as the Tablet PC, offer convenience for the mobile user. A variety of alternatives for entering data and instructions is available for these devices and computers.

iPod, iPads, eReaders and PDAs   A user enters data and instructions into an iPad, eReader or a PDA in many ways (Figure 5-14). iPads, eReaders and PDAs ship with basic stylus, which is the primary input device. With the stylus or your finger, you enter data in two ways: using an on-screen keyboard or using handwriting recognition software.

For users who prefer typing to handwriting, some iPads, eReaders and PDAs have a built-in mini keyboard. For iPads, eReaders and PDAs without a keyboard, user can purchase a keyboard that snaps on the bottom of the device. Other user type on a desktop computer or notebook computer keyboard and transfer the data to the iPad or PDA. To take photographs and view on an iPad or PDA, you can use your iPad or simply attach a digital camera directly to the PDA.

FIGURE 5-14 User input data into a PDA using a variety of techniques.

SMART PHONE Voice in one method of input for smart phone. Instead of voice, communicate with others. With text messaging, you type and send a short message to another smart phone by pressing buttons on the telephone's keypad. Some wireless Internet service providers (WISPs) partner with IM (instant messaging) services so you can use your smart phone to communicate via text with other smart phone or computer users with the same IM service. Users can send graphics, pictures, video clips, and sound files, as well as short text messages with picture messaging, to another smart phone with a compatible picture messaging service.

Most smart phones include PDA capabilities. Thus, input devices used with PDAs typically also are available for smart phones.

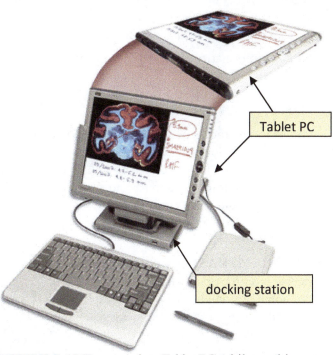

TABLET PCS The primary input device for a Tablet PC is a pressure-sensitive digital pen, which allows users to write on the device's screen. Both the slate and convertible designs of a Tablet PC provide a means for keyboard input. To access peripherals at their home or office, users can slide their Tablet PC in a docking station, which is an external device that attaches to a mobile computer, contains a power connection and provides connections to peripherals (Figure 5-15). The design of docking stations varies depending on the type of mobile computer or device to which they attached.

FIGURE 5-15 To use a slate Tablet PC while working at a desk, simply insert the Tablet PC in a docking station.

Digital Cameras

A **digital camera** allows users to take pictures and store the photographed images digitally, instead of on traditional film (Figure 5-16). Some digital cameras use internal flash memory to store images. Others store images on mobile storage media, including a flash memory card, memory stick, and mini CD/DVD.

Digital cameras typically allow users to review, and sometimes edit, images while they are in the camera. Some digital cameras can connect to or communicate wirelessly with a printer or television, allowing users to print or view images directly from the camera.

Often users prefer to download, or transfer a copy of, the images from the digital camera to the computer's hard disk, where the images are available for editing with photo editing software, printing, faxing, sending, via e-mail, including in another document, or posting to a Web site or photo community for everyone to see.

A digital camera often features flash, zoom, automatic focus, and special effects. Some allow users to record short audio narrations for photographed images. Others even record short video clips in addition to still images.

FIGURE 5-16 With a digital camera, users can view photographed images immediately through a small screen on the camera to see if the picture is worth keeping.

One factor that affects the quality of a digital camera is it resolution. **Resolution** is the number of horizontal and vertical pixels in a display device. A digital camera's resolution is defined in pixels. A **pixel** (short for picture element) is the smallest element in an electronic image. The greater the number of pixels the camera uses to capture an image, the better the quality of the image. Digital camera resolutions range from 1 million to more than 8 million pixels (MP).

For additional information about digital cameras, read Digital Images and Video Technology feature on the book's Web site

Video Input

Video input is the process of capturing full-motion images and storing them on a computer's storage medium such as a hard disk or DVD. Some video devices use analog video signals. A **digital video (DV) camera,** by contrast, records video as digital signals instead of analog signals. Many DV cameras have the capability of capturing still frames, as well as motion. To transfer recorded images to a hard disk or DC or DVD, users connect DV cameras directly to a USB port or a FireWire port on the system unit. After saving the video or a storage medium, such as a hard disk or DVD, you can play it or edit it using video editing software on a computer.

PC VIDEO CAMERAS   A **video camera**, or **PC camera**, is a type of digital video camera that enables a home or small business user to capture video and still images, send e-mail messages with video attachments, add live images to instant messages, broadcast live images over the Internet, and make video telephone calls. During a **video telephone** call, both parties see each other as they communicate over the Internet (Figure 5-17). The cost of PC video camera usually is less than $100.

WEB CAMS   A **Web cam** is any video camera that displays its output on a Web page. A Web cam attracts Web site visitors by showing images that change regularly.
Home or small business users might see Web cams to show a work in progress, weather and traffic information, employees at work, photographs of a vacation, and countless other images

FIGURE 5-17 Using a PC video camera, home users can see other as they communicate over the Internet.

VIDEO CONFERENCING   A **video conference** is a meeting between two or more geographically separated people who use a network or the Internet to transmit audio and video data (Figure 5-18). To participate in a video conference, you need conference software along with a microphone, speakers, and a video camera attached to a computer. As you speak, member of the meeting hear your voice on their speakers. Any image in front of the video camera, such as a person's face, appears in a window on each participant's screen.

As the cost of video conferencing hardware and software decrease, increasingly more business meeting, corporate training, and educational classes will be conducted as video conferences.

FIGURE 5-18 To save on travel expenses, many large businesses are turning to video conferencing.

Scanners and Reading Devices

Some input devices save users time by capturing data directly from a source document, which is the original form of the data. Example of source documents include time cards, order forms, invoices, paychecks, advertisements, brochures, photographs, inventory tags, or any other document that contains data to be processed.

Devices that can capture data directly from a source document include optical scanners, optical readers, bar code readers, FRID readers, magnetic stripe readers, and magnetic-ink character recognition readers.

OPTICAL SCANNERS An **optical scanner**, usually called **scanner,** is a light-sensing device that reads printed text and graphics and then translates the results into a form the computer can process. A **flatbed scanner** works in a manner similar to a copy machine except it creates a file of the document in memory instead of a paper copy (Figure 5-19). Once you scan a picture or document, you can display the scanned object on the screen, store it on a storage medium, print it, fax it, attach it to an e-mail message, include it in another document, or post it to a Web site or photo community for everyone to see.

Many scanners include OCR (optical character recognition) software, which can read and convert text documents into electronic files. OCR software converts a scanned image into a text file that can be edited, for example, with a word processing program.

FIGURE 5-19 A Flatbed Scanner that comes with a OCR Software for scanning documents and photos.

OPTICAL READERS An **optical reader** is a device that uses a light source to read characters, marks, and codes and then convert them into digital data that a computer can process. Two technologies used by optical readers are optical character recognition and optical mark recognition.

- **Optical character recognition (OCR)** involves reading typewritten, computer-printed, or hand-printed characters from ordinary documents and translating the images into a form the computer can process. Most **OCR devices** include a small optical scanner for reading characters and sophisticated software to analyze what is read. OCR devices range from large machines that can read thousands of documents per minute to handheld wands that reads one document at a time.

Many companies use OCR characters on turn-around documents. A **turnaround document** is a document that you return (turn around) to the company that creates and send it. For example, when consumers receive a bill, they often tear off a portion of the bill they return usually has their payment (Figure 5-20). The portion of the bill they return usually has their payment amount, account number, and other information printed in OCR character.

- **Optical mark recognition (OMR)** devices read hand-drawn marks such as small circles or rectangles. A person places these marks on a form, such as a test, survey, or questionnaires answer sheet.

FIGURE 5-20 OCR characters frequently are used with turnaround documents. With this bill, you tear off the top portion and return it with a payment.

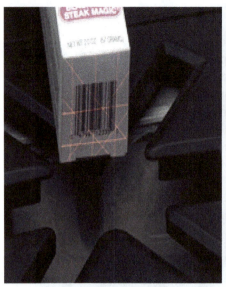

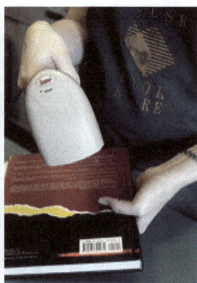

BAR CODE READERS   A **bar coder reader,** also called a **bar code scanner**, is an optical reader that uses laser beams to read bar codes (Figure 5-21). A **bar code** is an identification code that consists of a set of vertical lines and spaces of different widths. The bar code represents data that identifies the manufacturer and the item.

Manufacturers print a bar code either on a label that is affixed to a product. Read Discussion 5-2 for a related discussion.

FIGURE 5-21 A bar code reader uses laser beams to read bar codes on product such as groceries and books.

DISCUSSION 5-2
Scanner Error at the Checkout Counter?

Have you ever taken an item to a store's checkout and discovered that the price displayed when the item's bar code was scanned was different from the price shown on a shelf tag, sign, or advertisement? If you have, you are not alone. A government survey found that eight percent of the time, an item's scanned price is different from the price presented elsewhere. When an item is scanned at a store's checkout counter, a computer finds the item's price in the store's database. Store owners claim that discrepancies between the scanned price and a listed price are the result of human error – either failure to update the store's price database or incorrect or incorrect shelf tags, signs, or advertisements. Yet, some consumer advocates claim that the discrepancy sometimes is intentional. They accuse stores of scanner fraud, insisting that some stores advertise one price and then charge another, hoping buyers will not recognize the difference. Most state have laws that protect consumers against scanner fraud. Some laws even require stores to pay consumers an immediate reward, sometimes $5 against or more, if the consumer finds a scanner error. Who do you think is responsible for differences between scanned prices and posted cost? Why? Should stores be responsible for pricing error? Why or why not?

RFID READERS   **RFID** (radio frequency identification) is a technology that uses radio signals to communicate with a tag placed in or attached to an object, an animal, or a person. RFID tags, which contain a memory chip and an antenna, are available in many shapes and size. An **RFID reader** reads information on the tag via radio waves. RFID readers can be handheld devices or mounted in a stationary object such as a doorway.

Many retailers see RFID as an alternative to bar code identification because it does not require direct contact or line-of-site transmission. Each product in a store would contain a tag that identifies the product (Figure 5-22). As consumers remove products from the store shelves and walk through a checkout area, an RFID reader reads the tag(s) and communicates with a computer that calculates the amount due. Other uses of RFID include tracking times of runners in a marathon; tracking location of soldiers, employee wardrobes, and airlines baggage; checking lift tickets of skiers; gauging pressure and temperature of tires on a vehicle; checking out library books; and tracking payment as vehicles pass through booths on tollway systems. Read Looking Ahead 5-2 for a look at the next generation of RFID.

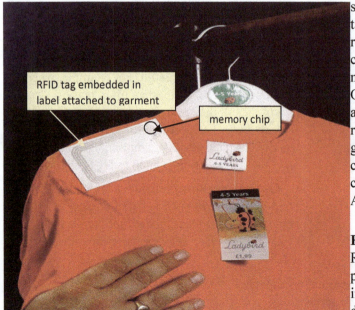

FIGURE 5-22 RFID readers read information. Stored on an RFID tag and then communicate this information to computers, which instantaneously compute payments and update inventory records. In this example, the RFID tag is embedded in a label attached to the garment.

MAGNETIC STRIPE CARD READERS

A **magnetic stripe card reader**, often called a mag-stripe reader, reads the magnetic stripe on the back of credit cards, entertainment cards, bank cards, and other similar cards. The stripe contains information identifying you and the card issuer (Figure 5-23). Some name, account number, the card's expiration date, and a country code.

When a consumer swipes a credit card through the magstripe reader, it reads the information store on the on the card. If the magstripe reader rejects your card, it is possible that the magnetic stripe is scratched, dirty, or erased. Exposure to a magnet or magnetic field can erase the contents of a card's magnetic stripe.

MICR READERS

MICR (magnetic-ink character recognition) devices read text printed with magnetized ink. An **MICR reader** converts MICR characters into a form the computer can process. The banking industry almost exclusively uses MICR for check processing. Each check in your checkbook has precoded MICR characters beginning at the lower-left edge (Figure 5-24). Banks in Liberia need to begin using MICR reader to improve banking security.

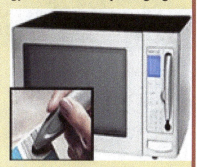

Looking Ahead 5-2

RFID Sensors Simplify Monitor Task

Burnt microwave meals may become a thing of the past with the development of RFID technology. Just wave the packaging in front of a food-enabled scanner and let the microwave determine how long to cook the food at a particular temperature.

Many uses for RFID sensors are planned. They could determine when a soccer ball crosses a goal line or a marathon runner crosses the finish line, signal when a child passes a doorway in his pajamas or an inmate enters restricted areas, and track packages by sensing and transmitting product locations. On the battlefield, they could sense vehicle and missile movement. In hospital, patient wristbands could monitor when a particular drug and dosage is administered. For more info, visit book's Web site and then click RFID Uses.

FIGURE 5-23 A magnetic stripe card reads information encoded on the stripe on the back of your credit card.

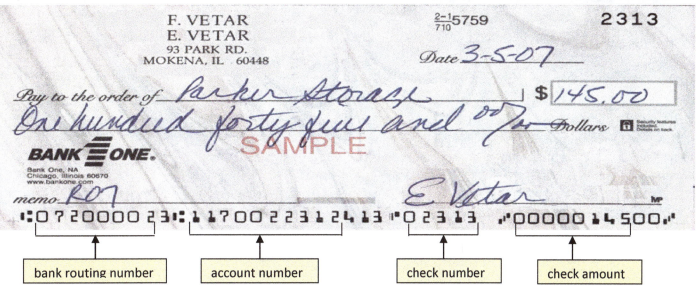

FIGURE 5-24 The MICR characters preprinted on the check represent the bank routing number, the customer account number, and the check number. The amount of the check in the lower-right corner is added after the check is cashed.

When a bank receives a check for payment, it uses an MICR inscriber to print the amount of the check in MICR characters in the lower-right corner. The check then is sorted or routed to the customer's bank, along with thousands of others. Each check is inserted in an MICR reader, which sends the check information – including the amount of the check–to a computer for processing.

Terminals (this may not be found in many stores in Liberia and other African countries)

A **terminal** consists of a keyboard, a monitor, a video card, and memory. These components often are housed in a single unit. Users enter data and instructions into a terminal and then transmit some or all of the data over a network to a host computer.

Special-purpose terminals perform specific task and contain features uniquely designed for use in a particular industry. Two special-purpose terminals are point-of-sale (POS) terminal and automated teller machines.

Point-of-Sale (POS this is currently in Liberia) Terminals – The location in a retail or grocery store where a consumer pays for goods or services is the point of sale (POS). Most retail stores use a POS terminal to record purchases, process credit or debit cards and update inventory.

Many POS terminals handle credit card or debit card payments and thus also include a magstripe reader. Once the transaction is approved, the terminal prints a receipt for the customer. A self-service POS terminal allows consumers to perform all the checkout-related activities (Figure 5-25). That is, they scan the items bag the items, and pay for the items themselves.

Automated Teller Machines – An **automated teller machine (ATM is in Liberia)** is a self-service banking machine that connects to a host computer through a network (Figure 5-26). Banks place ATMs in convenient locations, including grocery stores, convenience stores, retail outlets, shopping malls, and gas stations.

Using an ATM, people withdraw cash, deposit money, transfer funds, or inquire about an account balance. Some ATMs have a touch screen; others have special buttons or keypads for entering input. To access a bank account, you insert a plastic bankcard in the ATM's magstripe reader. The ATM asks you to enter a password, called a personal identification number (PIN), which verifies that you are the holder of the bankcard. When your transaction is complete, the ATM prints a receipt for you record.

FIGURE 5-25 Many grocery stores offer self-serve checkouts, where the consumers themselves use the POS terminals to scan purchases, scan their store saver card and coupons, and then pay for the goods.

FIGURE 5-26 An ATM is a self-service banking terminal that allows customers to access their bank accounts.

Biometric Input

Biometrics is the technology of authenticating a person's identity by verifying a personal characteristic. Biometric devices grant users access to programs, systems, or rooms by analyzing some physiological (related to physical or chemical activities in the body) or behavioral characteristic. Examples include fingerprints, hand geometry, facial features, voice, signatures, and eyes patterns.

The most widely used biometric device today is a fingerprint scanner. A **fingerprint scanner** captures curves and indentations of a fingerprint. With the cost of finger scanners dropping to less than $100, many homes and small businesses install fingerprint scanners to authenticate users before they can access a personal computer. To save on desk space, some newer keyboards and notebook computers have a fingerprint scanner built into them, which allows users to log on to Web sites via their fingerprint instead of entering a user name and password (Figure 5-27).

A face recognition system captures a live face image and compares it with a stored image to determine if the person is a legitimate user. Some buildings use face recognition systems to secure access to rooms. Law enforcement, surveillance systems, and airports use face recognition to protect the public.

Biometric devices measure the shape and size of a person's hand using a hand geometry system. Because their cost is more than $1,000, large companies typically use these systems as time and attendance devices or as security devices.

A voice verification system compares a person's live speech with their stored voice pattern. Larger organizations sometimes use voice verification systems as time and attendance devices. Many companies also use this technology for access to sensitive files and networks.

FIGURE 5-27 Keyboard with built-in fingerprint scanner.

A signature verification system recognizes the shape of your handwritten signature, as well as measures the pressure exerted and the motion used to write the signature. Signature verification systems use a specialized pen and tablet.

High security areas use iris recognition systems. The camera in an iris recognition system uses iris recognition technology to read patterns in the iris of the eye (Figure 5-28). These patters are as unique as a fingerprint. Iris recognition systems are quite expensive and are used by government security organizations, the military, and financial institutions that deal with highly sensitive data. Some organizations use retinal scanners, which work similarly but instead scan patterns of blood vessels in the back of the retina.

Sometimes, fingerprint, iris, retina, and other biometric data are stored on a smart card. A **smart card**, which is comparable in size to a credit card or ATM card, stores the personal data on a thin microprocessor that is embedded in the card.

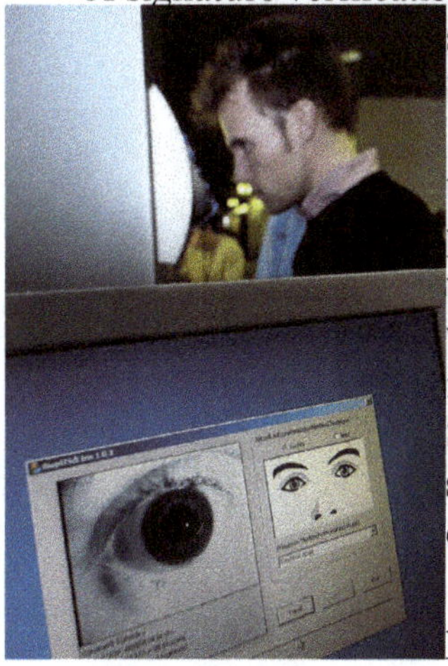

FIGURE 5-28 An iris recognition system.

Test your knowledge of pages 149 through 157 in Quiz Yourself 5-2

QUIZ YOURSELF 5-2

Instructions: Find the true statement below. Then rewrite the remaining false statement so they are true.

1. A digital camera allows users to take pictures and store the photographed images digitally, instead of on a traditional film.

2. A fingerprint scanner captures curves and indentations of a signature.

3. After swiping a credit card through MICR reader, it reads the information stored on the magnetic stripe on the card.

4. Instant messaging is the computer's capability of distinguishing spoken word.

5. Many smart phones today have POS capabilities.

6. RFID is a technology that uses laser signals to communicate with a tag placed in an object, an animal, or a person.

Quiz Yourself Online: To further check your knowledge of bits, voice input, input devices; scanner, PDAs, smart phones, biometric devices; and reading devices, visit www.clarkepublish.com or visit the Internet and then search www.google.com for more information.

WHAT IS OUTPUT?

Output is data that has been processed into a useful form. That is, computers process data (input) into information (output). Users view output on a screen, print it, or hear it through speakers, headphones, or earphones, or earphones. While working with a computer, a user encounters four basic categories of output: text, graphics, audio, and video (Figure 5-29). Very often, a single form of output, such as a Web page, includes more than one of these categories.

An **output device** is any hardware component that conveys information to one or more people. Commonly used output devices include display devices; printers; speakers, headphones, and earphones; fax machines and fax modems; multifunction peripherals; and data projectors.

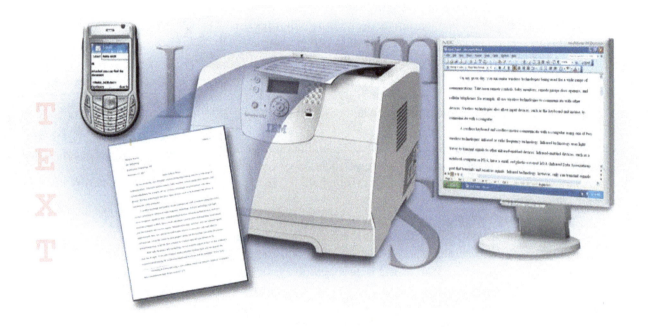

FIGURE 5-29 Four Categories of output are text, graphics, audio, and video.

DISPLAY DEVICES

A **display device** is an output device that visually conveys text, graphics, and video information. Desktop computers typically use a monitor as their display device. A **monitor** is a display device that is packaged as a separate peripheral. Most monitors have a tilt-and-swivel base that allows users to adjust the angle of the screen to minimize neck strain and reduce glare form overhead lighting. Monitor controls permit users to adjust the brightness, contrast, positioning, height, and width of images.

Most mobile computers devices integrate the display and other components into the same physical case.

FIGURE 5-30 Four Categories of output are text, graphics, audio, and video.

Display devices usually show text, graphics, and video information in color. Some however, are monochrome. Monochrome means the information appears in one color (such as white, amber, green, black, blue or gray) on a different color background (such as black or grayish-white). Some PDAs and other mobile devices use monochrome displays because they require less battery power.

Types of display devices include LCD monitors and screens, plasma monitors, and CTR monitors. The following pages discuss each of these display devices

LCD Monitors and Screens

An **LCD monitor**, also called a flat panel monitor, is a desktop monitor that uses a liquid crystal display to produce images (Figure 5-30). These monitors produce sharp, flicker-free images. LCD monitors have a small footprint; that is, they don not take up much desk space. LCD monitors are available in a variety of sizes, with the more common being 15, 17, 18, 19, 20, 21 and 23 inches – some are 30 or 40 inches. You measure a monitor the same way you measure a television, that is, diagonally from one corner to the other.

Mobile computers, such as notebook computers and Tablet PCs, and mobile devices, such as PDAs and smart phones, often have built-in LCD screens (Figure 5-31). Notebook computer screens are available in a variety of sizes, with the most common being from 14.1, 15, and 17 inches. PDA screens average 3.5 inches. On smart phones, screen sizes.

FIGURE 5-31 An LCD monitor is thin and lightweight.

FIGURE 5-32 Notebook computers and Tablet PCs have color LCD screen. Many PDAs and smart phones also have color displays.

LCD TECHNOLOGY AND QUALITY A **liquid crystal display (LCD)** uses a liquid compound to present information on a display device. Computer LCDs typically contain fluorescent tubes that emit light waves toward the liquid-crystal cells, which are sandwiched between two sheets of material.

The quality of an LCD monitor or LCD screen depends primarily on its resolution, response time, brightness, pixel pitch, and contrast ratio.

• Resolution is the number of horizontal and vertical pixels in a display device. For example, a monitor that has a 1600 X 1200 resolution displays up to 1600 pixels per horizontal row and 1200 pixels per vertical row, for a total of 1,920,000 pixels to create a screen image. A higher resolution uses a greater number of pixels and thus provides a smoother, sharper, and clearer image. As the resolution increases, however, some items on the screen appear smaller, such as menu bars, toolbars, and rulers.

With LCD monitors and screens, resolution generally is proportional to the size of the devices. That is, the resolution increases for larger monitors and screens. For example, a 17-inch LCD monitor typically has a resolution of 1280 X 1024, while a 20-inch LCD monitor has a resolution of 1600 X 1200. LCDs are geared for a specific resolution.

• Response time of an LCD monitor or screen is the time in milliseconds (ms) that it takes to turn a pixel on or off. LCD monitors' and screens' response time range from 8 to 25 ms. The lower the number, the faster the response time.

• Brightness of an LCD monitor or LCD screen is measured in nits. A nit is a unit of visible light intensity. The higher the nits, the brighter the image.

• Pixel pitch, sometimes called dot pitch, is the distance in millimeters between pixels on a display device. Average pixel pitch on LCD monitors and screens should be .28 mm or lower. The lower the number, the sharper the image.

• Contrast ration describes the difference in light intensity between the brightest white and darkest black that can be display on an LCD monitor. Contrast ratios today range from 400:1 to 800:1. Higher contrast ratios represent colors better.

PORTS AND LCD MONITOR A cable on a monitor plugs in a port on the system unit. LCD monitors use a digital signal to produce a picture. To display the highest quality images, an LCD monitor should plug in a DVI (Digital Video Interface) port, which enables digital signals to transmit directly to an LCD monitor.

Plasma Monitors

Large business users or power users sometimes have plasma monitors, which often measure more than 60 inches wide (Figure 5-33). A **plasma monitor** is a display device that uses gas plasma technology, which sandwiches a layer of gas between two glass plates.

Plasma monitors offer larger screen sizes and higher display quality than LCD monitors but are more expensive. These monitors also can hang directly on a wall.

FIGURE 5-33 Large plasma monitors can measure more than 60 inches wide.

CRT Monitor

A **CRT monitor** is a monitor that contains a cathode-ray tube (Figure 5-35). A cathode-ray tube (CRT) is a large, sealed glass tube. The front of the tube is the screen. CRT monitors for desktop computers are available in various sizes, with the more common being 15, 17, 18, 19, 21 and 22 inches. In addition to monitor size, advertisements also list a CRT monitor's viewable size. The viewable size is the diagonal measurement of the actual viewing area provided by the screen in the CRT monitor. A 21-inch monitor for example, may have a viewable size of 20 inches.

A CRT monitor costs less than a LCD monitor but also generates more heat and uses more power than an LCD monitor. To help reduce the amount of electricity

FIGURE 5-34 The core of a CRT monitor is a cathode-ray tube.

used by monitors and other computer components, the United State Department of Energy (DOE) and the United States Environmental Protection Agency (EPA) developed the **ENERGY STAR program.** This program encourages manufacturers to create energy-efficient devices that require little power when the devices are not in use. Monitors and devices that meet the ENERGY STAR guidelines display an ENERGY STAR label.

CRT monitors produce a small amount of electromagnetic radiation. Electromagnetic radiation (EMR) is a magnetic field that travels at the speed of light. Excessive amount of EMR can pose a health risk. To be safe, all high-quality CRT monitors comply with a set of standards that defines acceptable levels of EMR for a monitor. To protect yourself even further, sit at arm's length from the CRT monitor because EMR travels only a short distance.

QUALITY OF A CRT MONITOR   The quality of a CRT monitor depends largely on its resolution, dot pitch, and refresh rate.

- Most CRT monitors support a variety of screen resolutions. Standard CRT monitors today usually display up to a maximum of 1800 X 1440 pixels, with 1280 X 1024 often the norm. High-end CRT monitors (for the power user) can display 2048 X 1536 pixels or more.
- As with LCD monitor, text created with a smaller dot pitch, or pixel pitch, is easier to read. To minimize eye fatigue, use a CRT monitor with a dot pitch of .27 millimeters or lower.
- Electron beams inside a CRT monitor "draw" an image on the entire screen many times per second so the image does not fade. The number of times the image is drawn per second is called the refresh rate. A CRT monitor's refresh rate, which is expressed in hertz (Hz), should be fast enough to maintain a constant, flicker-free image. A high-quality CRT monitor will provide a vertical refresh rate of a least 68 Hz. This means the image on the screen redraws itself vertically 68 times in a second.

GRAPHIC CHIPS AND CRT MONITOR   Many CRT monitors use an analogy signal to produce an image. A cable on the CRT monitor plugs in a port on the system unit, which enables communications from a graphics chip. If the graphics chip resides on a video card, the video card converts digital output from the computer into an analog video signal and sends the signal through the cable to the monitor, which displays output on the screen. Some users place additional video cards in their system unit, allowing multiple monitors to display output from a single computer simultaneously.

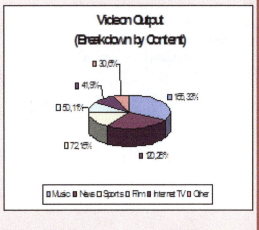
Test your knowledge of pages 158 through 163 in Quiz Yourself 5-3

QUIZ YOURSELF 5-3

Instructions: Find the true statement below. Then rewrite the remaining false statement so they are true.

1. A lower resolution uses a greater number of pixels and thus provides a smoother image.

2. An output device is any type of software component that conveys information to one or more people.

3. LCD monitors have a large footprint than CRT monitors.

4. You measure a monitor diagonally from one corner to the other

Quiz Yourself Online: To further check your knowledge of bits, voice input, input devices; scanner, PDAs, smart phones, biometric devices; and reading devices, visit www.clarkepublish.com or visit the Internet and then search www.google.com for more information.

PRINTERS

A **printer** is an output device that produces text and graphics on a physical medium such as paper or transparency film. Many different printers exist with varying speeds, capabilities, and printing methods. Figure 5-35 presents a list of questions to help you decide on the printer best suited to your needs.

The following pages discuss producing printed output and the various printer types including ink-jet printers, thermal printers, mobile printers, plotters, and large format printer.

1. What is my budget?
2. How fast must my printer print?
3. Do I need a color printer?
4. What is the cost per page for printing?
5. Do I need multiple copies of documents?
6. Will I print graphics?
7. Do I want to print photographs?
8. Do I want to print directly from a memory card or other type of miniature storage media?
9. What types of paper does the printer use?
10. What sizes of paper does the printer accept?
11. Do I want to print on both sides of the paper?
12. How much paper can the printer tray hold?
13. Will the printer work with my computer and software?
14. How much do supplies such as ink and paper cost?
15. Can the printer print on envelopes and transparencies?
16. How many envelopes can the printer print at a time?
17. How much do I print now, and how much will I be printing in a year or two?
18. Will the printer be connected to a network?
19. Do I want wireless printing capability?

FIGURE 5-35 Questions to ask when purchasing a printer.

Producing Printed Output

Although many users in Liberia today print by connecting a computer to a printer with a cable, a variety or printing options are available as shown in Figure 5-36.

Today, wireless printing technology makes the task of printing from a notebook computer, Tablet PC, PDA, smart phone, or digital camera much easier. Two wireless technologies for printing are Bluetooth and infrared. With Bluetooth printing, a computer or other device transmits output to a printer via radio waves. With infrared printing, a printer communicates with a computer or other device using infrared light waves.

Instead of downloading images from a digital camera to a computer, users can print images using a variety of other techniques. Some cameras connect directly to a printer via a cable. Others store images on media cards that can be removed and inserted in the printer. Some printers have a docking station, into which the user inserts the camera to print pictures stored in the camera.

Finally, many home and business users print to a central printer on a network. Their computer may communicate with the network printer via cables or wirelessly.

Various Ways Users Print Documents and Pictures

FIGURE 5-36 Users print documents and pictures using a variety of printing methods.

Nonimpact Printers

A **nonimpact printer** forms characters and graphics on a piece of paper without actually striking the paper. Some nonimpact printers spray ink, while others use heat or pressure to create images. Commonly used nonimpact printers are ink-jet printers, photo printers, laser printers, thermal printers, mobile printers, plotters, and large-format printers.

Ink-Jet Printers

An **ink-jet printer** is a type of nonimpact printer that forms characters and graphics by spraying tiny drops of liquid ink onto a piece of paper. Ink-jet printers have become a popular type of color printer for use in the home. Ink-jet printers produce text and graphics in both black-and-white and color on a variety of paper types (Figure 5-37). A reasonable quality ink-jet printer costs less than $100.

As with many other input and output devices, one factor that determines that quality of an ink-jet printer is its resolution. Printer resolution is measured by the number of dots per inch (dpi) a printer can print. Most ink-jet printers can print from 600 to 4800 dpi.

The speed of an ink-jet printer is measure by the number of pages per minute (ppm) it can print. Most ink-jet printers print from 3 to 26 ppm. Graphics and colors print at a slower rate.

FIGURE 5-37 Ink-jet printers are a popular type of color printer used in the home.

The print head mechanism in an ink-jet printer contains ink-filled cartridges. Each cartridge has fifty to several hundred small ink holes, or nozzles. The ink propels through any combination of the nozzles to form a character or image on the paper. When the print cartridge runs out of ink, you simply replace the cartridge. Most ink-jet printers have at least two print cartridges: one containing black ink and the other(s) containing colors. Read Discussing 5-3 for related discussion.

DISCUSSION 5-3
Is It Ethical to Refill an Ink-Jet Cartridge?

H In 1903, King Camp Gillette introduced an innovative product – a safety razor with disposable blades. Gillette accompanied his product with an even more innovative idea – sell the razor, which was purchased once, at or below cost, and rely on sales of the razor blades, which were purchased repeatedly, for profit. The idea made Gillette a millionaire. Manufacturers of ink-jet printers use a similar approach. The printers are inexpensive, often less than $100. The ink cartridges the printers use, however, can cost from $30 to $50 each time they are replaced. To avoid the high cost of cartridges, some people get cartridges refilled cheaply by a third party vendor. At least one printer company legally prohibits the practice, and violators may be breaking patent and contract law if they refill a cartridge. Additionally, some printer manufacturers have inserted special chips that keeps a cartridges from being refilled and , some claim, shut down a cartridge before it is really out of ink. Opponents of these practices say that the printer companies are gouging customers and that no legitimate reason exists why someone should not be able to refill an ink-jet cartridge in the same way a soap dispenser can be refilled. Should manufacturers be allowed to prevent people from refilling ink cartridges? Why? Would you have a cartridge refilled even if it violates the manufacturer's one-use-only policy? Why or why not?

Photo Printer

A **photo printer** is a color printer that produces photo-lab-quality picture (Figure 5-38). Some photo printers print just one or two sizes of images, for example, 3 X 5 inches and 4 X 6 inches. Other printer up to letter size, legal size, or even larger. Many photo printers use ink-jet technology. With models that can print letter-sized documents, users connect the photo printer to their computer and use it for all their printing needs.

Many photo printers have a built-in card slot so the printer can print digital photographs directly from the media card. That is, you do not need to transfer the images from the media card to the computer to print them. Some photo printers have built-in LCD color screens, allowing users to view and enhance the pictures before printing them.

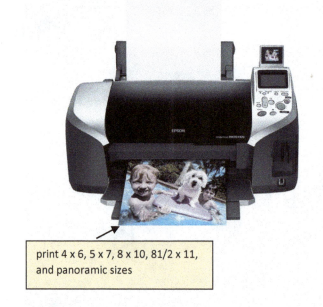

print 4 x 6, 5 x 7, 8 x 10, 81/2 x 11, and panoramic sizes

Laser Printers

A **laser printer** is a high-speed, high-quality nonimpact printer (Figure 5-39 on the next page). Laser printers for personally computers ordinarily use individual sheets of paper stored in one or more removable trays that slides in the printer case.

Laser printers print text and graphics in high-quality resolutions, usually ranging from 1200 to 2400 dpi. While laser printers usually cost more than ink-jet printers, they

FIGURE 5-38 Photo printers print in a range of sizes.

also are much faster. A laser printer for the home and small office user typically prints black-and-white text at speeds of 15 to 50 ppm. Color laser printers print 4 to 27 ppm. Laser printers for large business users print more than 150 ppm.

Depending on the quality, speed, and type of laser printer, the cost ranges from a few hundred to a few thousand dollars for the home and small office user, and several hundred thousand dollars for the large business user. Color laser printers are slightly higher priced than otherwise equivalent black-and-white laser printers.

Operating in a manner similar to a copy machine, a laser printer creates images using a laser beam and powdered ink, called toner. When the toner runs out, replace the toner cartridge.

black-and-white laser printer

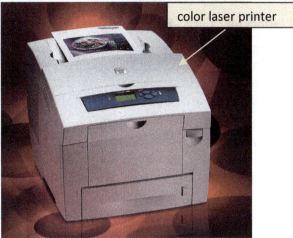

color laser printer

FIGURE 5-39 Laser printers are available in both black-and-white and color models.

FAQ 5-3

How do I dispose of toner cartridges?

Do not throw them in the garbage. The housing contains iron, metal, and aluminum that is not biodegradable. The ink toner inside the cartridges contains toxic chemicals that pollute water and soil if discarded in dumps. Instead, recycle empty toner cartridges. Contact your printer manufacturer to see if it has a recycling program here in Liberia. For more information, visit www.clarkepublish.com for information on how to dispose of used cartridges in Liberia or www.google.com

Thermal Printers

A **thermal printer** generates images by pushing electrically heated pins against heat-sensitive papers. Basic thermal printers are inexpensive, but print quality is low and the images tend to fade over time. Self-service gas pumps often print gas receipts using a built-in lower-quality thermal printer.

Some thermal printers have high print quality. A dye-sublimation printer, sometimes called a digital photo printer, uses heat to transfer colored dye to specially coated paper. Professional applications requiring high image quality, such as photography studios, medical labs, and security identification systems, use dye-sublimation printers. These high-end printers cost thousands of dollars and print images in a wide range of sizes.

Dye-sublimation printer for home or small business user, by contrast, typically print images in only one or two sizes and are much slower than their professional counterparts. These lower-end dye-sublimation printers are comparable in cost to a photo printer based on ink-jet technology (Figure 5-40).

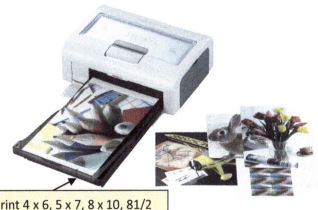

print 4 x 6, 5 x 7, 8 x 10, 81/2 x 11, and panoramic sizes

FIGURE 5-40 The printer shown in this figure uses dye-sublimation technology.

Mobile Printers

A **mobile printer** is a small, lightweight, battery-powered printer that allows a mobile user to print from a notebook computer, Tablet PC, PDA, or smart phone while traveling (Figure 5-41). Barely wider than the paper on which they print, mobile printers fit easily in a briefcase alongside a notebook computer. Mobile printers mainly use ink-jet or thermal technology.

Plotters and Large-Format Printers

Plotters are sophisticated printers used to produce high-quality drawing such as blueprints, maps, and circuit diagrams. These printers are used in specialized fields such as engineering and drafting and usually are very costly.

Using ink-jet printer technology, but on a much larger scale, a **large-format printer** creates photo-realistic-quality color prints. Graphic artists use these high-cost, high-performance printers for Signs, posters, and other professional quality displays (Figure 5-42).

FIGURE 5-41 A mobile printer.

FIGURE 5-42 Graphic artists use large-format printers to print signs, posters, and other professional quality displays.

Impact Printers

An **impact printer** forms characters and graphics on a piece of paper by striking a mechanism against an inked ribbon that physically contacts the paper. Impact printers are ideal for printing multipart forms because they easily print through many layers of paper. Two commonly used types of impact printers are dot-matrix printers and line printers.

A **dot-matrix printer** is an impact printer that produces printed images when tiny wire pins on a print head mechanism strike an inked ribbon (Figure 5-43). When the ribbon presses against the paper, it creates dots that form characters and graphics.

Dot-matrix printers typically use continuous-form paper, in which are connected together end to end. The pages have holes along the sides to help feed the paper through the printer. The speed of most dot-matrix printers ranges from 300 to 1100 characters per second (cps), depending on the desired print quality.

A **line printer** is a high-speed impact printer that prints an entire line at a time. The speed of a line printer is measured by the number of lines per minute (lpm) it can print. Some line printers print as many as 3,000 lpm.

OTHER OUTPUT DEVICES

In addition to monitors and printers, other output devices are available for specific uses and applications. These include speakers, and earphones; fax machines and fax modems; multifunction peripherals; and data projectors.

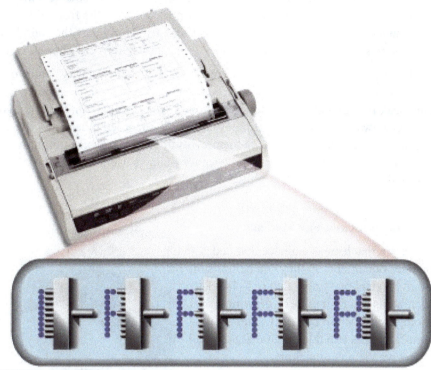

FIGURE 5-43 A dot-matrix printer produces printed images when tiny pins strike an inked ribbon.

Speakers, Headphones, and Earphone

An **audio output device** is a component of a computer that produces music, speech, or other sounds, such as beeps. Three commonly used audio devices are speakers, headphones, and earphones.

Most personal computers have a small internal speaker that usually emits low-quality sound. Thus, many personal computer users add surround sound **speakers** to their computers to generate a higher-quality sound (Figure 5-44). Most surround sound computer speaker systems include one or two center speaker and two or more satellite speakers that are positioned so sound emits from all directions. Speakers typically have tone and volume controls, allowing users to adjust settings. To boost the low bass sounds, surround sound speaker system also include a subwoofer. In many cases, users connect the speakers and subwoofer to ports on the sound card. With wireless speakers, however, a transmitter connects to the sound card, which wirelessly communicates with the speakers.

FIGURE 5-44 Most personal computer users add high-quality surround sound speaker systems to their computers.

In a computer laboratory or other crowded environment, speakers might not be practical. Instead, users can plug headphones in a port on the sound card, in a speaker, or in the front of the system unit. With headphones or earphones, only the individual wearing the headphones or earphones hears the sound from the computer. The difference is that **headphones** cover or are placed outside of the ear, whereas **earphones**, or **earbuds**, rest inside the ear canal.

Electronically produced voice output is growing in popularity. **Voice output** occurs when you hear a person's voice or when the computer talks to you through the speakers on the computer. In some software applications, the computer can speak the content of the document through voice output. On the Web, you can listen to (or download and then listen to) interviews, talk shows, sporting events, news, recorded music, and live concerts from many radio and television stations. Some Web sites dedicate themselves to providing voice output, where you can hear songs, quotes, historical lectures, speeches, and books. Internet telephony allows users to speak to other users over the Internet using their computer or mobile devices.

Fax Machines and Fax Modems

A **fax machine** is a device that codes and encodes documents so they can be transmitted over telephone lines (Figure 5-44). The documents can contain text, drawings, or photographs, or can be handwritten. The term fax refers to a document that you send or receive via a fax machine.

Many computers include fax capability by using a fax modem. A fax modem transmits computer-prepared documents, such as a word processing letter, or documents that have been digitized with a scanner or digital camera. A fax modem transmits these faxes to a fax machine or to another fax modem.

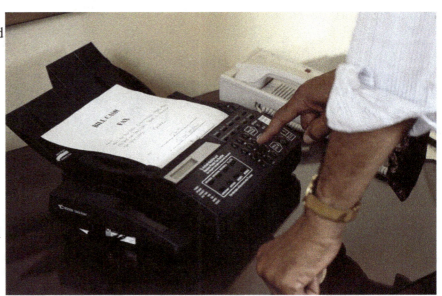

FIGURE 5-45 A stand-alone fax machine. Currently in Liberia, fax machines are not available to the public. In fact, many offices do not use fax machine to send and receive documents and messages.

Multifunction Peripherals

A **multifunction Peripheral** is a single device that looks like a copy machine but provides the functionality of a printer, scanner, copy machine, and perhaps a fax machine (Figure 5-46). Some use color ink-jet printer technology, while others include a black-and-white laser printer. An advantage of these devices is they are significantly less expensive than if you purchase each device separately.

If the device breaks down, however, you lose all four functions, which is the primary disadvantage.

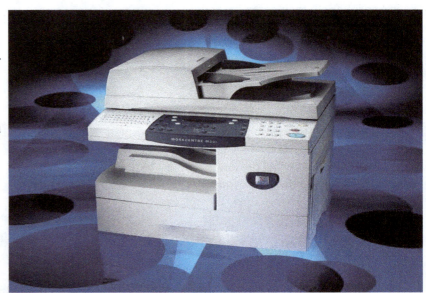

FIGURE 5-46 This multifunction peripheral is a color printer, scanner, copy machine, and fax machine all-in-one device.

Data Projectors

A **data projector** is a device that takes the text and images displaying on a computer screen and projects them on a larger screen so an audience can see the image clearly. Some data projectors are large devices that attach to a ceiling or wall in an auditorium. Others are small portable devices (Figure 5-46). Read Looking Ahead for a look at the next generation of digital cinema projectors.

computer

data projector

FIGURE 5-47 Data projector can produce sharp, bright images.

Looking Ahead 5-3

The Future of Digital Cinema

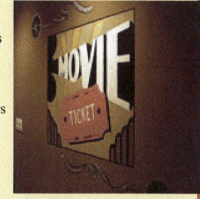

Computers have influenced the motion picture business by modifying how movies are produced, distributed, and exhibited. Major movie studios are part of the Digital Cinema Initiative (DCI), and they plan to release all of their theatrical feature films world in digital format. The new technology's superior sound and visual clarity have been heralded as the greatest innovations since talkies replaced silent movies 80 years ago.

The seven larger Hollywood movie studios have developed final system requirements and specifications that enable manufacturers to develop standardized digital theater equipment. These uniform standards were created along with a compression scheme, which allows the prints, thus saving millions of dollars annually.

With the equipment and compression standards in place, manufacturers now can intensify their efforts to develop digital cinema projectors. For more info, visit book's Web site and then click Digital Cinema.

PUTTING IT ALL TOGETHER

Many factors influence the type of input and output devices you should use: the type of input and output desired, the hardware and software in use, and the anticipated cost. Figure 5-47 outlines several suggested input and output devices for various types of computer users.

User	Input Device	Output Device
HOME 	• Enhanced keyboard or ergonomic keyboard • Mouse • Stylus for PDA or smart phone • Joystick or wheel • Color scanner • 3-megapixel digital camera • Headphones that include a microphone • PC video camera	• 17- or 19-inch color LCD monitor • Ink-jet color printer; or • Photo printer • Speakers • Headphones or earphones
SMALL OFFICE/ HOME OFFICE 	• Enhanced keyboard or ergonomic keyboard • Mouse • Stylus and portable keyboard for PDA or smart phone, or digital pen for Tablet PC • Color scanner • 3-megapixel digital camera • Headphones that include a microphone • PC video camera	• 19- or 21-inch LCD monitor • Color LCD screen on Tablet PC, PDA, or smart phone • Multifunction peripheral; or • Ink-jet color printer; or • Laser printer (black-and-white or color) • Fax machine • Speakers
MOBILE 	• Wireless mouse for notebook computer • Touchpad or pointing stick on notebook computer • Stylus and portable keyboard for PDA or smart phone, or digital pen for Tablet PC • 3- or 4-megapixel digital camera • Headphones that include a microphone • Fingerprint scanner for notebook computer	• 15.7-inch LCD screen on notebook computer • Color LCD screen on PDA or smart phone • Mobile color printer • Ink-jet color printer; or • Laser printer, for in-office use (black-and-white or color) • Photo printer • Fax modem • Headphones or earphones • Data projector
POWER 	• Enhanced keyboard or ergonomic keyboard • Mouse • Stylus and portable keyboard for PDA or smart phone • Pen for graphics tablet • Color scanner • 6- to 8-megapixel digital camera • Headphones that include a microphone • PC video camera	• 23-inch LCD monitor • Laser printer (black-and-white or color) • Plotter or large-format printer; or • Photo printer; or • Dye-sublimation printer • Fax machine or fax modem • Speakers • Headphones or earphones
LARGE BUSINESS 	• Enhanced keyboard or ergonomic keyboard • Mouse • Stylus and portable keyboard for PDA or smart phone, or digital pen for Tablet PC • Touch screen • Light pen • Color scanner • OCR/OMR readers, bar code readers, or MICR reader • Microphone • Video camera for video conferences • Fingerprint scanner or other biometric device	• 19- or 21-inch LCD monitor • Color LCD screen on Tablet PC, PDA, or smart phone • High-speed laser printer • Laser printer, color • Line printer (for large reports from a mainframe) • Fax machine or fax modem • Speakers • Headphones or earphones • Data projector

FIGURE 5-48 This table recommends suggested input and output devices for various types of users.

INPUT AND OUTPUT DEVICES FOR PHYSICALLY CHALLENGED USERS

The ever-increasing presence of computers in everyone's lives has generated an awareness of the need to address computing requirements for those who have or may develop physical limitations. The **Americans with Disability Act (ADA)** requires any company with 15 or more employees to make reasonable attempts to accommodate the needs of physically challenged workers. Read Discussion 5-4 for a related discussion.

Besides voice recognition, which is ideal for blind or visually impaired users, several other input devices are available. Users with limited hand mobility who want to use a keyboard have several options. Keyboards with larger keys are available. Still another option is the on-screen keyboard, in which a graphic of a standard keyboard is displayed on the user's screen. As the user clicks letters on the on-screen keyboard, they appear in the document at the location of the insertion point. An option for people with limited hand movement is a head-mounted pointer to control the pointer or insertion point (Figure 5-49). To simulate the functions of a mouse button, a user works with switches that control the pointer. The switch might be a had pad, a foot pedal, a receptor that detects facial motions, or a pneumatic instrument controlled by puffs or air.

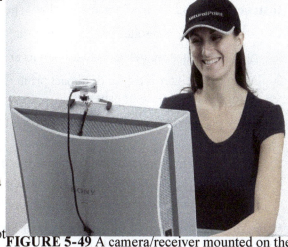

FIGURE 5-49 A camera/receiver mounted on the monitor tracks the position of the head-mounted pointer, which is reflective material that this user is wearing on the brim of her cap.

For uses with mobility, hearing, or vision disabilities, many different types of output devices are available. Hearing-impaired users, for example, can instruct programs to display words instead of sounds.

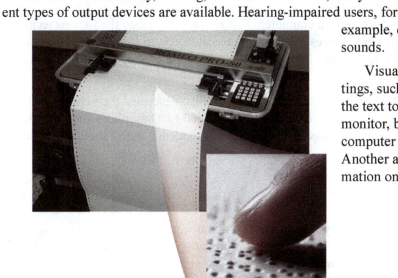

Visually impaired users can change Windows XP settings, such as increasing the size or changing the color of the text to make the words easier to read. Instead of using a monitor, blind users can work with voice output. That is, the computer reads the information that appears on the screen. Another alternative is a Braille printer, which outputs information on paper in Braille (Figure 5-50).

FIGURE 5-50 A Braille printer prints texts for the blind.

DISCUSSION 5-4

Should Web Sites Be Held Account able for Accessibility Level for Physically Challenge People?

The World Wide Web Consortium (W3C) has published accessibility guidelines for Web sites. The guidelines specify measures that Web site designers can take to increase accessibility for physically challenged users. Among its guidelines, the W3C urges Web site designers to provide equivalent text for audio or visual content, include features that allow elements to be activated and understood using a variety of input and output devices, and make the user interface follow principles of accessible design.

A recent report found that most Web sites do not meet all of the W3C guidelines. This failure is disappointing, because many physically challenged users could benefit from the Web's capability to bring product and services into the home. Should the government require that all Web sites meet the W3C accessibility guidelines? Why or why not? What can be done to encourage people to make their Web sites more accessible?

Test your knowledge of pages 163 through 173 in Quiz Yourself 5-4

QUIZ YOURSELF 5-4

Instructions: Find the true statement below. Then rewrite the remaining false statement so they are true.

1. A laser printer generates images by pushing electrically heated pins against heat-sensitive paper.

2. A photo printer creates images using a laser beam and powdered ink, called toner.

3. An ink-jet printer is a type of impact printer that forms characters and graphics by spraying tiny drops of liquid nitrogen onto a piece of paper.

4. Many personal computer users add surround sound printer systems to their computers to generate a high-quality sound

5. Multifunction peripherals require more space than having a separate printer, scanner, copy machine, fax machine.

6. 6. The American with Disabilities ACT (ADA) requires any company with 15 or more employees to make reasonable attempts to accommodate the needs of physically challenged workers.

Quiz Yourself Online: To further check your knowledge of types of printers, other output devices, and input and output options for physically challenged user, visit www.clarkepublish.com or visit the Internet and then search www.google.com for more information.

CHAPTER SUMMARY

Input is any data and instructions you enter into the memory of a computer. This chapter described the various techniques of entering input and several commonly used input devices. Topics included the keyboard; mouse and other pointing devices; voice input; input for PDAs, smart phones, and Tablet PCs; digital cameras; video input; scanners and reading devices; terminals; and biometric input.

Computers process and organize data (input) into information (output). This chapter also described the various methods of output and several commonly used output devices. Output devices presented included LCD monitors and screens; CRT monitors; printers; speakers, headphones, and earphones; fax machines and fax modems; multifunction peripherals; and data projectors.

Graphics Designer/Illustrator

CAREER CORNER

A Graphic designer are artists, but many do not create original works. Instead, they portray visually the ideas of their clients. Illustrators create pictures for books and other publications and sometimes for commercial products, such as greeting cards. They work in fields such as fashion, technology, medicine, animation, or even cartoons. Illustrators often prepare their images on a computer. Designers combine practical skills with artistic talent to convert abstract concepts into designs for products and advertisements. Many use computer-aided design (CAD) tools to create, visualize, and modify designs. Designer careers usually are specialized in particular areas, such as:

- Graphic designer – book covers, stationery, and CD covers, commercial, etc.
- Fashion designer – clothing, shoes, and other fashion accessories, interior design, etc.

Certificate, two-year, four-year, and masters-level educational programs are available within design areas. About 30 percent of graphic illustrators/designers choose to freelance, while others work with advertising agencies. Salaries range from $30,000 to $$80,000-plus, based on experience and educational background. This salary may not be the same for Graphic Designer in Liberia. For more info, visit book's Web site and then click Computer Engineer.

Logitech

Personal Interface Products Leader

The average Internet user has more than 40 inches of cords or his desktop, according to a Logitech survey. This company is working to reduce desktop clutter with a variety of cordless peripherals, including mouse devices, keyboards, mobile headphones and earphones, and game controller.

A market leader, Logitech has sold more than 50 million wireless devices. It also designs, manufactures, and markets corded devices. The company's retail sales accounts for more than 85 percent of its revenue.

Two engineering students from Stanford University, Italian-born Pierluigi Zappacosta and Swiss-born Daniel Borel, launched Logitech in 1981. today, the corporation is the world's largest manufacturer of the mouse, having sold more than 50 million since the company's founding. For more info, visit book's Web site and then click Logitech.

Hewlett-Packard

Technology for Business and Life

If you have printed a document recently, chances are the printer manufacturer was Hewlett-Packard (HP). Market analysts estimate that 60 percent of printers sold today bear the HP logo, and HP says it ships one million printers each week.

HP is noted for a range of high-quality printers, disk storage systems, UNIX and Windows servers, and notebook, desktop, and handheld computers. In 2005, HP acquired Snapfish, an online photo service, and also unveiled the world's fastest photo printing devices.

William Hewlett and David Packard started the company in a one-car garage in 1939 with the goal manufacturing

test and measurement equipment. HP has been developing personal devices, including eReaders, Tablets calculators and computers, for more than 30 years. For more info, visit book's Web site and click HP.

Douglas Engelbart

Creator of the Mouse

The phrase "point and click" might not be part of every computer user's vocabulary if Douglas Engelbart had not pursued his engineering dreams. In 1964, he developed the first prototype computer mouse with the goal of making it easier to move cursor around a computer screen.

Ten years later, engineers at Xerox refined Engelbart's prototype and showed the redesigned product to Apple's Steve Jobs, who applied the concept to his graphical Macintosh computer. The mouse was mass produced in the mid 1980s, and today it is the most widely used pointing device. Engelbart currently serves as director of the Bootstrap Institute, a company he founded With his daughter to form strategic alliances and consequently improve corporations' performance. For more information, visit www.google.com.

Donna Dubinsky

Palm Cofounder

PDAs are ubiquitous, partly due to the efforts of Donna Dubinsky. In the mid-1990s, she sensed that people wanted to own an electronic version of their paper appointment books. She and Jeff Hawkins introduced the original Palm Pilot prototype of mahogany and cardboard at Palm Computing in 1996. sales of more than two million units made the Palm Pilot the most rapidly adopted new computing product ever manufactured.

Dubinsky and Hawkins left Palm in 1998 to cofound Handspring, where they introduced several successful products, including the Treo smart phone. In 2003, Handspring merged with Palm hardware group to create PalmOne, now called Palm.

Dubinsky currently serves as CEO and chairman of Numenta, Inc., which develops computer memory. For more information, visit book's Web sit and then click Donna Dubinsky.

Chapter Review

The Chapter Review section summarizes the concepts presented in this chapter. To obtain help from other students regarding any subject in this chapter, visit book's Web site.

1. **Why Are the Characteristics of a Keyboard?**

   Any hardware component that allows users enter data and instruction is an **input device**. A **keyboard** is an input device that contains keys users press to enter data and instructions into a computer. Computer keyboards have a typing area that includes letters of the alphabet, numbers, punctuation marks, and other basic keys. An enhanced keyboard also has function keys programmed to issue commands, a numeric keypad, arrow keys, and additional keys and buttons.

2. **How Do Pointing Devices Work?**

   A **pointing device** allows users to control a small symbol, called a **pointer,** on the computer screen. A **mouse** is a pointing device that fits under the palm of your hand. As you move the mouse, the pointer on the screen also moves. A **trackball,** is a stationary pointing device with a ball that you rotate to move the pointer. A **touchpad** is a flat, pressure-sensitive device that you slide you finger across to move the pointer. A **pointing stick** is a pointing device positioned on the keyboard that you push to move the pointer. A **joystick** is a vertical lever that you move to control a simulated vehicle or player. A **wheel** is a steering-wheel-type device that you turn to simulate driving a vehicle. The **control pad** on an audio player is a pointing device that enables users to scroll through and play music, adjust volume, and customize settings. A **gamepad,** sometimes called a game controller, is a pointing device that controls the movement and actions of players or objects in video games or computer games. A **light pen** is a light-sensitive device that you press against or point at the screen to select objects. A touch screen is a touch-sensitive display device that you interact with by touching areas of the screen. A s**tylus** and **digital pen** use pressure to write text and draw lines.

3. **What Are Other Types of Input?**

   Voice input is the process of entering input by speaking into a microphone. Mobile users employ a basic stylus to enter data and instructions into a PDA, or sometimes use a built-in keyboard or snap-on keyboard. The primary input device for a Tablet PC is a digital pen. A **digital camera** allows users to take pictures, store the images digitally, and download the images to a computer's hard disk. Video input is the process of capturing full-motion pictures and storing them on a computer's storage medium. A **digital video (DV) camera**, a **PC video camera,** and a **Web cam** are used for video input. A **scanner** is a light-sensing input device that reads printed text and graphics and translates the results into a form a computer can process. Reading devices use a light source to read characters, marks, and codes and convert them into digital data. **OCR (optical character recognition)** devices use a small optical scanner and software to analyze characters from ordinary documents. OMR (optical mark recognition) devices read hand-drawn marks on a form. A bar code reader uses laser beams to read bar codes. An **RFID** reader reads information on an embedded tag via radio waves. A **magnetic stripe** card reader reads the magnetic stripe on the back of credit, entertainment, bank, and other similar cards. A **MICR (magnetic-ink character recognition)** reader reads text printed in magnetizes ink. A **terminal** consists of a keyboard, a monitor, a video card, and memory and often is used to perform specific tasks for a particular industry. **Biometrics** is the technology of authenticating a person's identity by verifying a physical characteristic. Biometric input can include fingerprints, hand geometry, facial features, voice, signatures, and eye patterns.

4. **What Are the Characteristics of LCD Monitors, LCD Screens, and CTR Monitors?**
   Any hardware component that conveys information to one or more people is an **output device**. A **display device** is a commonly used output device that visually conveys text, graphics, and video information. An **LCD monitor,** also called a flat panel monitor, is a desktop display that uses a liquid crystal display. A **liquid crystal display (LCD)** uses a liquid compound to present information on the screen. A **CTR monitor** is a desktop display device that contains a cathode-ray tube.

5. **What Are Various Types of Printers?**
   A **printer** is an output device that produces text and graphics on a physical medium. A **nonimpact printer** forms characters and graphics without striking the paper. Several types of nonimpact printers are available. An **ink-jet printer** forms characters and graphics by spraying tiny drops of ink onto paper. A **photo printer** produces lab-quality pictures. A **laser printer** is a high-speed, high-quality printer that operates in a manner similar to a copy machine. A **thermal printer** generates images by pushing electrically heated pins against heat-sensitive paper. A **mobile printer** is a small, battery-powered printer used to print from a notebook computer, Tablet PC, PDA, or smart phone. Plotters are used to produce high-quality drawings in specialized fields. A **large-format printer** creates large, photo-realistic-quality color prints. An **impact printer** forms characters and graphics by striking a mechanism against an inked ribbon that physically contacts the paper. A **dot-matrix printer** is an impact printer that produces an image when tiny wire pins on a print head strike an inked ribbon. A **line printer** is an impact printer that prints an entire line at a time.

6. **What Are the Characteristics of Speaker, Headphones, and Earphones; Fax Machines and Fax Modes; Multi function Peripherals; and Data Projection?**
   Speakers are an **audio output device** added to computer to generate higher-quality sound. With headphones and earphones, only the individual wearing the headphones or earphones hears the sound from the computer. The difference is that **headphones** comes or are placed outside of the ear, whereas **earphones**, or **earbuds**, rest inside the ear canal. A **fax machine** is a device that codes and encodes documents so they can be transmitted over telephone lines. Many computers have a fax modem that transmits computer-prepared documents. A **multifunction peripheral** is a single device that provides the functionality of a printer, scanner, copy machine, and perhaps a fax machine. A **data projector** is a device that takes the text and images displaying on a computer screen and projects them onto a larger screen for audience.

7. **What Are Input and Output Options for Physically Challenged Users?**
   Voice recognition, which is the computer's capability of distinguishing spoken words, is an ideal input option for visually impaired users. Input options for people with limited hand mobility include keyboards with larger keys, on-screen keyboards, and head-mounted pointers. Hearing-impaired users can instruct programs to display words instead of sound. Visually impaired users can change windows Vista setting such as the size and color of text to make words easier to use. Instead of a monitor, blind users can use voice output and a Braille printer.

Key Terms

You should know the Key Terms. Use the list below to help focus your study. To further enhance your understanding of the Key Terms in this chapter, visit book's Web site and click the chapter 1 link.

American with Disability Act
  (ADA) (173)
audio input (149)
audio output (169)
automated teller machine (156)
bar code (154)
bar code reader (154)
biometrics (157)

Click Wheel (147)
control pad (147)
CRT monitor (162)
data projector (171)
digital camera (151)
digital pen (148)
digital video (DV) camera (152)
display device (159)
dot-matrix printer (168)

earbuds (170)
earphones (170)
ENERGY STAR program (162)
ergonomics (144)
fax machine (170)
fingerprint scanner (157)
flatbed scanner (153)
gamepad (147)
graphic designers (144)

graphic illustrators (174)
graphics tablet (148)
headphones (170)
impact printer (168)
ink-jet printer (165)
input (142)
input devices (142)
joystick (147)
keyboard (144)
large-format printer (168)

LCD monitor (160)
light pen (147)
line printer (169)
liquid crystal display (161)
magnet stripe card reader (155)
MICR (155)
MICR reader (155)
mobile printer(168)
monitor (159)
mouse (145)
mouse pad (145)
multifunction peripheral (170)
nonimpact printer (165)

OCR devices (153)
optical character recognition OCR (153)
optical mark recognition (153)
optical mouse (1445
output (158)
output device (158)
PC camera (152)
PC video camera (152)
pen input (148)
photo printer (166)
pixel (152)
plasma monitor (161)
plotters (168)

pointer (143)
pointing device (143)
pointing stick (146)
POS terminal (156)
printer (163)
resolution (151)
RFID (154)
RFID reader (154)
scanner (153)
    smart card (157)
speakers (169)
speech recognition (149)
stylus (148)
terminal (156)
thermal printer (167)

touch screen (147)
touchpad (146)
trackball (146)
turnaround document (153)
video conference (152)
video input (152)
video telephone call (152)
voice input (149)
voice output (170)
voice recognition (149)
Web cam (152)
Wheel (147)

Checkpoint

Use the Checkpoint exercises to check your knowledge level of the chapter.

True/False — Mark T for True and F for False. (see page numbers in parentheses.)

_____ 1. On notebook and some handheld computers, PDAs, and smart phones, the keyboard is built in the top of the system unit.

_____ 2. Touchpads are found most often on mainframe computers.

_____ 3. Resolution is the number of horizontal and vertical pixels in a display device.

_____ 4. A flatbed scanner works in a manner similar to a copy machine except it creates a file of the document in memory instead of a paper copy.

_____ 5. Plasma monitors offer larger screen sizes and higher display quality than LCD monitors.

_____ 6. While laser printers usually cost more than ink-jet printers, they also are much faster.

_____ 7. A line printer is a high-speed impact printer that prints an entire line at a time.

_____ 8. The advantage of a multifunction peripheral is that it is significantly more expensive than if if you purchase each device separately.

Multiple Choice — Select the best answer (see page numbers in parentheses.)

1. An ergonomic keyboard _____.
a. is used to enter data into a biometric device
b. transmits data using wireless technology
c. has a design that reduces wrist and hand injuries
d. is built into the top of a handheld computer

2. A _____ is a pointing device that controls the movement and action of players or objects in video games or computer games.
a. control pad
b. gamepad
c. pointing stick
d. touchpad

3. Two types of pen input are _____.
a. digital pen and touch screen
b. digital pen and stylus
c. trackball and stylus
d. pointing stick and digital pen

4. A _____ is any video camera that displays its output on a Web page.
a. digital video camera
b. Web cam
c. PC camera
d. video conference

5. Display devices; printer, headphones, fax machines, multifunction peripherals are examples of commonly used_____ devices.
a. input   b. digital
c. output   d. POS terminal

6. The speed of an ink-jet printer is measure by the number of _____ it can print.
a. pages per minute (ppm)
b. dots per inch (dpi)
c. characters per second (cps)

d.   lines per page (lpp)

7.   A(n) _____ is device that takes the text and images displaying on a computer screen and projects them on a larger screen so an audience can see the image clearly.

a.   data projector   b. scanner

c.   copy machine   d. LCD monitor

8.   A(n)_____ is an output device for blind us-ers.

a.   Braille printer

b.   head-mounted pointer

c.   on-screen keyboard

d.   all of the above

Short Answer	Write a brief answer to each of the following questions.

_____ 1. control pad

_____ 2. bar code

_____ 3. magnetic stripe card reader

_____ 4. smart card

_____ 5. LCD monitor

a.   reads information on back of credit cards, bank cards, etc

b.   stores data on a thin microprocessor that is embedded in a credit-card-size cards

c.   self-service banking machine that connects to a host computer through network

d.   a pointing device on an audio player that enables users to scroll through and play music, adjust volume, and customize settings

e.   identification that consists of a set of vertical lines and spaces of different widths

f.   a desktop monitor that uses a liquid crystal display to produce images

Short Answer	Write a brief answer to each of the following questions.

1.   How are a mechanical mouse an optical mouse, and a wireless mouse different? ¬¬¬_____ What is a mouse pad? _____

2.   What is the difference between a digital video camera and one that uses analog video signals? _____ How can digital video be transferred to a PC? _____

3.   How are optical character recognition (OCR), optical mark recognition (OMR), and magnetic ink character recogni-tion (MICR) different? _____ How is RFID reader used? _____

4.   What factors determine the quality of a CRT monitor? _____ What is EVERGY STAR program? _____Wh

5.   at are two common types of impact printers? _____ What are the differences between the two types? ____

Working Together	Working in a group of your classmates, complete the following team exercise.

1.   Stores, libraries, parcel carriers, and other organizations use optical codes. Some people mistakenly believe that an optical code contains the name of a product or its price, but the codes are only a link to a database in which this in-formation, and more, is stored. Have each member of your team visit an organization that uses optical code. Note: (I am not sure if this technology is being presently used in Liberia, but if it is?). How are the optical codes read? What information is obtained when the code is read? What information is recorded? How is the information used? Meet with the members of your team to discuss the results of your investigations. Then, use PowerPoint to create a group presentation and share your findings with the class.

180

Web Research

Use the Internet-based Web Research exercises to broaden your understand of the concepts presented in this chapter. Visit book's Web site to obtain more information pertaining to each exercise. To discuss any of the Web Research exercises in this chapter with other students, post your thoughts or questions at the

1. Journaling   Respond to your readings in this chapter by writing at least one page about your reactions, evaluations, and reflections about input devices. For example, do you recall the first time you used a mouse? What experiences have you had with voice recognition? Do you own a PDA or Tablet PC, digital camera, or smart phone? Have you ever participated in a video conference? How do you reduce the chances of experiencing repetitive strain injuries? You also can write about the new terms you learned by reading this chapter. If required, submit your journal to your instructor or teacher

2.   Scavenger Hunt   Use one of the search engines listed in Figure 2-8 in chapter 2 on page 46 or your own favorite search engine to find the answer to the question below. Copy and paste the Web address from the Web page where you found the answer. Some question may have more than one answer. If required, submit your answer to your instruction or teacher. (1) The inventor of the first commercial typewriter wanted to persuade people to buy and use the device, so he ordered the keys to allow users to type as quickly as possible. Who was the QUERTY keyboard's primary inventor? (2) What are reasonable accommodations that employers must make to comply with the Americans with Disabilities ACT? Please note that the later is a legislation that was passed in the United States several decades age, and this may not be the same for disable employees in Liberia and elsewhere in Africa. (3) Who holds patents awarded in the 1950s for automatic video scanning and inspection and inspection methods, which led to bar code technology?

3. Search Sleuth   Typical search Web sites, such as Google and Ask Jeeves, maintain their own internal database of links to Web pages. MetaCrawler (metacrawler.com) is a different type of search Web site because it returns combine results from these and other leading search engines. Visit this Web site and then use your word processing program to answer the following questions. (1) Click the Tools & Tips link at the top of the page Browse and then explore some of the tools, such as Search Tips and FAQs. (2) Scroll down and then read some of the information contained in the Popular Searches section. What are some of the popular MetaCrawler search terms? (3) Click your browser's Back button or press the BACKSPACE key twice to return to the MetaCrawler home page. What are the six most popular searches today? Click a link for one of these popular searches and scroll through the results MetaCrawler returns. (4) Click your browser's Back button or press the BACKSPACE key to return to the MetaCrawler home page. Click the Search text box and then type what are the top selling digital cameras? As the keywords in the Search text box. (5) Scroll through the links MetaCrawler returns and then click one that provides the information requested. What are three popular digital camera? Read the information and then write a 50-word summary.

Learn How To

Use the Learn How To activities to learn fundamental skills when using a computer and accompanying technology. Complete the exercises and submit them to your instructor or teacher.

LEARN HOW TO 1: Adjust the Sound on a Computer

Every computer today contains a sound card and associated hardware and software that allow you to play and record sound. You can adjust the sound by completing the following steps:
1. Click the Start button on the Windows taskbar and the click Control Panel on the Start menu.
2. When the Control Panel window opens, click Sounds, Speech, and Audio Devices and then click Adjust the system volume; or double click Sounds and Audio Devices. The sounds and Audio Devices Properties dialog box is displayed (Figure 5-50).
3. To adjust the volume for all devices connected to the sound card, drag the Device volume slider left or right to decrease or increase the volume.
4. If you want to mute the sound on the computer, click the Mute check

Recording Control

Options   Help

CD Player   Microphone   Line In

Balance: Balance: Balance:

Volume: Volume: Volume:

☐ Select   ☑ Select   ☐ Select

SoundMAX Digital Audio

box so it contains a ckeckmark, and then click the OK button or the Apply button.

5.   To place the volume icon on the Windows taskbar, click the Place icon in the taskbar check box so it contains a checkmark, and then click the OK button or the Apply button. You can click the icon on the taskbar to set the volume level or mute the sound.

6.   To make sound and other adjustments for each device on the computer, click the Advanced button in the Device volume area. The Play Control or Recording Control window opens, depending on prior choices for the window (Figure 5-51).

7.   If the Recording Control window is opened, click Options on the window menu bar, click Properties on the Options menu, click the Playback option button, and then click the OK button.

8.   In the Play Control window, Play Control volume is the same as the volume adjusted in the Sounds and Audio Devices Properties dialog box. The other columns in the Play Control window refer to devices found on the computer. To select the columns that are displayed, click Options on the menu bar and then click Properties. With Playback selected, place checkmarks in the check boxes for those devices you want to be displayed in the Control window.

9.   To adjust volumes, drag the Volume sliders, To adjust speaker balance, drag the Balance sliders.

10. If the Advanced button is not displayed in the Play Control window, click Options on the menu bar and then click Advanced Controls on the Options menu. Click the Advance button. You can control the Bass and Treble settings by using the sliders in the Tone Controls area of the Advanced Controls for Play Control dialog box.

Exercise

1.   Open the Control Panel window and the display the Sounds and Audio Devices Properties dialog box. What kind of sound card is on the computer? Click the Place volume icon in the taskbar check box and then click the Apply button. What change did you notice on the Windows taskbar? Do the same thing again. What change occurred on the Windows taskbar? Click the Advanced button in the Device volume area. Ensure the Play Control window is open. What devices are chosen for control in the Play Control window? How would you change what devices are chosen? Submit your answer to your instructor or teacher.

SPECIAL NOTE

To All Students and Teachers:

To bring down the cost of printing this textbook and other instructional resources, the publisher of this text has made available Chapter 6 of this book and other related resource as referenced within this textbook along with it's complementing lab manuals on the company's website at, www.clarkepublish.com. Please visit the website in order to access resources that will help you reenforce all that has been presented and learned in this book along with the lab manual. Materials that are available to teachers and students include:

1. **Discussions Topics**   2. **Looking Ahead**   3. **How To** 4. **Quiz Yourself Answers**
5. **Career in Technology**   6. **Frequently Asked Questions, FAQ**   7. **Making Transition to the Workplace,** and many other resources.

This Page Was Intentionally Left Blank

INDEX

manufactured. **121**

Fixed disk, 186

Fixed wireless: Microwave transmissions that send signals from one microwave station to another. **40**

Flame wars, 62

Flames, 62

Flash memory: Type of nonvolatile memory that can be erased electronically and rewritten. **121**

Flash memory card: Removable flash memory device that allows users to trans-fer data and information from mobile devices to their desktop computers. **121**, 123

Flatbed scanner: Type of light sensing input device that scans a document and creates a file of the document in memory instead of a paper copy. **153**

Flat-panel display, 160-61

Floppy disk: Potable, inexpensive storage medium that consists of a thin, circular, flexible plastic Mylar film with a magnetic coating, enclosed in a square shaped plastic shell. **7**

bays and, 126

Font: Name assigned to a specific design of characters. **80**

Font size: Size of the characters in a particular font. **80**

Font style: Font design, such as bold, italic, and underline, that can add emphasis to a font. **80**

Footprint, 160

Form: Window on the screen that provides areas for entering or changing data in a database. Also called data entry form. **82**. See also Data entry form

Format: To change a document's appearance. **80**

Formular, 81

Freeware: Copyrighted software provided at no cost to a user by an individual or a company that retains all rights to the software. **75**

Frequently asked questions. See FAQ

FTP (File Transfer Protocol): Internet standard that permits file uploading and downloading with other computers on the Internet. **60**

FTP server, 60

Function, 80

Function keys, 144

Game console: Mobile computing device designed for single-player or multiplayer video games. **16**

Gamepad: Pointing device that controls the movement and actions of players or objects in video games or computer game. Sometimes called a game controller. **147**

interactive,94

pointing devices for, 147

GB, 118. See also Gigabyte

GHz, 114. See also Gigahertz

GIF, 53

Gigabyte (GB): Approximately 1 billion bytes. 118

Gigahertz (GHz): One billion ticks of the system clock per second. **114**

Google, 49, 64

Government computer used in, 24

Internet structure and, 38

Graphics: Digital representation of nontext information such as a drawing, chart, or photograph. **53**. See also Graphical image

Graphic designer/illustrator: Employee who creates visual impressions of products and advertisements in the field of graphics, theater, and fashion. **174**.

Graphic illustrator. See Graphic designer/illustrator

Graphical image, 53. See also Graphic

Graphical user interface (GUI): Type of user interface that allows a user to interact with software using text, graphics, and visual images, such as icons. **10**

Graphics, 53

application software and, 86-87

business software and, 78-79

multimedia and, 53

Graphics card: Adapter card that converts

computer output into a video signal that travels through a cable to the monitor, which displays an image on the screen. 123. See also Video card

Graphics chip, 162

Graphics tablet: Flat, rectangular, electronic, plastic board that is used to create drawings and sketches. **148**

Hand geometry system, 157

Handheld computer: Computer small enough to fit in one hand. **15** See also Handtop computer, ultra personal computer (uPC)

keyboards, 143

Handhelds: Computers small enouth to fit in one hand. See also handtop computer; handheld computer. **15**

Handtop computer: Com puter small enough to fit in one hand. **15**. See also Handheld computer, ultra personal computer (uPC)

Handwriting recognition software, 80, 150

Hard disk: Type of storage device that contains one or more inflexible, circular platters that store data, instructions, and information. 7

bus connection for, 127

downloading from digital camera, 150

Hard drive, Internet. See Internet hard drive

Hardware: Electric, electronic, and mechanical components contained in a computer. **6-8**

Head-mounted pointer, 173

Headphones: Audio output device that covers or is placed outside the ear. **169**

CRT monitor, 162

disadvantage in computer, 5

keyboard, 143

radiation, 162

Hearing impaired user, out-put devices for, 173

Help application software and, 96-97

Online. See Online Help

Web-based, 96-97

Help Desk Specialist:

Employee who answers hardware, software, or networking questions in person, over the telephone, and/or in a chat room. 98

Hertz, 114

Hewlett-Packard (HP), 175

Home design/landscaping, software: Application software that assists users with the design, remodeling, or improvement of a home, deck, or landscape. 93

Home page: First page that Web site displays. **43-44**

Home user: User who spends time on a computer at home. **18-19**

application software for, 9-94

inpu devices, 173

output devices, 166, 173

printers, 165

processor selection, 114, 129

RAM needs, 120

storage and, 7

Web cams, 151

Host: Any computer that provides services and connection to other computers on a network. **38**

http: A set of rules that defines how pages transfer on the Internet. **44**. See Hypertext Transfer Protocol

Hyperlink: Built-in connection to another related Web page or part of a Web page. **45-46**. See also Link

Hypertext Transfer Protocol, 45. See also http

Icon: Small image displayed on a computer screen that represents a program, an instruction, a document, or some other object. 10, **76**.

Illustration software, 87. See also Paint software

IM, 61-62. See also Instant messaging

Image editing software: Application software that provides the capabilities of paint software and also includes the capability to enhance and modify existing images and pictures. 87

Images, 54, 55

as links, 46

personal DTP software, 91

that content aggregators use to distribute content to subscribers. **54**

Run: Process of using software. **2**

Satellite companies
Internet structure and, 39
wireless Internet access, 40
Satellite modem: Internet connection that communicates with a satellite dish to provide high-speed Internet connections via satellite. **40**
Save: To transfer a document from a computer's memory to a storage medium. **80**
Scanner: Light-sending input device that reads printed text and graphics and then translates the results into a from the computer can process. 6, **153**-55 See also
Optical scanner bar code, 154
flatbed,153
optical, 153
Scanner fraud, 154
School connecting to the Internet through, 39
Science computers used in, 25
Screen, 162
Security biometric devices and, 157
Serial port: Type of interface that connects a device to the system unit by transmitting data one bit at a time. **125**
Sever: Computer that control access to the hardware, software, and other resources on a network and provides a centralized storage area for programs, data, and information. **38**
processors, 115
Shareware: Copyrighted software that is distributed at no cost for a trial period. 75
Sharing copyrighted music, 88
copyrighted video, 88
resources, 8
Shopping e-commerce used for, 57
Shopping cart: Element of an electronic storefront that allows a customer to collect purchases. **57**
Signature verification system, 157
Small office/home office

(SOHO): Describes any company with fewer than 50 employees, as well as the selfemployed who work from home. **20**, 22
input devices, 172
output devices, 166, 172
printer, 166
processor selection, 130
Smart card: Card, similar in size to a credit card or ATM card, that stores data on a thin microprocessor embedded in the card. **157**
Smart card (biometric): Card that stores personal biometric data on a thin microprocessor embedded in the card. **157**
Smart dust, 155
Smart phone: Internet-enabled telephone that usually also provides PDA capabilities. **16**
flash memory and, 121, 124
mobile users, 21
screen on, 160
wireless service provider and, 40
Society
computer applications in, 24-29
development of, 12
suite, 90
system, 10-11
Software suite: Collection of individual programs sold as a single package. Business software suites typically include word processsing, spreadsheet, e-mail, and presentation graphics software. **85**, 90
Son, Masayoshi, 100
Sound, 53, 149. See also
Audio; Microphone, Music,
Sound card; Speakers
Sound card: Adapter card that enhances the sound generating capabilities of a personal computer by allowing sound to be input through a microphone and output through external speakers or headphone. 110, **123**
MIDI standard, 126
Source document, 153
Spam: Unsolicited e-mail message or newsgroups posting sent to many recipi-

ents or newsgroups at once. **62**
Speakers: Audio output devices that generate sound. 7, **169**
Special-purpose terminal, 156
Speech, 53
Speech recognition: Computer's capability of distinguishing spoken words. See also Voice recognition. **149**
Speed
advantage in computer, 5
access times, 122
bus, 127
bus width, 127
cache, 120-21
processor, 115
RAM, 119-20
of storage devices and memory, 121
system clock influence on, 114
Spelling checker, 80
Spoiler, 64
Spreadsheet software: Application software that allows a user to organize data in rows and columns and to perform calculations on the data. 11, **80-81**
SRAM, 120. See also Static RAM
Client operating system
Stand-alone utility programs, 96
Start button (Windows XP), starting application using, 77
Starting application software, 77, 78
See also Booting
Startup instructions, flash memory holding, 121
Static RAM (SRAM), 120
Storage, 118
clipboard used for, 80
digital cameras using, 151
saving document and, 80
Storage device: Hardware used to record (write and/or read) items to and from storage media, 7, 118
Storage Media: The physical material on which a computer keeps data, instructions, and information, 7, 118
Streaming: Process of transferring data in a continuous and even flow. **54**
Streaming audio, 54
Streaming video, 55

Stylus: Small metal or plastic device that looks like a ballpoint pen, but uses pressure instead of ink to write, draw, or make selections. 16, **148**, 149. See also Digital pen
Subject directory: Search tool that classifies Web pages in an organized set of categories. 47, 48
Submenu, 77
Subscribe (mailing list): Process of a user adding his or her e-mail name and address to a mailing list. **60**
Supercomputer: Faster, most powerful, and most expensive computer, capable of processing more than 100 trillion instructions in a single second. **17**
Support tools, for application software, 96-98
Surfing the Web: Activity of using links to explore the Web. **45**
System board, 11. See also Motherboard
System bus: Bus that is part of the motherboard and connects the processor to main memory. **127**
System clock: Small quartz crystal circuit that is used by the processor to control the timing of the computer operations. **114**
System software: Programs that control or maintain the operations of a computer and its devices. 11-12, **75**
System unit: Case that contains the electronic components of a computer that are used to process data. 7, **110**-12
adapter cards, 123-24
bays, 127
buses, 127
cleaning, 131
connectors, 124-26
data representation and, 116-17
expansion slots, 123
hard disk in, 118
memory and, 117-122
mobile computers and

that appears as a three dimensional (3-D) space. **55**
multimedia and, 53
Virus: Potentially damaging computer program that affects, or infects, a computer negatively by altering the way the computer works without a user's knowledge or permission. **59**, 96
Visually impaired users, output devices for, 173
Voice chat, 61
Voice input: Process of entering data by speaking into a microphone. **149**
Voice output: Audio output that occurs when a user hears a person's voice or when a computer talks to the user through the speakers on the computer. **170**
Voice over IP: Technology that allows users to speak to other users over the Internet using their desktop computer, mobile computer, or mobile device. **62**. See also Internet telephony
Voice recognition: Computer's capability of distinguishing spoken words. See also Speeh recognition. 80, **149**
RAM needed for, 120
See also Speech recognition.
Voice verification system, 157
Volatile memory: Type of memory that loses its contents when a computer's power is turned off. **118**, 120

Web: Worldwide collection of electronic documents called Web pages, the Web is one of the most popular services on the Internet. Also called the World Wide Web. **43**, 38, 42-57
addresses, 44
e-commerce on, 57
freeware on, 75
multimedia on, 53-57
navigating, 45
processors and, 115

public domain software on, 75
publishing Web pages on. See Web publishing
searching for information on, 45-50
shareware on, 75
surfing, 44
types of Web sites, 50-52
See also Internet
Web address: Unique address for a Web page. Also called a URL (Uniform Resource Locator). **44**
Web browser: Application software that allows users to access and view Web pages. Also called a browser. **43**
online service provider, 40
software, 11, 95
Web cam: Video camera that displays its output on a Web page. **152**
We developer, 64
Web filter, 96
Web log, 52. See also blog
mobile, 52
Web pages: Electronic document on the Web, which can contain text, graphics, audio, and video and often has built-in connections to other documents, graphics, Web pages, or Web sites. 10, **43**
downloading, 43-44
multimedia on, 53
number of visits per month, 44
searching for, 45-50
Web page authoring software: Software used to create Web pages that include graphical images, video, audio, animation, and other special effects with interactive content. **89**
Web publishing: Development and maintenance of Web pages. **56**-57
Web server: Computer that delivers requested Web pages to a computer. **43**
Web site: Collection of related Web pages and associated

items, such as documents and pictures, stored on a Web server. 10, 23, **43**
creating, 56, 57
deploying, 56, 57
directories, 48
evaluating, 52
maintaining, 56, 57
planning, 56 ,57
posting photographs on, 151
types of, 50-53
Web-based help, 96
Web-based training (WBT): Computer-based training that uses Internet technology and consists of application software on the Web. **97**
Wheel: Steering-wheel-type input device that is used to simulate driving a vehicle. **147**
Wiki: Collaborative Web site that allows users to add to, modify, or delete the Web site content via their Web browser. **52**
Window: Rectangular area of a computer screen that displays data or information. **77**
Windows operating system, 11
Windows Media Player, 53
Windows 7 and 8: Microsoft's fastest, most reliable and efficient operating systems, offering quicker application start up, built-in diagnostics, automatic recovery, improved security, and enhanced searching and organizing capabilities. **11**
Windows XP: Version of the Windows operating system, which is a fast, reliable operating system. **11**
date and time and, 122
desktop, 76
role of, 75
Wireless Internet access, 40
Wireless Internet service
provider (WISP): Internet service provider that provides

wireless Internet access to computers with wireless modems or access devices or to Internet-enabled mobile computers or devices. **40**
Wireless mouse. See cordless mouse Wireless network
Wireless port, 126
WISP, 40, See also Wireless Internet service
Word processing software: One of the more widely used types of application software; allows a user to create and manipulate documents containing mostly text and sometimes graphics. 11, **79**-80. See also
Word processor
developing document using, 80
Word processor, 79-80. See also Word processing software
Wordwrap, 79
Workgroup computing, 52
Worksheet: Rows and columns used to organize data in a spread sheet. 80
World Wide Web (WWW): Worldwide collection of electronic documents. **43**-56. See also Web organizations from around the world that oversees research and sets standards and guidelines for many areas of the Internet. 39, 65
accessibility guidelines and, 153
WWW, 43. See also World Wide Web
WYSIWYG (what you see is what you get), 77
xD Picture Card: Type of miniature mobile storage media that is a flash memoriy card capable of storing between 64 MB. 121

Xeon, 115

Yahoo!, 50, 64

PHOTO CREDITS

Chapter 1: © Free Stock photo/www.sxc.hu, © Digital Vision/Getty Images, © Sandisk Corporation, Google image gallery, Yahoo image gallery, targe.com, www.bankofamerica.com, www.saintleo.com, www.shockwave.com, www.rhapsody.com, www.fastlaneblog.com, © Dell Computer Corporation, © Apple Incorporated, www.mapquest.com, www.imperialcapitalbank.com, www.golfonline.com, © Xerox Corporation, © 3com Corporation **Chapter 2:** © Free Stock photo/www.sxc.hu, www.businessweek.com, www.e-zine.com, www.yahoo.com, www.us-park.com, www.msn.com, www.weather.com, www.disney.go.com, www.cnn.com, www.excite.com, www.nlm.nih.com, www.kraftgood.com, www.howstuffworks.com, www.realarcade.com, www.act-az.org, www.gizmodo.com, www.newsgator.com, www.wikipedia.com, www.discovery.com, www.ebay.com, Microsoft Corporation. **Chapter 3:** © Free Stock photo/www.sxc.hu, Google image gallery, © Adobe systems Inc., © Corel Corporation, © Autodesk Inc. © Cakewalk Inc. © SumTotal Systems Inc. © Lotus Software, © Sony Corporation, © Intuit Inc. © Broderbund, © Dell Computer Corporation, © Roxio, www.howstuffworks.com **Chapter 4:** © Free Stock photo/www.sxc.hu, © Intel Corporation, © Advanced Micro Devices Inc. © SanDisk Corporation, © Dell Inc. ATI Technologies Inc. © Sony Ericsson Mobile Communicationss, © Acer America Corporation., © Apple Computers Inc. © Herrington Photography, © Cisco Corporation, © Kingston Technology Corporation, © Logitech Inc. © Lexar Media Inc. © 3M Corporation. **Chapter 5:** © Free Stock photo/www.sxc.hu, © Logitech Inc. © Microsoft Corporation, © IBM Corporation, © Palm Inc. © Chase Bank/Continental Airlines, © American Express Corporation, © Bank One, © Apple Inc. © Epson America, Inc. © ViewSonic Corporation, © Sony Ericsson Mobile Corporation, © BenQ Corporation, © NEC Corporation, © www.clickz.com, © Xerox Corporation, © Canon U.S.A. Inc. © Hewlett-Packard Development Company, L.P. **Chapter 6:** © Free Stock photo/www.sxc.hu, © Seagate Technology LLC, © SanDisk Corporation, © Iomega Corporation, © Lexar Media Inc. © Kingston Technology Corporation, © www.filesanywhere.com, © Memorex Products Inc. © Eastman Kodak Company, © Sony Ericsson Mobile Corporation, © Toshiba Corporation.

A SPECIAL THANK YOU!

Dear Student:

It was a great pleasure serving you. We look forward to meeting you in the not so far future. Please do not forget to access Chapter 6 of this books on our website at: www.clarkepublish.com. Once there, you should click the "Support" link. On the Support page, kindly navigate to the Chapter 6 link and read the chapter right in your Web browser.

While this might be it for now, we hope to meet you again when you begin your university, college or professional journey. For us at Clarke Publishing and Consulting Group, Inc. we want to be a part of your academic success. This is why we'll be with you every step of the way until you can find that career you so deserve.

Thank you for choosing us as your technology learning partner.

The Clarke Team

2 0 1 4

JANUARY
Mo		6	13	20	27
Tu		7	14	21	28
We	1	8	15	22	29
Th	2	9	16	23	30
Fr	3	10	17	24	31
Sa	4	11	18	25	
Su	5	12	19	26	

FEBRUARY
Mo		3	10	17	24
Tu		4	11	18	25
We		5	12	19	26
Th		6	13	20	27
Fr		7	14	21	28
Sa	1	8	15	22	
Su	2	9	16	23	

MARCH
Mo	31	3	10	17	24
Tu		4	11	18	25
We		5	12	19	26
Th		6	13	20	27
Fr		7	14	21	28
Sa	1	8	15	22	29
Su	2	9	16	23	30

APRIL
Mo		7	14	21	28
Tu	1	8	15	22	29
We	2	9	16	23	30
Th	3	10	17	24	
Fr	4	11	18	25	
Sa	5	12	19	26	
Su	6	13	20	27	

MAY
Mo		5	12	19	26
Tu		6	13	20	27
We		7	14	21	28
Th	1	8	15	22	29
Fr	2	9	16	23	30
Sa	3	10	17	24	31
Su	4	11	18	25	

JUNE
Mo	30	2	9	16	23
Tu		3	10	17	24
We		4	11	18	25
Th		5	12	19	26
Fr		6	13	20	27
Sa		7	14	21	28
Su	1	8	15	22	29

JULY
Mo		7	14	21	28
Tu	1	8	15	22	29
We	2	9	16	23	30
Th	3	10	17	24	31
Fr	4	11	18	25	
Sa	5	12	19	26	
Su	6	13	20	27	

AUGUST
Mo		4	11	18	25
Tu		5	12	19	26
We		6	13	20	27
Th		7	14	21	28
Fr	1	8	15	22	29
Sa	2	9	16	23	30
Su	3	10	17	24	31

SEPTEMBER
Mo	1	8	15	22	29
Tu	2	9	16	23	30
We	3	10	17	24	
Th	4	11	18	25	
Fr	5	12	19	26	
Sa	6	13	20	27	
Su	7	14	21	28	

OCTOBER
Mo		6	13	20	27
Tu		7	14	21	28
We	1	8	15	22	29
Th	2	9	16	23	30
Fr	3	10	17	24	31
Sa	4	11	18	25	
Su	5	12	19	26	

NOVEMBER
Mo		3	10	17	24
Tu		4	11	18	25
We		5	12	19	26
Th		6	13	20	27
Fr		7	14	21	28
Sa	1	8	15	22	29
Su	2	9	16	23	30

DECEMBER
Mo	1	8	15	22	29
Tu	2	9	16	23	30
We	3	10	17	24	31
Th	4	11	18	25	
Fr	5	12	19	26	
Sa	6	13	20	27	
Su	7	14	21	28	

2 0 1 5

January
Su	Mo	Tu	We	Th	Fr	Sa
				1	2	3
4	5	6	7	8	9	10
11	12	13	14	15	16	17
18	19	20	21	22	23	24
25	26	27	28	29	30	31

February
Su	Mo	Tu	We	Th	Fr	Sa
1	2	3	4	5	6	7
8	9	10	11	12	13	14
15	16	17	18	19	20	21
22	23	24	25	26	27	28

March
Su	Mo	Tu	We	Th	Fr	Sa
1	2	3	4	5	6	7
8	9	10	11	12	13	14
15	16	17	18	19	20	21
22	23	24	25	26	27	28
29	30	31				

April
Su	Mo	Tu	We	Th	Fr	Sa
			1	2	3	4
5	6	7	8	9	10	11
12	13	14	15	16	17	18
19	20	21	22	23	24	25
26	27	28	29	30		

May
Su	Mo	Tu	We	Th	Fr	Sa
31					1	2
3	4	5	6	7	8	9
10	11	12	13	14	15	16
17	18	19	20	21	22	23
24	25	26	27	28	29	30

June
Su	Mo	Tu	We	Th	Fr	Sa
	1	2	3	4	5	6
7	8	9	10	11	12	13
14	15	16	17	18	19	20
21	22	23	24	25	26	27
28	29	30				

July
Su	Mo	Tu	We	Th	Fr	Sa
			1	2	3	4
5	6	7	8	9	10	11
12	13	14	15	16	17	18
19	20	21	22	23	24	25
26	27	28	29	30	31	

August
Su	Mo	Tu	We	Th	Fr	Sa
30	31					1
2	3	4	5	6	7	8
9	10	11	12	13	14	15
16	17	18	19	20	21	22
23	24	25	26	27	28	29

September
Su	Mo	Tu	We	Th	Fr	Sa
		1	2	3	4	5
6	7	8	9	10	11	12
13	14	15	16	17	18	19
20	21	22	23	24	25	26
27	28	29	30			

October
Su	Mo	Tu	We	Th	Fr	Sa
				1	2	3
4	5	6	7	8	9	10
11	12	13	14	15	16	17
18	19	20	21	22	23	24
25	26	27	28	29	30	31

November
Su	Mo	Tu	We	Th	Fr	Sa
1	2	3	4	5	6	7
8	9	10	11	12	13	14
15	16	17	18	19	20	21
22	23	24	25	26	27	28
29	30					

December
Su	Mo	Tu	We	Th	Fr	Sa
		1	2	3	4	5
6	7	8	9	10	11	12
13	14	15	16	17	18	19
20	21	22	23	24	25	26
27	28	29	30	31		

www.ingramcontent.com/pod-product-compliance
Lightning Source LLC
Chambersburg PA
CBHW080410060326
40689CB00019B/4198